WITHDRAWN FROM
TSC LIBRARY

TALLAHASSEE
LIBRARY
COMMUNITY COLLEGE

D1563834

Demons of Disorder
Early Blackface Minstrels and Their World

DALE COCKRELL

Vanderbilt University

CAMBRIDGE
UNIVERSITY PRESS

PUBLISHED BY THE PRESS SYNDICATE OF THE UNIVERSITY OF CAMBRIDGE
The Pitt Building, Trumpington Street, Cambridge CB2 1RP, United Kingdom

CAMBRIDGE UNIVERSITY PRESS
The Edinburgh Building, Cambridge CB2 1RU, United Kingdom
40 West 20th Street, New York, NY 10011-4211, USA
10 Stamford Road, Oakleigh, Melbourne 3166, Australia

© Cambridge University Press 1997

This book is in copyright. Subject to statutory exception
and to the provisions of relevant collective licensing agreements,
no reproduction of any part may take place without
the written permission of Cambridge University Press.

First published 1997

Printed in the United States of America

Typeset in Ehrhardt

Library of Congress Cataloging-in-Publication Data
Demons of disorder: early blackface minstrels and their world / Dale Cockrell
p.   cm. – (Cambridge studies in American theatre and drama)
Includes bibliographical references (p.)
ISBN 0-521-56074-8 (hardback). – ISBN 0-521-56828-5 (paperback)
1. Minstrel shows – History.
2. Minstrel music – United States – History and criticism.
3. Blackface entertainers – United States.   4. Dixon, George Washington, 1808–1861.
5. United States –   Social conditions – 19th century.
6. United States – Race relations.   I. Title.   II. Series
ML1711.C63   1997
791'.12'0973 – dc21   96-45566
CIP

A catalog record for this book is available from the British Library

ISBN 0 521 56074 8 hardback
ISBN 0 521 56828 5 paperback

Publication of this book was supported by a grant from the
Sonneck Society for American Music.

For Lucinda and Sam

Contents

List of Illustrations

Figures

viii

Preface

ORLDS ARE THREE-DIMENSIONAL, stretching forever into an infinitude of directions. They are very unlike narratives, which try to line up the points and progress inexorably, step by step toward conclusion and closure. This is a book about a world – urban, brotherhood-based, American, from the time of Jackson through 1843 – in which popular musical and theatrical entertainments by men in blackface first found nurture and meaning. I attempt here to map some of the directions taken by blackface minstrelsy but not necessarily to connect them, although I do notice some of the intersections. All of which is to say that this is not a history of early blackface minstrelsy; it is not a rigidly chronological narrative that documents the significant moments when nineteenth-century white men put on black makeup and more or less mocked black people through song, dance, and speech. I believe that to extrapolate such a linear story from lives that fought against the whole idea of a logical, reasonable, contiguous statement of quasi-scientific facts would be to indulge in a form of misrepresentation and leave me in the awkward position I explore and deplore toward the end of this study, where perspective dictates the "facts," and intrusive real-world concerns be damned!

Nevertheless, there are some basic, "real-world" issues with which I deal in this study. For instance, one can reconstruct a world of vapors only in theory; historicizing demands something more. This presented me with a problem: Most of those who supported the development of blackface minstrelsy lived their lives below "the horizon of record." My subjects tended not to leave diaries, letters, novels, newspapers, paintings, busts, or monuments (although, when they did, I rushed to examine the trail). However, fortunately for me if not for them, those at the bottom were constantly subjected to ridicule, derision, and patronization. The "better sorts" found common people instructive exemplars of depravity, criminality, and lustful behavior. One of the best ways for those up the higher rungs of the ladder to indulge those on the lower was through the reports of court proceedings filed daily in some of the larger metropolitan newspapers. Here one can read about the manifestly debauched, unsocial behavior of those dragged in by the watch. Unintentionally, these columns become a kind of gloss on many of the things that make urban lower-class life different from that of the urban middle class.[1] Luckily for my project, music and dancing play much more extensive parts in "Police Court" proceedings than I would have expected. Reading day by day, column by column through multiple titles for New York and Boston, and in selected runs for other cities, I have collected stories, facts, trials, and data of a magnitude such that this book represents only the tip. With these files I am thus able to arrive at conclusions that I believe, somewhat immodestly, have not been supportable previously. With such a focus, I was freed to concentrate on the contexts out of which minstrelsy developed and spread, and to buttress (not construct) my findings with the texts of minstrelsy: songs, songsters, playlets, handbills, posters, and articles.

Other forms of "suspicious" evidence I use here are the symbolic and the anecdotal. Of the former, if images, sounds, or icons are manipulated in certain ways in certain situations, which can then be shown to resemble behaviors in other contexts, then one can state something about relationships (although not as directly as one could in the presence of clear intentions and explicit connections). For example, it is now clear to me that bells meant something quite different to the early nineteenth century than they mean today; context glosses meaning, and by the end of this book I hope these bells (which are to be found throughout this book in surprising places) peal out to readers in a different way. Brooms, too, play a surprising part in my story. They and their function are, of course, common symbols of pollution and depollution. (They can also be used as weapons, as one instance will show.) Sometimes the function of a broom can be inverted, allowing it to dirty, as we shall also see; and sometimes the whores of Boston (who are, of course, "unclean") arrive with brooms to freshen an area for dancing. These images resonate in a way similar to folk theatricals and early blackface minstrelsy. Although scholarly standards of evidence would compel a disregard of much of this, it seems to me little different than accepting autobiography as an accurate, objective chronicle of a necessarily subjective life. The symbols and metaphors that make up social rites and traditions swim around in the collective imagination and join and reappear in places and times often ungraspable by the disciplined methodologies of history, which is precisely why the history of ritual is generally delegated to the anthropologist and folklorist.

In somewhat like ways can anecdotes be useful. Much of the most interesting information I present here is probably inaccurate – as in, it never actually happened! Often I flag these occurrences, but at other times I let the story stand by itself, for anecdotal evidence can be a form of social myth and thus at least as powerful as fact. It is for this reason, for example, that I begin this study around 1829. Not that this is when blackface minstrelsy actually commenced, for one could probably build an equally strong case for ca. 1815[2] or for 1832, when T. D. Rice first jumped "Jim Crow" in New York City. For that matter, as Robert Winans has pointed out, most of the components that came to make up minstrelsy were "evident in American popular culture of the 1780s and 1790s, . . ."[3] However, the mythmakers of the Jacksonian era (generally, newspaper editors) believed that "Coal Black Rose" was the beginning, a song of around 1829, first heard at the time of the inauguration of the president who gave name to the epoch. Blackface minstrelsy began in myth, and the myth must be treated with great courtesy.

By letting the mythmakers tell me what to study I hope to avoid certain presentist views about minstrelsy that have, I believe, polluted our understanding of the early period. Especially problematic was much writing on minstrelsy before the past decade or so. Carl Wittke (1930), Robert Toll (1974), and Sam Dennison (1982) have all to some extent stretched their era's understanding of minstrelsy back over the whole thing, to 1829 and before, representing attitudes and meanings to be monolithic, particularly in regards to race. Robert Cantwell (1984), Sean Wilentz (1984), Eric Lott (1993a), and a few others have helped us recomplicate that period, especially in how those who lived then related to matters of race. Lott in particular has shown convincingly that the racist content of antebellum minstrel shows was never so absolute as the hideous blackface mask would seem to indicate, but was slippery and problematic. Even the writers of this distinguished latter group, however, have not been careful with race and minstrelsy in the earlier period, and have tended to treat 1832 and 1845 as subject to the same laws and contracts (although they would never do so politically, socially, or economically). This book affirms that those who told the stories back then, and made a big deal about 1843 being different from 1832, did so for very good reasons. The time span covered in this book thus embodies much more than just fifteen years of 365 days each: it is of attitudes and worlds, histories and myths, rituals and methods, words and acts. I confess that it is with considerable trepidation that I approach the world of ambiguity, and hope that my mediation makes for greater understanding.

✳✳✳✳✳

THE MOST PROBLEMATIC WORD for me in this whole study is "minstrel." It is a word first applied to blackface entertainment in late 1842 for good self-conscious reasons that must have resonated broadly, for it was quickly picked up by others and became a popular convention within months of its initial employment. The reasons, as I show in Chapter 5, have to do with economics, politics, status, and music. It is a word of its time, and is appropriately transforming in its impact. I try to make the case that 1842–3 was a substantially different time from 1829. What word do I then use to characterize the music, dance, and theatre treated in this book before late 1842, which does, after all, make up the bulk of my study? Would I not, by using the word "minstrel," project anachronistically a context of understanding onto something (often) quite different? I am afraid, alas, the answer is yes; but there seems no ready alternative to the word, and after trying "blackface dialect," "blackface entertainment," and just "blackface," I rejected each for various reasons, and have resorted to the convention. Forbearance is begged.

Demons of Disorder is, in part (for worlds can never be a single thing), an attempt to comprehend the role of music in cultural history. This study embraces a range of music made by common Jacksonians, holds music's antonym – noise – to be a legitimate form of cultural expression, and asks questions of meaning following analysis of sound's place in society. My approach to the study of music bridges between those who would decontextualize music in a search for an autonomous, aesthetic-based musical canon, and those who would ignore musical sound altogether, opting only for text and context. This book is also a number in the growing literature on the ways in which theatre reflects and instills social values. My topic is especially apt in this regard, for minstrelsy was a highly popular enterprise powerfully expressive of the common person's politics. This, then, is a study of class and race. Here I attempt to take the long view, which sees class relations in urban Jacksonian America as connected to a premodern set of strictures and mores, and to define the frame, which sets off relations between common people and the middle class through the image and reality of race. In the end of this revisionist work, the inevitable question confronted is "How is it that our received view of early blackface minstrelsy was so widely off the mark?" By setting the historiography of minstrelsy within its own social context, which was generally white, northern, liberal, middle class, and academic, I bring my story into the present and ponder, "Did any one group or class benefit from the fabrication?" Could it be that the powerful misrepresented traditions and meanings special to the powerless in a wild search for scapegoats?

✳✳✳✳✳

ALL SIX WORDS of my subtitle make up a form of tribute to Mikhail Bakhtin and his *Rabelais and His World*. I have found his study to be a primary source of insight, method, and support. Bakhtin's contributions are many, but primary among them was his situating of Rabelais in the light of folk humor and outside that of the official culture of power. He discovered that Rabelais had tapped into an incredibly rich world of humorous, grotesque metaphors employed and lustily enjoyed by the common people of that period, a language that was intentionally obscure to those in power. Rabelais wrote for readers newly emerged from an "ear culture" (about which, more later), who carried with them in their collective memories the symbols that defined and enriched heritage. Not surprisingly, given the brilliance of the work, Bakhtin anticipated my line of reasoning, which argues for the continued existence of ancient European folk theatricals well into nineteenth-century America and for a tradition of modes of behavior and knowing that infected contemporary means of expression. "[Folk humor] continues to live and to struggle for its existence in the lower canonical genres (comedy, satire, fable) and especially in non-canonical genres (in the novel, in a special form of popular dialogue, in burlesque). . . . [and] on the popular stage . . ."[4] Not content, however, just to point to source and lineage, Bakhtin lays bare process and significance:

[T]he system of popular-festive images was developed and went on living over thousands of years. This long development had its own scoria, its own dead deposits in manners, beliefs, prejudices. But in its basic line this system grew and was enriched; it acquired a new meaning, absorbed the new hopes and thoughts of the people. It was transformed in the crucible of the people's new experience. The language of images developed new and more refined nuances.

Thanks to this process, popular-festive images became a powerful means of grasping reality; they served as a basis for an authentic and deep realism. Popular imagery did not reflect the naturalistic, fleeting, meaningless, and scattered aspect of reality but the very process of becoming, its meaning and direction. Hence the universality and sober optimism of this system.[5]

Far from being disappointed that my primary point and the shape of my conclusion has received previous articulation, I am comforted and somewhat relieved; for, like Bakhtin's, my research flies in the face of some parts of our canon. I would be honored to see this work stand as a buttress to the monument that is his.

Acknowledgments

HOW CAN I EVER HONOR all those who have helped me toward my measure of understanding? Well, truth be known, I cannot; undaunted, though, I shoulder the effort. Let me begin appropriately by expressing my gratitude to the Sonneck Society for American Music. The first tentative public presentations of my findings were at the Society's conferences. The colleagues and friends that constitute this body of believers in American music supported me then and at many turns since, both formally and informally. I am especially thankful for the display of confidence in my work shown by the award to Cambridge University Press of an H. Earle Johnson Book Publication Grant.

Many institutions have opened their files to me, and without their cooperation this would be a much lesser book. Wayne Everard, archivist at the Louisiana Division, New Orleans Public Library; Jessica Travis, reference librarian, Historic New Orleans Collection; and the Louisiana and Lower Mississippi Valley Collections at Louisiana State University Libraries all devoted critical time and services. Kenneth R. Cobb, Director of the Municipal Archives, City of New York, provided me with everything I needed to work there. Rosemary Cullen, Curator of the Harris Collection, The John Hay Library, Brown University, treated me as if I were the only person in the library. Michael Dumas, Harvard Theatre Collection, Harvard College Library, on several occasions made me feel welcome in that splendid collection. The Wisconsin Historical Society made available to me issues of newspapers that I would not have been able to consult otherwise. Virginia Smith at the Massachusetts Historical Society enthusiastically helped me find what I needed from their collection. Elizabeth C. Bouvier at the Massachusetts Archives helped me through the Massachusetts court records. The New York Public Library allowed me access to vital and unique documents.

Four institutions, though, stand out. One is the Commonwealth Center for the Study of American Culture, which provided me with a quiet place to work, resources, and stimulating colleagues during the formative stages of this work. (Alas, my encomium has a bittersweet knell about it, for politicians in their infinite wisdom regarding matters intellectual have determined that the Center is expendable, and it is at this writing no more.) I wish also to thank the College of William and Mary, which supported my work at several turns by making available time and resources. It was my academic home during most of this work and nurtured me in untold ways. Vanderbilt University was my haven during the final push to publication, and has also provided financial support and intellectual nourishment. Regarding the American Antiquarian Society, I fear that I might be accused of exaggeration. The granting of an AAS–National Endowment for the Humanities Fellowship quite simply made this work possible – "simply" because I could not have done this work anywhere else. What a truly great place to live and work, and what a wonderful, rich collection of resources – the most valuable of these being not the seemingly endless collections of primary source material, but the people. I suspect they too have trouble conceiving of themselves as "employees." Staffers seem to like working there, and stay for a good long spell, often a lifetime. Accordingly, they have a depth of knowledge about the collection that surpasses extraordinary, and all are perfectly willing to share what they know! Many aided me in some way, from the maintenance guys, to the business office, to cataloguing, to Nancy Burkett, librarian, and Ellen Dunlap, the president. However, to limit myself to those those who helped put the materials I needed into my hands (or the ideas I stole into my head), I would like to express my thanks to Georgia Barnhill, Joanne Chaison, Sarah Heinser, John Hench, Tom Knoles, Marie Lamoureux, Dennis

Laurie, Jim Moran, Caroline Sloat, Joyce Tracy, Laura Wasowicz, and Caroline Wood. Extra special thanks go to Gigi, Caroline, Susan, and Lee for conferring upon me "honorary girl" status, and, as a result, coming to put up with my "most recent discovery" at the coffee hour.

As for individuals, and with the certainty that I have overlooked at least one friend or colleague who contributed a key piece of understanding, let me intone the names of those who can lay claim to a part of this work (assuming they would wish to do so). They are Karen Ahlquist, Joyce Appleby, Chris Ballantine, Jay Blair, Bill Brooks, Chandos Brown, Steve Bullock, Martha Burns, Betty Ch'maj, Chris Clark, Dan Cohen, Pat Cohen, Mary Jane Corry, Richard Crawford, Barbara Cutter, Bill DeFotis, John Dougan, Ken Emerson, Dena Epstein, Wayne Franklin, Bob Gross, Grey Gundaker, Dan Gutwein, Lee Heller, David Horn, Phyllis Hunter, Carol Karlsen, Bill Kearns, Virginia Kearns, Kitty Keller, Arthur Knight, Bruce Laurie, Rip Lhamon, Eric Lott, Bill Mahar, David Napier, Ron Pen, Dan Preston, Kitty Preston, Anne Rasmussen, John Reilly, Carol Rifelj, Tom Riis, Brenda Romero, Deane Root, Howard Sacks, Kirk Savage, Art Schrader, Regina Sweeney, Jeff Titon, George A. Thompson, Jr., Mark Tucker, Alden Vaughan, Rob Walser, Paul Wells, Glenn Wilcox, Edgar Williams, Kit Wilson, and Bob Winans.

Let me single out a few colleagues for special thanks. Bruce McConachie has provided me with warm, friendly support and encouragement throughout this project. Stephen Nissenbaum is responsible for the seed idea from which it all sprang and for tending what grew from it. George Harris has been both a good friend and a good critic, and has dragged me away for a day of fellowship and fishing at the most appropriate times. Finally, to my mentor (if he will claim me) Charles Hamm, I express unending gratitude for his advice, insight, encouragement, criticism, and, most important, for his being perhaps the finest person ever to write an intelligent word on popular music. Let me also thank the students in my 1996 seminar on "Blackface Minstrelsy," for they endured in good humor the forced reading of my draft manuscript, and offered me a semester's worth of dialogue, insight, and constructive criticism.

Cambridge University Press has given me much support. My series editor, Don Wilmeth, believed in this research when it was still in its infancy, and has guided and advised me at many turns. My senior editors, first Susan Chang, later Anne Sanow, provided steady, encouraging editorial support. Michael Gnat has been much more than production editor *extraordinaire;* he is to be credited with much of the sense in my syntax and a great deal of the sensibility. I hope they all take pride in our work.

On a softer note, my parents, Elliott and Jo Ann Cockrell, nurtured and instructed me through so many formative moments, a debt that I now see (as a parent, myself) I can never repay. Finally, there's Lucinda and Sam, who overwhelm me daily with the meaning, beauty, and love of living. They have endured much at the hands of this project. (At the moment I write this I could – and probably should – be playing catch with a promising five-year-old right-hander.) My dedication of this book to them is a start toward making up for lost joint time.

As for failings and errors, I've always admired how my colleague Bruce McConachie handled them in his *Melodramatic Formations:* "Of course, the blame for any mistakes in the book rests entirely with them, not me" (1992: viii). So, since Bruce was my friend, critic, and guide through much of this work, and since he is by now surely wanting of correction, let me pass on any mistakes or failings in this book to him, for they were surely of *his* making! . . . However, having momentarily slipped the harness of responsibility that attends to a right, I must again crib from Bruce: "having written such a sentence myself, I am no more able to endorse its wise crack than any other scribbling pedant. My mistakes, alas, are my own."

Dictionariana[1]

ABSTRACT REASONING – Reasoning from principles, as distinguished from the ratiocination of weak minds, who can only reason directly from matters of fact.

ACCOMPLISHMENT – Any acquisition that improves the manners without necessarily strengthening the mind, which renders one more agreeable without increasing his intelligence.

BIGOTRY – The veneration of ones opinions.

DANCING – An active employment of the understanding.

DEVIL – A word used, in comparison, as a climax for every extreme.

EYES – The windows and mirrors of the soul.

FABLES – Fictions invented for the illustration of truths – or, lies in fact, and truths in principle.

FACTS – Lies, well supported by testimony.

FINE – A means by which the wealthy may atone for a crime, for which the poor must suffer punishment, from their inability to pay it.

FREEMAN – An individual who cannot discern the limits of his imprisonment, or the fetters of his bondage.

HARMONY (IN MUSIC) – Scientific discord.

HISTORY – Well authenticated fiction; a catalogue of hypocrisy, crimes and misfortunes.

HOLIDAYS – Those seasons of pastime which the puritanical selfishness of the Americans has nearly banished from the calendar.

HOPE – A mistress whom we still love and still believe, though she has often deceived us, because we cannot be happy without her.

HORRIBLE – Exceedingly interesting.

ILLOGICAL – Contrary to the decisions of the schools.

INFERIORS – Those who possess less wealth than ourselves.

LEARNED – Ignorant of common things.

LIFE – A monotonous repetition of eating and drinking, sleeping and waking, occasionally relieved by the perusal of the daily papers.

MANNERS – The language of action.

MISREPRESENTATION – The art of falsifying, without lying.

MUSIC – The most social of all the arts, which has the misfortune to be ridiculed by Mammon-worshippers, because it sometimes leads to unthriftiness, and by the unmusical, because they cannot appreciate its value.

PARADOX – A startling truth.

PEN – The chief implement of modern warfare.

POETRY – Literary vomit.

PREFACE – An introductory essay by which the author endeavors to recommend or apologize for the nonsense which follows.

PROFOUND – Unintelligible.

REASON – A faculty used by men when they wish to apologize for their errors and to defend their prejudices.

RESPECTABILITY – Conformity to all the customs both good and bad that are sanctioned by public opinion.

SELF – An individual who is of the greatest consequence to each, and of the least consequence to all of the human race.

Prologue

Oh! I'se from Lucianna, as you all know.
Dar whare Jim along Josey's all de go,
Dem niggars all rise when de bell does ring,
And dis is de song dat dey do sing.
Hey get along, get along Josey,
Hey get along Jim along Joe!
Hey get along, get along Josey,
Hey get along, Jim along Joe![1]

    When lo! a Harlot form soft sliding by,
With mincing step, small voice, and languid eye:
Foreign her air, her robe's discordant pride
In patch-work flutt'ring and her head aside:
By singing Peers up-held on either hand,
She tripped and laughed, too pretty much to stand;
Cast on the prostrate Nine a scornful look,
Then thus in quaint Recitativo spoke.
    "O *Cara! Cara!* silence all that train:
Joy to great Chaos! let Division reign:
Chromatic tortures soon shall drive them hence,
Break all their nerves, and fritter all their sense:
One Trill shall harmonize joy, grief, and rage,
Wake the dull Church, and lull the ranting Stage;
To the same notes thy sons shall hum, or snore,
And all thy yawning daughters cry, encore.
Another Phoebus, thy own Phoebus, reigns,
Joys in my jigs, and dances in my chains.
But soon, ah soon, Rebellion will commence,
If Music meanly borrows aid from Sense."[2]

I

O N THE 18TH OF APRIL 1842 George Magnus was charged in
New York City's Court of General Sessions for assault and
battery on John Jacob Wintringham, who was in turn charged
five days later for the same on James L. Magnus, George's father.[3] Before either of these cases could be tried, however, another related suit,
John Wintringham (John J.'s father) v. *James L. Magnus* for slander, was
heard before the Court of Common Pleas commencing on 7 May 1842,
Judge Inglis presiding. In opening statements Wintringham was shown
to be "highly respectable"; Magnus was more complexly characterized
as a "native of Germany, a member of the Jewish persuasion" who had
immigrated to the United States some six or seven years earlier, and
was recently widowed with "two fine boys" in tow to which "he had
been both father and mother." Magnus had established a merchant
business after arriving in New York and been successful until a "hurri-
cane" hit the city, wiping out his business. He rebuilt and by 1842 again
held property, "but [was] in debt for it." His dry goods business, at 125
William Street, was located in a building owned by Wintringham, one
that had been divided into a commercial rental and, on the other side,
a family dwelling where Wintringham and his family resided. The
prosecution opened by swearing in Margaret A. C. Richards, "a young
rosy cheeked woman" who was a servant at Wintringham's residence.
Richards claimed that on 20 December 1841 she had been crossing a
public space when she bumped into Magnus; during the brief encoun-
ter she related that Magnus "called me [a trull] and asked me if I was
going to Wintringham's brothel." She alleged that he carried "his opposition and abuse so far as to create serious injury to the reputation of
Mr. Wintringham and his family." Mrs. Eliza Grosebeck, the daughter of Wintringham and also resident in the building, testified that
Magnus had "called my mother a common prostitute. He has called
my mother a wh___ twenty times, and told my father to look out how
she went to certain places." Magnus assumed his own defense in cross-
examining the witness. He drew out of Grosebeck that she had agreed
once to go "to the Battery" with him and that there they shared soda
waters at Rushton's and Aspinwall's. Magnus: "I will show dat woman
had a notion to marry me [and claimed to be divorced]. . . . She thought
I was rich, yet she was a married woman." He asked her if she could
"recollect calling me up stairs, and putting your hands on me so –
(Magnus here put his hands on the lower part of his sides) – and ask

me if I was ticklish," at a time when no one else was at home? Magnus
built to what he considered the most damaging testimony in the following exchange.

> MAGNUS: When you found I was not to be catched, did you not try to
> annoy me in every way possible?
> WITNESS: Never.
> MAGNUS: You do not remember annoying me and singing out Jim-
> along-Josey?
> WITNESS: No, never. We sometimes played on the piano.
> MAGNUS: Oh, you play on de piano do you?
> WITNESS: No I don't, but we sing.
> MAGNUS: You sing – oh yes, I know you can sing – you sang Jim-
> along-Josey, and danced, and raised de devil to annoy me.

Magnus then attacked with his own witnesses. Mrs. Saltus swore to the
bad character of Mrs. Richards, and claimed that "she cohabitated with
a black man!" Margaret Ball and Bridget McGann stated something
similar. Theo. Magnus, son of the defendant, then took the stand. He
swore that "Mrs. Richards has called my father an old beast, and said
that I was a rascal." He also corroborated that Richards would try to
annoy the Magnus family by singing and dancing "Jim Along Josey."
He asserted too that Richards had tried to force him to kiss her; upon
his refusal, she "called my father an old state's prison bird, and claimed
that he had cheated and swindled his creditors." George Magnus, the
other son, about twenty-two years old, testified that his father was a sober man and confessed that "his blood had boiled since being in court
to hear assertions to the contrary." He exclaimed that he would rather
someone stab him "to the heart, than say so." He too gave "rather a
hard account of the Jim-along-Josey." To build further his case Magnus called Amelia White, a "pretty little black-eyed girl"; she "claimed
to have seen Mrs. Richards make faces at [Magnus] through the glass-
window of the door, and sweep dirt into [his] store." Mrs. Richards was
then called again and testified before Magnus that she "never put my
tongue out at you, nor called you a beast. I never heard Mrs. Grosebeck threaten to broomstick you, . . . I never swept the dirt in your
door, nor made faces at you." In an attempt to impugn Mrs. Richards's
character, Magnus called her husband, "Mr. John D. Richards, a young

man," who, however, denied saying to Mr. Magnus "that he would let
him have his wife for half a dollar and a dinner to boot. He declared it
to be a lie." Before the case went to the jury, the judge instructed them
that "[c]haracter was a most sacred thing, and it was for the Jury to
guard it."

The Jury returned a decision in favor of Wintringham, for clearly
there had been slander; but the victory was virtually in name only, for
it carried damages of only $100, much reduced from the $2,000 in pu-
nitive damages that Wintringham had claimed.[4]

On the 23rd of May the double assault and battery cases were
brought up. Court proceedings show that on 5 March 1842 John Jacob
Wintringham sought restitution for attacks on his family's honor by
knocking down "old Magnus twice." George Magnus then "beat young
Wintringham in return." The court declared the fight a draw; each was
found guilty and fined $25.[5]

✳✳✳✳✳

ON ITS SURFACE, there would appear to be nothing about "Jim Along
Josey" (Figure 1) that suggests its working in such an extraordinary
way. There are seven published verses, the first of which appears at the
head of this chapter. That first is, in some ways, the most "logical" of
them all: Slaves are expected to rise "when de bell does ring" and then
line up alongside the others.[6] The other verses are less narrative than
this and are on occasion so abstracted as to acquire poetic qualities.

> My sister Rose de oder night did dream,
> Dat she was floating up and down de stream,
> And when she woke she began to cry,
> And de white cat picked out de black cat's eye.

This last line notwithstanding, there is a general sense pervading the
text that is sympathetic to the plight of the slave, although it is sometimes hard to pin down. Musically, there is less equivocation. The melody of the verse is predictable, even static; but for one passing tone all
pitches derive from a C major chord (Musical Example 1). It is, however, heard as structurally unbalanced (two related but different three-
measure phrases), giving it a kind of awkward energy. The chorus is

Figure 1. "Jim Along Josey." Sheet music cover by Firth & Hall (New York), 1840. Courtesy, American Antiquarian Society.

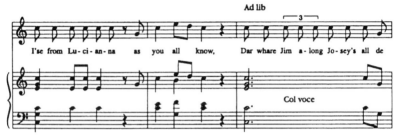

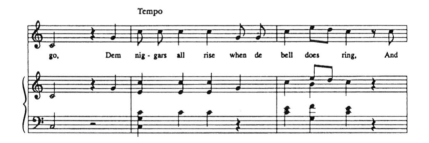

Musical Example 1 (above and facing). "Jim Along Josey" (New York: Firth & Hall, 1840).

Musical Example 1 (cont.)

both more unusual and more ordinary: It is based upon a pentatonic scale (c-d-e-g-a-C) – often an element associated with the "exotic" or oral tradition – but is classically balanced in phrase length and structure. Range throughout is precisely one octave. It is only in the rhythm that one finds much reason for "Jim Along Josey's" great popularity. Unusual for minstrel songs of the period, tempos actually change from

Moderato to *Allegro* at the chorus, and the last measure of each of the verse's phrases is marked *Ad Lib*. Most telling, though, is the eight-measure postlude, marked simply "Dance." Here the accompaniment moves up into the bright treble range and the rhythms become more spritely. This section – which is literally beyond words – is, in a real way, the heart of the song.

✳✳✳✳✳

The month after Magnus's trial an account was published in a New York weekly newspaper of a dance competititon between the two best-known prostitutes in Boston, Nancy Holmes and Susan Bryant, and ti-tled the "Dance on Long Wharf – Boston" (Figure 2). At nine o'clock, the reporter

noticed a crowd of females coming down under a small trot, and as we ex-pected, they were the rival parties, arm in arm, closely followed by Julia Carr, Julia King, Lucy Bartlett, Miss Dunbar, Kate Hall, Harriet Motley, Elmira Lewis, all giggling and talking as fast as woman can.[7]

Mysteriously, each cyprien carried a broom. "However, we were soon enlightened, for at the word of command, they all commenced sweeping Long Wharf for a clean spot which was soon done." For music there was a fiddler employed for just this occasion, "a half white negro barber." Two men were selected as judges.

The first dance on the list was a hornpipe, and the one who took the most steps was to come off victor. It was Bryant's first turn, and as she entered the ring, she made three courtesies to the spectators who formed three sides about her. The word was given; the negro fiddler struck up Fisher's Hornpipe, and Susan commenced – and the way she put in the big licks was a "sin to Moses." Shouts of applause rent the air, whenever she changed a step. Every move was grace, her limbs moved as if guided by machinery. She now came to the heel and toe business – and done it to a nail, with which she wound up the horn-pipe.

There was general admiration of her performance, when a voice was heard.

"Make way for old Nance, she'll make some of you howl." "Yes, indeed, hoss," cried she as she entered. "Come," she said, funnily clapping Bryant on the shoulder, "get off the floor, and see how soon I will make the grease come – and give us some chalk, for see how wet Suse has made it. Why old gal you

Figure 2. "Grand Trial Dance between Nance Holmes and Suse Bryant, on Long Wharf, Boston." From *The Libertine*, 15 June 1842. Courtesy, American Antiquarian Society.

have sweat a gallon; I guess you over-fed yourself. Come strike up, white nigger."

"What tune?" enquired Cuffey.

"Why, the same to be sure, I ain't going to give that gal any advantage," quoth Nance.

"Well, I only thought you were goin to put in your fancy licks on de Elssler music."[8]

"No, no, keep them back," said she, "so here goes."

And so it did. As soon as the music struck the air, Holmes struck the wharf, and the way she made her body move was a caution to French bedsteads. Every step the Bryant took Nance repeated – and all [conceded] that it would be hip and thigh between them, which is a tie. "If the Holmes can only last," cried one of the idlers, and as the words fell on our ears, she dropped, not flat, no indeed, but in a position which looked much like a squat – when she was forced to take the step which was to decide all, and which was no more or less than the famous "Taylor's Hop," and that did decide all. Every time Holmes struck out that leg, the old wharf shook again. "Quit, Holmes, quit," cried her friends; but it was no go; all h_ll couldn't stop her, and the only way it was effected was by Jule King and Carr rushing in and seizing her under the arm pit, and raising her up, they carried her in the fresh air, she shouting, "Go away old gal, you can't take this child's time, no how."

After the performance by Holmes, there were general refreshments passed around – "gin and round hearts" – and everyone was set for the finishing dance, a "Virginia breakdown," in which the women would dance against each other, one-on-one. After the participants had been sponged off, they began.

The negro struck up the Camptown Hornpipe and the gals struck the wharf. It was hard to decide who was to come off victor notwithstanding that the knowing odds were offered in favor of Bryant. From the Camptown the tune was changed to the Grape Vine; yet both went it, as the change had no effect on them. From this they changed to
"Take your time Miss Lucy,"
and the way they went it was a caution – even the change to
"Where did you come from, knock a nigger down,"
and "Jenny get your hoe cake done my lady," did not affect them – the sweat run down their faces, as if all within was on fire; perhaps occasioned by the gin taken in the recess. But now came the tug of war – the tune was changed to one of Sandford's jigs – "Go it Nance," "Go it Suse," came in from all sides. They danced – the sweat poured, and now the fatigue of the delicate Nance became apparent, but amid the cheers of her friends she yet kept pace with the Bryant; but she couldn't stand it much longer, and after one of the closest contested dances on record Nance Holmes gave out, and the Bryant came off victorious! Nance was carried home on a cart, procured for the purpose, while Suse footed it, amid shouts of joy from her friends.

It is surely significant that blackface minstrelsy provided all the music for the climax. "Miss Lucy Long" was the most often programmed minstrel song of its era;[9] "Whar Did You Come From?," subtitled "Knock a Nigger Down," was performed first (and often) by banjoist Joel Sweeney,[10] who also made famous "Jenny Get Your Hoe Cake Done."[11] The last unidentified tune is explicitly associated with James

Sanford, one of the most-renowned dancers of "negro extravaganzas" of that time.

*****

I BELIEVE THAT THESE TWO EVENTS – one real enough, one perhaps apocryphal, both at a critical juncture in the history of the United States – frame the ideas, metaphors, images, concepts, movements, and sounds that gave meaning to what we call early blackface minstrelsy. Music here is about the sweating corpulence of Nancy Holmes and about a man's character; it is both body and mind. It is joyous, entertaining and uplifting, yet also threatening and frightening. It promises sex and ecstasy and it is an incentive to violence. It is dirt and it is light. It is a reward and it is a weapon. These stories are also about music that mattered.

This is a book about many things – blackface, music, cities, newspapers, theatres, sexuality, class, race, gender – but throughout it is about this passion, about believing in ideas and experiences that are sticking points, and about how that passion can be tragically lost, stolen, or denied.

The form that I have fashioned to deal with these issues is sometimes smoothly contoured, and sometimes ragged, recursive, or disjunctive – similar, I believe, to the ways of the worlds that occupy me here. I first attempt to establish a baseline by examining in the opening two chapters how blackface was used in American culture through 1843. Blackface was often to be found in legitimate theatre,[12] and Chapter 1 is largely concerned with such, both its productions and its audience. However, because blackface was also used and known by Americans of this period outside the stage, I investigate in Chapter 2 a whole range of folk ritual theatricals that employ this device. Here I wish to establish that these rituals did not so much feed into blackface minstrelsy (although there is some oblique evidence that they did) as coexist with it – two worlds in sympathetic resonance. To unlock the door to one lost world is to unlock it to the other, and everything that follows in this study is affected to some extent by the pull of folk theatricals on the development of popular culture. Chapter 2 thus offers a corrective to the current historiography. Quite typically, William Torbert Leonard's *Masquerade in Black* (1986), which purports to be a "history of whites in blackface,"[13] concentrates exclusively on the legitimate stage. Leonard's book, Joseph Boskin's *Sambo: The Rise and Demise of an American Jester* (1986), and most other studies that touch on the subject either miss entirely or show no interest in the theatricals where blackface was most richly and anciently expressed: in the folk dramas, deep in the oral histories of common people.

Once I have established my poles – blackface among the uncommon and the common – I proceed to analyze the cultural artifacts and to overlay these with their functions. Manifestly, nothing could be more important to my topic than the songs that were sung and danced, and the people who gave life to them or who loved and used them. Accordingly, Chapters 3–5 treat expansively three important minstrel songs of the period and the people associated with them. In composite I hope to establish the world of blackface minstrelsy, delineate its audience, and show how "Jim Crow" (and T. D. Rice) in 1832 differed substantially from "Old Dan Tucker" (and the Virginia Minstrels) in 1843 in ways that foretell developments in minstrelsy thereafter. Burning his way across nearly all the worlds I uncover is George Washington Dixon, probably the central figure in this study, the man I believe most deserves the title "father of blackface minstrelsy" and surely one of celebrity's all-time heavyweight eccentrics – a bonafide "demon of disorder." Throughout, I try never to disturb my material, even if embedded in the muck and muss of society. (In fact, I've rather come to like its redolence.) With the fragrance fresh in my nostrils, I turn in the Epilogue to the stretch of American society (and music) from 1843 to the day (on the cusp of the twenty-first century) when I write these words, for I believe deeply in a constant, ongoing, and enrichening dialogue between the present and the past. History – especially music history, I like to think – is not just something we study; it's something we live.

I

Blackface on the Early American Stage

Sentiment is a simple common-place business;
But cutting a Joke is the most serious undertaking this side the grave.[1]

THEATRICAL BLACKFACE was not limited to the minstrel stage. Othello is only the most obvious character to have been, in almost all cases, a white actor in blackface. Since this study, in the end, is as much a study of the historiography of blackface as of blackface itself, let me summarize at the onset the narrative most commonly fixed for blackface minstrelsy's pre- and early history:[2]

Blackface has long had a place on the legitimate stage. In addition to *Othello*, American eighteenth-century theatre-goers knew plays like *Oroonoko, The Padlock,* and *Inkle and Yarico,* all of which feature blackfaced characters.

In the early nineteenth century, audiences continued to see these plays, and theatres added a few newer ones featuring blackface, such as *The Aethiop* and *The Africans.*

There matters stood until the 1820s, when actor Charles Mathews play-mocked an American black he claimed to have observed butchering the role of Hamlet.

At the commencement of the Jacksonian period, some American actors were blacking up and singing comic dialect songs about "Coal Black Rose" and a few other such stereotypes.

In 1832, Thomas Dartmouth Rice came to New York with
his portrayal of Jim Crow, and thus began the full development of the phenomenon called blackface minstrelsy.

Quite simply, in this chapter, I ask anew the questions that implicitly
undergird what has become accepted wisdom. Just how common was
the representation of blackness on the American stage before the first
so-called minstrel "show" (a misnomer, as I will point out later) in
1843? Did American theatregoers regularly see white actors (and actresses) in blackface? Under what circumstances? What did they understand "blackness" to be? Was it inevitably a reference to those of African descent? What was the context for audience reception? and What
understandings can be garnered from the answers to these questions?

✳✳✳✳✳

TO UNRAVEL SOME of the most fundamental of my problems, I have
established a chronology of stage performances in America that include
characters in blackface. My list is incomplete, for I have by no means
exhausted the resources for establishing stage annals from 1716 through
1843, a herculean task indeed and probably impossible. The *New York
Courier and Enquirer* of 18 February 1832 estimated that there were thirty to forty theatres then in the United States (and nearly eight hundred
actors and actresses). The annals to a few of these are published, principally for theatres in New York, Philadelphia (after 1834), and New
Orleans (through 1842).[3] Other large, important theatregoing cities, like
Boston and Baltimore, have not had systematically collected stage histories, and Charleston only has one for the pre-eighteenth-century period.[4] A few smaller towns and cities have received such treatment (although none of these is complete for the period up to 1843);[5] but many,
perhaps most, have not, including such then-active theatre towns as
Portland, Mobile, St. Louis, Louisville, Cincinnati, and Pittsburgh. To
compile my list I have thus drawn from many of the bibliographies
available to me, then fleshed the list with information winnowed from
newspaper ads and extant playbills. However, before I could do this (in
practice, often along the way), I had to identify the plays, farces, melodramas, operas, endpieces, extravaganzas, songs, and so on that included representations of Africans, West Indians, or African Americans.

James V. Hatch's *Black Image on the American Stage* (1970) provided a starting place but is not complete. I have looked at many plays and character lists to add titles to those provided by Hatch; undoubtedly, I have overlooked a number.

Altogether, I expect that my research has captured something on the order of one-quarter of all blackface performances in America through 1843. Nevertheless, although the list is necessarily incomplete and will always be incomplete, it is surely statistically representative. My chronicle begins with 23 December 1751 and goes to the very end of 1843; it is about twice the length of this book and includes, by estimate, more than five thousand productions involving blackface on American stages. If this represents 25 percent of the total, then there might have been more than twenty thousand opportunities for Americans to see staged blackface before 1844. This order of magnitude quite frankly surprised me, and I trust I am not alone. The facts are that blackface theatre was extremely common, and Americans had ample opportunities to see it, often had to choose between competing performances on the same night, and attended blackface performances with enthusiasm.

Only about half of the blackface performances I document are of the "minstrel" variety, mostly songs and "extravaganzas" (songs that featured more than just singing – typically, some dancing and perhaps playacting). That leaves, very roughly, ten thousand performances of legitimate blackface, still a staggering total. This number includes at least 168 legitimate plays, operas, melodramas, farces, endpieces, set pieces, pantomimes, and entr'actes, none with any obvious minstrel characteristics, nor any that featured renowned minstrel performers.[6]

An analysis of this list should reveal much about the nature and meanings of staged legitimate blackface. There is, for example, a full range from comedy to tragedy. There are straight dramas and musical theatre. There are serious pieces and quasi-novelty pieces. (*The Planter and His Dogs* of 1835, e.g., is one of a number of trained-dog novelty acts common to the mid-1830s; in this skit, the planters' dogs are used to round up runaway slaves.) Most can be learned though, I believe, first by developing a "core" repertory of blackface theatrical productions, and then by proceeding to an analysis of qualities and characteristics from that platform.

To limit myself usefully, although somewhat arbitrarily as well, to the ten most-performed legitimate blackface productions, I derive the

Table 1. *Most-performed legitimate blackface productions in America*

Play	Author	First Am. prod.	Doc'd. perfs.
Othello	Shakespeare	1751	425
Jonathan in England; or,	Hackett	1828	180
John Bull at Home	(after Colman)		
The Forest Rose; or,	Woodworth	1825	126
American Farmers			
The One Hundred-Pound Note	Peake	1827	109
Laugh When You Can	Reynolds	1799	107
The Irishman in London	McCready	1793	101
The Kentuckian	Bernard	1833	100
The Green Mountain Boy	Jones	1833	80
The Yankee Pedlar; or,	Barnett	1834	76
Old Times in Virginia			
The Padlock	Bickerstaffe	1769	66

list shown in Table 1.[7] The total number of performances on this list is 1,370, suggesting that one of the "top ten" was billed in about every four productions featuring blackface (which, of course, includes minstrel songs and plays), or more than half of the total legitimate productions (since about half of my roughly five thousand documented performances were of a minstrel type).[8] Clearly, each of these pieces was significant, not only enjoying widespread and frequent production, but also exhibiting staying power: At the end of 1843, all ten were still being produced regularly.

Before proceeding to an analysis of the pieces, a word about playgoers, on whom some excellent research has been conducted.[9] Most urban American theatres before 1843 were the domains of privileged Americans, whether through wealth, status, education, race, or gender. They were, generally, places where educated, well-off, often elite, white men gathered, although there are important exceptions (about which more later). The houses, which in the larger urban centers often held two to three thousand patrons, were constructed so that there was a floor-level area – the pit – where general, inexpensive admission was procured by clerks, mechanics, apprentices, and the petite bourgeoisie. The first and second tiers contained most of the seats, arranged into boxes, priced higher than elsewhere in the house, often by a factor of 2 but sometimes more. The sociology of the third tier would be the most alien to modern-day playgoers, for this was the "service tier," significantly populated by prostitutes, their pimps, and their clients; Jacksonian-era theatre managers actively encouraged prostitute attendance in the belief that their marks were ticket purchasers as well.[10] The topmost part of the house was the gallery, occupied by the lower sorts, including some African Americans. A theatre's well-being depended upon keeping the first and second tiers full and happy; hence playbills were generally pitched at those levels. Theatre managers, then, must have thought that the "top ten blackface productions" would somehow appeal to these patrons of the muse.

With no excuse greater than a desire to understand something of how the audience perceived representations of blackness, I turn to the nine of the ten plays that I have managed to locate.[11]

Of all of these, the most problematic is *The One Hundred-Pound Note*. The role of Billy Black appears to have been played largely in blackface in the United States, although there is no reason for this inherent to the role. In English productions it was played by a boy in sooty face. (Billy's response to an admonition to "go down stairs . . . and wash your face" was: "Sir, it's no use – it's dirty again in five minutes."[12]). Smut face was, logically enough I suppose, transliterated to blackface in America. However, there was another reason for the leap across the color line: Billy Black was a bootblack – a function often assumed by blacks in northern American cities, a profession that received stage blackface treatment in no less a personage than Jim Crow. Billy was, thus, a "low" character and appropriate for further blackening. The most interesting aspect of Billy Black's character was that he was a punster: "I love a conundrum better than anything in the world."[13] Punning, of course, becomes a key feature of the later minstrel show, usually in the form of repartee between the "endmen" (Mr. Bones, typically) and the "interlocutor" (Mr. Johnson). There was an easy and common popular association made between Billy Black and punning in the 1830s; when Rice played "Black Billy" in 1833, the *Spirit of the Times* published an article entitled "Conundrums Given by Mr. Rice in Billy Black, as Black Billy."[14] In league with Billy's blackness we have here a possible source for an important tradition, but one that did not fully develop until after the advent of the minstrel show in 1843. Through the period under study here, conundrums were the domain of Billy Black, the audience that enjoyed *The One Hundred-Pound Note* in the legitimate theatre, and the newspaper editors and readers that published and encouraged the developing tradition. Blackness to the patrons of this play was about comedy and commonness.

Frederick Reynolds's comedy *Laugh When You Can* enjoyed a long and lasting run. A central, major role is assigned to Sambo, a freed slave and a servant to Delville, a skirt-chasing lawyer. Sambo is the primary facilitator and expediter in a play of romantic intrigue. He is also the only musician. Counter to the blackface stereotype, however, he is the moral beacon, the one who sees through the fool's gold around him to the real stuff: "[My master] . . . made me a present of myself! – and poor as you may think the gift, I'll not sell it for all the gold in the universe."[15] Sambo's character is cut from the same cloth as the countless wise and knowing servants in eighteenth-century European plays and operas, who manage through their commonsense intelligence to see the path to a happy resolution and bring such about. There is no intrinsic reason for Sambo to function in this way, but his blackness (referred to constantly) does serve to deny him access to the erotic atmosphere that perfumes the play, which begins with Sambo searching for conveniently adjoining hotel rooms for Delville and his desired, whose husband is in Gibraltar (supposedly, of course). Like many servants in comedies of upper-class romantic intrigue, Sambo is sexually neuter; his romantic notions are not at stake in any way. One might ask, Why is he portrayed as a black at all? The answer in part is the novelty of it all, but more than this, his blackness envelops Sambo and separates him from those around him, who may like and respect him (as they do), but who do not love or desire him. He is, throughout, a catalyst, important to be sure, but incapable of entering into any of the emotional reactions he effects. By such forms of patronization Sambo assumes his rightful place in the world: always on the outside looking in. *Laugh When You Can* is thus one of the more subtle indictments of attitudes toward race held by those in the box seats to be found anywhere on the early-nineteenth-century stage.

The Irishman in London features a stereotypical representation of blackness, one recognizable as part of a sad stage tradition that continued into the near present. The farce by William McCready[16] is subtitled *The Happy African,* a reference to the central role of Cubba, a black female servant played by a white actress in blackface, and the only "black" character in the play. Predictably, Cubba is deferential, child-like, and natively wily. She is also happy to be a slave.

CUBBA: Me name Cubba, me only so many year old (holding up her fingers) when cross Bochro man catch me – me going walk one day, did
  take me from all my friend – me shall never see dem again – but missee
  so good since she buy me, me no wish to go back, though my fader great
  king.[17]

In this scene between the two characters that give the play its titles, the dimwitted white Irishman (Murtoch Delaney) – the play is a two-pronged advocate for the status quo in matters both racial and ethnic – cannot believe that Cubba's father could be a real king. Instead, he real-izes (he thinks): "Oh! it's king of the Mummors [*sic*] she manes; ay, ay, that fellow had a black face – I saw him yesterday."[18] Murtoch has in mind in this scene a romantic entanglement with Cubba – proof of his degeneracy – but in what is seemingly a turn on another stereotype, Cubba is the site of moral turpitude, and stands in opposition to the whole notion of miscegenation.

CUBBA: Me love a you dearly – but me no want you love me – dat be very
  wrong – your face white, me poor negro – me only tell you make me
  easy, den me pray for you be happy.
MURTOCH: . . . the milk of compassion rises within me for poor Cubbah –
  I wish she was not sooty – who knows – may be the journey will bleach
  her – troth it's a shame your mistress never found out that fellow, that
  advertises to whiten ladies' hands and faces, the limping Jew, he'd make
  you fair as a daisy.[19]

McCready has effectively used the blackness of Cubba to color Mur-doch, the Irishman. To the audience, Murdoch and Cubba are linked in decadence, degradation, and darkness. It is transparently the case that neither Murdoch nor Cubba belongs in London, the seat of refine-ment and white culture.

Only one of these plays incorporates significant music: the comic opera *The Padlock* by Isaac Bickerstaffe, music by Charles Dibdin. A major role is assigned to Mungo, played originally by Dibdin himself. Mungo is at least a black servant, probably a slave, but one who ex-presses resentment of his servitude and the conditions under which he labors.

Dear heart, what a terrible life am I led!
A dog has a better, that's shelter'd and fed;
   Night and day, 'tis de same,
   My pain is dere game:
Me wish to de Lord me was dead.
   Whate'ers to be done,
   Poor blacky must run;
   Mungo here, Mungo dere,
   Mungo every where;
   Above and below,
   Sirrah, come; sirrah, go;
   Do so, and do so.
   Oh! oh!
Me wish to de Lord me was dead.[20]

Severely oppressed – his "Massa" beats him daily with a rattan – Mungo does manage some small tactical victories, among which he counts being encouraged to sing and dance for the white folks, an activity that is the subject of an Act 2 aria. Other than the release offered through song, though, Mungo is a straightforward black servant role.

＊＊＊＊＊

TWO FEATURES OF MY LIST leap out for attention: Half of the plays are English, and the other half, all by or manifestly for Americans, are "Yankee" plays. *Jonathan in England* (based in turn on an English play), *The Forest Rose, The Kentuckian, The Green Mountain Boy,* and *The Yankee Pedlar* were all stage vehicles for one or the other of the period's impersonators of backcountry "down-easters." James Henry Hackett (1800–71), known also as one of the period's finest comedic Shakespeareans, was loved by audiences most for his Yankee roles, and was the most important early practitioner of the genre.[21] Among his most popular roles were those of Solomon Swap in *Jonathan in England* (sometimes called *John Bull at Home*), and Nimrod Wildfire in *The Lion of the West* (later rewritten as *The Kentuckian*), who was a Westerner but based on the down-east model. George Handel ("Yankee") Hill (1809–49) earned greater popularity than Hackett. Indeed, he was renowned as the finest Yankee interpreter of his period.[22] Hill, too, featured Solomon Swap, but also played widely Jedediah Homebred (*The*

Green Mountain Boy) and Hiram Dodge (*The Yankee Pedlar*). He interpreted, as well, Jonathan in *The Forest Rose,* although Dan Marble (1810–49), the third of the period's great Yankee interpreters, came eventually to be associated with the role.[23]

On occasion, the representation of blackness in the Yankee plays is minor and fairly benign. *The Kentuckian* is of this sort.[24] Caesar, "a free black waiter at the hotel," is a prototypical comic servant role; only in his pride in his free-black status is there any special identity. His part is small, however, and he takes his exit early, in the second scene of Act 1.

The Yankee Pedlar; or, Old Times in Virginia apparently first premiered in Boston's Tremont Theatre on 9 June 1834.[25] There were blackface parts for Pompey, a Virginia slave, and a pack of supernumeraries – "a flock of niggers!" – obviously intended to represent plantation slaves.[26] The jokes, and there are several, are of the sort that we would today call "minstrel," but seen here before they show up on the minstrel stage. For example, early in the play, Hiram (played by "Yankee" Hill) is reminded by the slaves of "Phil Water's darkey," whose "mouth was so big that he had to get it made smaller for fear he'd swaller his own head."[27] Otherwise, the blackface roles are ones of acquiescence and subservience.

The Green Mountain Boy; or, Love and Learning (also known as *Jedediah Homebred*) was written by the Boston actor and playwright (later, physician) Joseph S. Jones, and premiered on 25 February 1833 at the Walnut Street Theatre in Philadelphia. In this play,

[p]atriarch, social-snob Mr. Tompkins resolves to offer his daughter, Ellen, to a supposedly rich English peer, Lord Montague, despite her professed love for her cousin, Edward Merton of the U.S. Navy. Merton arrives in the nick of time and plans to elope with Ellen, but is stopped by his friend Sandfield. In the denouement Lord Montague, alias Wilkins, is proved not only an impostor but the scoundrel who forced Sandfield to a prison term in his stead. All ends happily when Merton finds a wife in Ellen and a long-lost father in Sandfield.[28]

Blackface is certainly more important to this comedy than to *The Kentuckian,* but in a way that says less about the characters than about how the Yankee character (and the blackface one) was perceived by the audience. The "Green Mountain" Yankee, Jedediah Homebred, personifies the pure, simple, unaffected virtues of country life; but as a result, he remains uneducated in spite of futile and comic efforts at autodidacticism. His thinking is oddly old-fashioned, and his speech patterns confirm for the audience his backwardness: "Wal, I swow this grammar's awful hard stuff to larn. I've been trying all the morning to parse chowder. Now, clam is a noun, third person spoken of."[29] When Jedediah confronts a black man (Bill Brown, a servant) for the first time in his life (thereby establishing his unsullied naturalness), the exchange, which occurs right at the beginning of the play at a critical moment in plot and character development, reveals much about Jedediah's character – and audience perceptions.

> JEDEDIAH: Halloo. Say, you, when did you wash your face last; can't tell, can you?
>
> BILL: Who's you sarsen dere, you know?
>
> JEDEDIAH: Are you a nigger? I never seen a real one, but I guess you be. Ar'nt ye – you?
>
> BILL: Who's you call nigger?
>
> JEDEDIAH: Well, I only ask'd you. Why he's mad as a hen a'ready. Did your mother have any more on you?
>
> BILL: Dere child, you better keep quiet, and mind what you say to me, you little bushwacker; if you am saucy I'll spile your profile, you mind dat now. . . . You only just trying to breed a scab on your nose, you up country looking ball face.
>
> JEDEDIAH: Look here, I'm es good a mind to take right hold and pound your black hide, as ever I had to eat. I'm like the rest of the Yankees. I don't like to begin fightin, but if I once get at it, I don't mind going on with the job no more than nothin. I'm full of grit as an egg is full of meat and yaller stuff, when the dander's raised.[30]

Humor, in this case, confirms the (seemingly) innocent nature of manifold forms of difference – between the characters and between each of them and the audience. For playgoers Jedediah's superiority, a birthright of whiteness, is questioned, and Jedediah is brought somewhat near the level of the spunky Bill Brown. In this way, *The Green Mountain Boy* and *The Irishman in London* are of a genre.

Other Yankee plays featured blackface more prominently than did *The Green Mountain Boy*. Samuel Woodworth's *The Forest Rose; or, American Farmers* (1825) – "the first 'hit' show of the American theatre"[31] – is one of the truly germinal plays in the history of Yankee impersonations, as well as one of the earliest. An (imagined) overture sets the scene:

[E]arly dawn, in the country, commencing at that hour of silence when ever the ticking of the village clock is supposed to be heard. It strikes four, and a gentle bustle succeeds, indicating the first movements of the villagers. A confused murmur gradually swells on the ear, in which can be distinguished the singing of birds, the shepherd's pipe, the hunter's horn, . . . until the united strength of the band represents the whole village engaged in their rustic employment.[32]

The play paints a benignly bucolic American paradise, where values are based in traditions. Woodworth reminded his audience at the premiere of *The Forest Rose* to "remember that while we are lords of the luxuriant soil which feeds us, there is no lot on earth more enviable than that of American Farmers."[33] Of the play itself, historian Alexander Saxton has written that "Woodworth's creation is, in certain respects, a gem of early Victorian sentimentality. It is sprightly, funny, loving. Especially its young women sparkle with . . . sensuous independence. . . ."[34] The Yankee role (Jonathan) is the comic centerpiece, the only character who shows significant growth (from exclusion to inclusion), and is involved in the play's most telling moments of "humor." While "legitimate" expressions of romantic involvement are shared between the others of the play's couples, Jonathan, who carries significant cultural baggage as an interloper and a merchant (instead of being from the rural aristocracy), receives different treatment from his romantic interest, the Deacon Forest's saucy daughter Sally. After a spat, Sally offers Jonathan a kiss, to which he willingly agrees.

SALLY: . . . [L]et me cover your eyes with my shawl, for Love, you know is blind as a bat. There, now, step a little this way, because the window is open. *(She places Rose between herself and Jonathan.)* Now! I am ready. Give me a good hearty squeeze. *(Jonathan embraces and kisses Rose.)*
JONATHAN: Now, that's a dear, sweet, kind, good girl! – Will you always love me so?
ROSE: Yes, Massa Jonathan, me lubber you berry bad.

. . .

JONATHAN: Darnation! if I have not been bussing Lid Rose! Now, Sal Forest, that is too bad! I would not serve a negro so. *[exit Sally]*

ROSE: But you did serve poor negro so, and ax me to lubber you, and now you desert me. *[exit]*

JONATHAN: Be off with you, garlic chops! Darn me, if ever I speak to Sal Forest again; but will take Granny Gossip's advice, and court Harriet Miller. Whew! how the wench smelt of onions. *[exit]*[35]

The denouement finds a parallel trick played on the villain, a lusty Englishman named Bellamy. He is set up for a tryst in the grove with the squire's daughter, or so he thinks. "Discovered" with his veiled paramour by the villagers, Bellamy asserts that the lady has come to him of her own volition.

BELLAMY: This lady is doubtless her own mistress; and since she prefers me to you, sir, I cannot see by what right you seek to control her actions. Permit me to remove this veil, lovely girl, that they may all see on whom you look with the eye of affection.

ROSE: *(Throwing aside the veil.)* On you, Massa Bellamy; cause you kissee me so sweet, in the grove, just now.

JONATHAN: Lid Rose! Ha! ha! ha!

BLANDFORD: This, then, is the Forest *Rose*, . . .[36]

The point of *The Forest Rose* is the maintenance of racial distinction, not even subtly camouflaged. Over it all is a cruel mantle of grotesque humor, woven some two or three years before the initial popularity of blackface minstrelsy. Saxton gives Woodworth the just credit for "transforming the convention of theatrical make-up into a collusion between white audiences and white performers."[37]

Historians have long noticed that the Yankee impersonators preceded minstrel impersonators in their emphasis on lower-class, working people as worthy subjects for ridicule or containment by the audience. It has not been widely observed that many of their most popular plays (and the five treated here would be right at the head of the list) involved blackface as well as "Yankee-face." In this light, some important aspects of theatrical minstrelsy should be seen as a direct spinoff of the Yankee plays.

There was, though, an important and apparently distinguishing difference between the Yankee plays and minstrel acts: venue. Theatres in the major cities were associated with genres and audiences. This was most apparent in New York City, where houses like the Park Theatre attracted a much more upscale audience than did the Bowery Theatre or the Chatham Theatre (which, according to one report in 1843, was patronized by "boys of six, eight, ten and twelve, to fifteen, sixteen and eighteen years of age").[38] If the Italian opera was in town, it typically played at the Park; opera was infrequently heard at the Chatham. Perhaps it is thus surprising that Hackett, Hill, and their plays were usually billed at the Park Theatre, as were many other examples of blackface from the legitimate repertory. To put this in perspective, George Washington Dixon and Thomas Blakeley had performed the minstrel song "Coal Black Rose" and other such songs at the Park in 1829, but there were no performances of minstrel material at the Park in 1830 or 1831. The next three years found widely scattered performances of minstrel songs by Blakeley, and "Jim Crow" Rice appeared for a single performance at the Park in 1833 – the exceptions that suggest the rule. After Blakeley's "Coal Black Rose" on 1 August 1834, there were no minstrel-type performances advertised for more than four years, this right at the early height of the craze. The next date for minstrel blackface at the Park was 27 September 1838, when Rice was billed to dance "Jim Crow" for a gala benefit for Edmund Simpson. He did not do so, however; nor was it likely he ever had real intentions of doing so, for he was on that date deep in an engagement at Boston's National Theatre. The management (likely with the contrivance of Rice) appears to have used the immensely popular actor's name to swell the house for the benefit, but without the prospect of actually sullying the Park's stage. Another benefit for Simpson (who must have been a friend of Rice's) on 8 January 1841 provided the first occasion in more than eleven years for the appearance of minstrel blackface. This night, Rice played in his *The Virginny Mummy; or, The Sarcophagus,* an exceptional event so acknowledged in the *New York Herald* for the next day. The next month, on the 18th, Rice performed again at the Park. The *Spirit of the Times,* which was purportedly a journal of theatrical news, but in fact by 1841 typically covered only the Park, filed this report.

On Thursday evening, a squad came down [from] the Bowery [Theatre] and played all manner of antics. We ventured into the house "on the sly," but found it so full of "smoke and brimstone"[39] that we made an immediate retreat. There was an immense array of talent "up" for the occasion; . . . The attraction was considered so immense that the prices were raised to the

old rates, which leads us to speak of a recent change in policy of the Park
Theatre in this particular; merely adding as to the result of the Thursday
night's work, that the pit was full, but the other parts of the house [i.e., the
boxes] disappointed the hopes of the projectors of the entertainments of that
night.[40]

From this time forth, however reluctantly, the Park made minstrel
blackface a more or less regular feature of its billing, precisely at the
time that some of its former patrons began to cry that the house was
doomed.

If the Park was the "status" theatre in New York, opera was the high
form.[41] In this light, it is instructive to look at the full program on
evenings that featured opera. (Unlike today, there were always several
pieces on a bill, even if one of them was a full-length opera.) In short,
virtually any form, genre, or style then current might be found billed
with opera, including Yankee plays, Shakespeare, comedies, farces,
songs, and melodramas – except for minstrelsy. On 31 March 1835 at the
American Theatre in New Orleans, Meyerbeer's *Robert le Diable* was
heard, as was Rice in *Oh Hush!*, and on 28 September 1841, Rice did
jump "Jim Crow" at the benefit for Clara Fisher, who sang some scenes
from *Zampa;* but these are noteworthy because truly exceptional, the
only two occasions I have been able to document in this period when
opera and blackface minstrelsy shared a billing. It must surely be that
theatre managers believed the audiences for opera and the audiences for
minstrelsy did not easily overlap.

Some quick summary generalizations about blackface on the legitimate stage through 1843.

> Blacks almost never appeared on the legitimate American
> stage during this period (unless the theatres were specifi-
> cally for blacks); blackface was a synecdoche for a black
> person.
> Most blackface characters were servants who acted like ser-
> vants; often they were mute or near-mute roles; they fre-
> quently had names like Sambo, Pompey, and Caesar.
> If the roles were more fully developed, they tended to be
> either clearly comic or clearly tragic, more commonly the
> former. Often the nature of the role was determined by
> the type of play; blackface in a farce guaranteed a happy,
> comic character, even if that character was a slave.

In almost all cases, blackness was a way of signaling "intruder" or "interloper" to the audience.
The plight of the black was not generally treated with any sensitivity or sympathy.

Throughout the plays studied here the representations are simple, if deeply felt; the characterizations are flat, with no surprising twists of character; the roles are the stuff of what we today call stereotypes.

*****

WHAT, HOWEVER, OF SHAKESPEARE'S *Othello*, a giant of a play, the most popular legitimate blackface entertainment by a factor of 3, and a work that vied with "Jim Crow" as the most performed of any blackface piece during the period? Surely *Othello* is a play of great richness, subtlety, and complexity? It is all these things, of course, and even more; but was it these things to Jacksonian audiences as well? What did it mean at the time?

Perhaps the fullest analysis of *Othello* published in the United States during the period is that by his great, gray eminence, former president (then congressman) John Quincy Adams, who wrote of "The Character of Desdemona" in the *American Monthly Magazine* of March 1836. Adams began by laying out a common defense for Desdemona's character.

There are critics who . . . defend her on the ground that Othello is not an Ethiopian, but a Moor; that he is not black, but only tawny; . . . To *them*, therefore, Desdemona is a perfect character; and her love for Othello is not unnatural, because he is not a Congo negro but only a sotty Moor, and has royal blood in his veins.[42]

Of course, Adams is employing a rhetorical device that implicitly reveals his own position, which he begins to develop more fully in the third paragraph.

My objections to the character of Desdemona arise . . . from what she herself *does*. She absconds from her father's house, in the dead of night, to marry a blackamoor. She breaks a father's heart, and covers his noble house with shame, to gratify . . . [an] unnatural passion; it cannot be named with delicacy.[43]

He asks, "[I]f Othello had been white, what need would there have been for [Desdemona to run] away with him? She could have made no better match." But he counters:

I must believe that, in exhibiting a daughter of a Venitian [*sic*] nobleman of the highest rank eloping in the dead of the night to marry a thick-lipped wool-headed Moor, opening a train of consequences which leads to her own destruction by her husband's hands, and to that of her father by a broken heart, [Shakespeare] did not intend to present her as an example of the perfection of female virtue.

He concluded this passage with "the deadly venom which inflicted immedicable wound . . . [was] but the color of Othello." At the close of the article, he stated that "the passion of Desdemona for Othello is *unnatural*, solely and exclusively because of his color." In other words, to John Quincy Adams, *Othello* is a parable, primarily about the moral dangers of miscegenation.

Adams was not alone in his belief. One of the most influential men in the theatrical circles of Jacksonian America was William T. Porter, editor of New York's *Spirit of the Times* during much of the 1830s and 1840s. His lively weekly carried sporting news, frequently involving horse races, and news of theatricals. It was a journal that appealed to those Americans with the time and money to dabble in horses and race-tracks and a subscription for a box at the Park. There is nothing to suggest that he challenged the shape of his readers' minds when he wrote in 1837:

Shakespeare was a good anatomist, and therefore made the African the easy dupe of the designing, crafty Iago, and gave him a corporeal and physical development suited to his nature, not the finesse and subtlety of a highly wrought intellect, which would have been utterly misplaced.[43]

All of which helps explain why so many of the period's finest actors chose to play Iago instead of Othello, for, although Othello was capable of great passion, according to the prevailing wisdom he was at heart a simpleminded, hulking black man given primarily to despoiling white womanhood.

*****

THE CONCLUSIONS ARE INESCAPABLE. To those better sorts in the first two tiers, the comprehension of theatrical blackface was simple: To be black was to be, at best, comic and happy, perhaps musical, and, at worst, unfortunate; to be black was to be, at best, patronized, and, at worst, condemned for the color of skin. Blackness was always understood to be fundamentally different from and lesser than the whiteness of the audience. New York Mayor Philip Hone, a regular theatregoer, helped contextualize this matter when, in his 1826 speech celebrating the opening of the first Bowery Theatre, he asserted: "It is therefore incumbent upon those whose standing in society enables them to control the opinions and direct the judgment of others, to encourage, by their countenance and support, a well-regulated theatre."[44] New York's *Courier and Enquirer*, one of the most influential papers of the time, certainly intended that there would be no ambiguity on issues of race. It reviewed at great length a production of *The Slave* at the Park Theatre in 1833, and concluded in this manner:

The opera of the *Slave* is beneath criticism, and beneath contempt. It seems to have been written for the anti-slavery society; the hero is a gentleman of colour, whose love, heroism, and disinterestedness, far surpasses anything which the degenerate whites have been able to exhibit for centuries past, and whose inflated declamations are almost too much for any body whose gravity is not like that of the Chinese philosopher, within one degree of absolute frigidity.[45]

It is not unfair to say that the representation of race on the legitimate stage was what we would today call "racist"; and it was so by very nearly official decree, emanating from the mouths of the powerful. It appears, then, that much of our conventional understanding of the relationship between blackface and race was a fixture of, if not also fixed in, the legitimate theatre – often before there even was such a thing as blackface minstrelsy.

2

Blackface in the Streets

The choir and office were left to the lay-brothers, the *quêteurs* [church-warden's assistants], cooks and gardeners. These put on the vestments inside out, held the books upside down, and wore spectacles with rounds of orange peel instead of glasses. They blew the ashes from the censers upon each other's faces and heads, and instead of the proper liturgy chanted confused and inarticulate gibberish.[1]

Night is the time when Demons meet
    To laugh at mortal sin
Each other's hellish acts to greet,
    And raise their hellish din.[2]

AFTER THE TIME OF Andrew Jackson's election to the presidency in 1828, theatrical blackface became a much more problematic cultural symbol. No longer in this era of populism was it as easy for the elite to control the actions of the stage, for audience (and political and social) dynamics underwent radical change. The best that the old guard could expect under the new circumstances was to live in a major city and have a single theatre that was identifiably *theirs*. In American metropolises that boasted two or more theatres, a kind of segregation by audience and, to some degree, repertory in fact occurred, although there was considerable fluidity. In no place was this stratification more sharply defined than in New York City, where the Park stood at the "high" end and the Chatham (sometimes called the "People's Theatre"[3]) at the "low," with the Bowery in the middle. We have already seen how the Park treated minstrel blackface; know too that the Chatham seldom billed opera or ballet. When the uses of the streets and commons, traditionally public spaces for ordinary folk, were increasingly restricted by municipal regulations – which were enforced vigorously by the watch, who got paid by the arrest – common people turned to the theatre, out of the shot of the watch, and constructed there a new public space.

First, however, they had to make the theatre their own. As class was implicitly at issue in the legitimate representation of blackness, so was it also at the crux of the battle for Jacksonian theatre, waged between, basically, the boxes and the pit (in league with the gallery). The mass media of the period are filled with the war news. No better source can be found than the *Spirit of the Times,* which by the end of the decade regularly featured articles on expensive horses, fox hunting, and fly-fishing (thus serving to fix these activities in the popular imagination as upper-class pursuits), while more and more coming to cover theatre at the Park and nowhere else. Occasionally editor Porter "slummed" and patronized (in both senses of the word) other theatres. He described with barely concealed revulsion his time at the Bowery in 1832:

By reasonable computation there were about 300 persons on the stage and wings alone – soldiers in fatigue dresses – officers with side arms – a few jolly tars, and a number of "apple-munching urchins." The scene was indescribably ludicrous. Booth played [Richard III] in his best style, and was really anxious to make a hit, but the confusion incidental to such a crowd on the stage, occasioned constant and most humorous interruptions. It was every thing, or any thing, but a tragedy. In the scene with Lady Anne, a scene so much admired for its address, the gallery spectators amused themselves by throwing pennies and silver pieces on the stage, which occasioned an immense scramble among the boys, and they frequently ran between King Richard and Lady Anne, to snatch a stray copper. In the tent scene, so solemn and so impressive, several curious amateurs went up to the table, took up the crown, poised the heavy sword, and examined all the regalia with great care, while Richard was in agony from the terrible dream; and when the scene changed, discovering the ghosts of King Henry, Lady Anne and children, it was difficult to select them from the crowd who thrust their faces and persons among the Royal shadows.

The Battle of Bosworth Field, capped the climax – the audience mingled with the soldiers and raced across the stage, to the shouts of the people, the roll of the drums and the bellowing of the trumpets; and when the fight be-

tween Richard and Richmond came on, they made a ring round the combat-
ants to see fair play, and kept them at it for nearly a quarter of an hour by
"Shrewsberry clock."[4]

Eight years later, Porter acknowledged the implicit antonym to the
whole notion of "legitimate" theatre, as well as the context for understanding, when he wrote that the "Bowery, . . . is to be transmogrified
into a Circus shortly, the 'Bowery boys' having lost their taste for the
illegitimate drama, and they never had any other."[5]

Lower-class audiences fought back against the attitudes of Porter and
his powerful friends; fought quite literally they did, for manifold are
the accounts of "theatre riots" during this period, ostensibly fomented
by working-class mobs, and generally against the more privileged or
their agents.[6] One of their weapons was economic, especially before the
ruinous depression that began with the panic of 1837. Some theatre
managers recognized the ticket power of the underclasses and began
during the 1830s to tailor bills for their patronage. No one was more
successful at this than Thomas S. Hamblin, the English-born actor and
longtime manager of the Bowery Theatre, the one in charge on the
night Porter visited. Hamblin programmed Shakespeare,[7] the newest
farces from England, American melodramas,[8] circus acts, and blackface
theatre and song – sure indications of appeal to class.

✳✳✳✳✳

HAMBLIN'S AUDIENCES, HOWEVER, entered the Bowery with experiences of blackface quite different from those in the lower tiers at the
Park. For one thing, some of them had donned it themselves; not onstage, to be sure, but in the streets. An instructive example is that of
the working-class callithumpian bands. *Callithumpians,* often masked in
chimney soot and grease, regularly took to the byways of New York,
Philadelphia, Boston, and elsewhere during the 1820s–1840s, generally
at the time of New Year's. Dressed in everything and anything (from
the outlandish to ordinary clothing worn inside out), they made "night
hideous" with their drums, whistles, horns, pots, pans, and kettles,
taunting both their social superiors and inferiors. They pelted houses
and persons with lime, flour, and other white powders, and intimidat-
ed and jousted both with free African Americans (who were nominally
below them on the social scale) and with their betters. If possible, they

managed to extract food and drink from their "victims" and ended their saturnalia on a caloric and alcoholic high.[9]

Callithumpians followed from an ancient line of three overlapping social rituals, all of which lived in folk culture and have theatrical components:[10] (1) the rite of passage, (2) that of communal regulation, and (3) that of role inversion.[11] Of these, the most discrete is the rite of passage, which usually marks the move from an age of adolescence to the period of adulthood. It is thus significant that the callithumpians, like many other such groups involved in a century of social riot, were almost always males in early adulthood.[12] The conflation of mob violence and a rite of passage is old and widespread in the West, no less a feature of the nineteenth-century social landscape than of the sixteenth or the twentieth.

The ritual of communal regulation is known generically as the *charivari*. In Anglo-American culture of the past century, it has often been called the skimmington, shivaree, or rough music, but in the period under study here it was known by many Americans as, simply, charivari.[13] In this ritual, young adult, generally unmarried males take upon themselves the well-being of the community and mark out those adjudged to be undermining the social cohesion of the community.[14] Once a fallen one was indicted by the community (informally, of course) of adultery, wanton sexuality, philandering, childlessness, condescension toward the community, wife beating, husband beating, or other such social vices, he or she would be visited in the middle of the night (and sometimes several in a row) by raucous, masked intruders, intent upon short-term destruction of the domestic peace to ensure long-term communal security. Attendant shame – the noise would alert the whole community – was meant to encourage future proper behavior.[15]

Rites governing community behaviors were not necessarily seasonal, nor were they pegged to a calendrical festival. Seasonality, though, is characteristically a feature of the third ritual form, the ritual of role inversion. This has several important forms and subforms, but the parent of them all is the feudal Lord of Misrule rite, often part of the Feast of Fools and usually held, like callithumpian parades, during the Christmas or pre-Lenten period – the one time of year in which there were enough calories available to the underclasses for indulging in a play of serious folly. In this ritual a commoner would be selected to be, essentially, "King for a Day." Not only did the feudal masters agree to such, they were generally willing participants, serving the whims of the symbolic lord, even enduring his taunts, sarcasms, and criticisms. A safety-valve simile is appropriate, for here was a chance for the underclass to blow off steam; but more than this, it served as an opportunity for rulers to hear their subjects, and perhaps redress grievances before it was too late. In this way, callithumpians, Lords of Misrules, and the rest of this lot are all dynamic indicators of social change.[16]

The Lord of Misrule ritual of inversion received its highest development in the West within the context of Carnival. That period immediately before Ash Wednesday, which might be as short as a single day or as long as two or three weeks, has fostered especially vivid forms of celebration. When Pieter Brueghel the Elder painted his famous *The Quarrel between Carnival and Lent* in 1559 (Figure 3), so rich were the traditions, theatricals, and symbols available to him that he packed them tightly onto the canvas, requiring art historians to have an extensive knowledge of the period's folk culture to unload them. The painting divides more or less in half, with Carnival on the left and Lent on the right. As Lent follows Carnival, so too, in the painting, is Lent moving into Carnival's domain. There are two Lords of Misrule represented, one of Carnival and one of Lent, for the spirit of Carnival is still dominant. In fact, their jousting confrontation characterizes the quarrel: Carnival's Lord, corpulent and surrounded by figures of excess, rides a keg; Lord Lent, emaciated and accompanied by symbols of denial, rides an uncomfortable prayer chair.

Carnival, to most Americans from the 1830s on, has meant Mardi Gras, specifically the one held in New Orleans. Social historian Samuel Kinser, who has written most intelligently about the American Carnival, enumerated the five disparate elements that came together to form the New Orleans Mardi Gras:[17]

> white plantation society's winter festivities;
> black society's need to adapt African customs in order to preserve them;
> the Gulf Coast's proximity to and influence of Caribbean festivities;
> a similar influence due to the festive practices of Anglo-Americans migrating westward; and
> the Spanish and then American commercialization of leisure time.

Figure 3. Pieter Brueghel the Elder, *The Quarrel between Carnival and Lent.* Courtesy, Kunsthistorisches Museum, Vienna.

Stewing together, these ingredients by about 1840 had produced something recognizable to modern-day revelers, a festival neither white nor black, neither sacred nor secular – if anything, an enculturated phenomenon. Appropriately, the "Lords" are the most conspicuous characters of Mardi Gras. Already by 1826, there are descriptions of black "Kings" leading the way.

> Every thing is license and revelry. Some hundreds of negroes, male and female, follow the king . . . , who is conspicuous for his youth, size, the whiteness of his eyes, and the blackness of his visage. For a crown he has a series of oblong, gilt-paper boxes on his head, tapering upwards, like a pyramid. From the ends of these boxes hang two huge tassels, like those on epaulets. He wags his head and makes grimaces. By his thousand mountebank tricks, and contortions of countenance and form, he produces an irresistible effect upon the multitude. All the characters that follow him, of leading estimation, have their own peculiar dress, and their own contortions. They dance, and their streamers fly, and the bells that they have hung about them tinkle.[18]

This description is remarkably similar to the black Mardi Gras Kings that parade still today. Whites too evolved a similar parading tradition, but called their king "Rex" and provided him with a retinue of western pseudonobility: queens, dukes, and duchesses.

Development of a full Carnival tradition in Mobile, Alabama, actually preceded the one in New Orleans. Its history is less complicated, in large part because it began and remained throughout the nineteenth century a white festival. The legend of the inception of Mobile's Carnival, probably not wholly apocryphal, has it that a young cotton broker, Michael Krafft, who had migrated there from near Philadelphia, on Christmas Eve 1831 toasted the well-being of his friends to such an extent that he lost his sense of propriety. Drunkenly, he then introduced to Mobile an old German (and Pennsylvania Dutch) Christmas tradition, that of the *belsnickel* – a form of the charivari but one pegged to a season. A belsnickel was a man masqueraded in a fur coat and cap who made his rounds on Christmas Eve frightening and delighting small children. The bells attached to his clothing or to a pole jangled diabolically as he went along, in a manner that dates back at least to the fourteenth century.[19] Typically he dispensed small presents, candy, and nuts, but then would slash at the children with a whip or rod as they went to take up their treats. Before allowing them to approach he would require from them a promise to "be good." The belsnickel was then treated to libation or food. His role was to enforce community codes of behavior, and in turn he was treated by the community.[20] Krafft, in a larkish mood and in the spirit of the season, attached bells to a rake, shook them in an annoying way, and invited others to join his "Cowbellion de Rakin Society." More than forty young male Mobilians took him up at his invitation, and turned out the next week for New Year's Eve. Outfitted in grotesque costumes and masks, they made wild, noisy "music" and behaved uproariously before the homes of upstanding Mobilians likely to advance them more drink and food. Within a decade, these street demonstrations were sanctioned by local authorities with official parades and balls. Shortly after the Civil War, the Cowbellions and other reveling societies moved their celebrations from New Year's to the season of Mardi Gras.[21]

Lord of Misrule festivities were also common in the North. In fact, northern misrule rituals by African Americans seem to have predated those in New Orleans, and are better documented. Shane White's work has laid open many of the traditions whereby eighteenth-century northern slaves elected, inaugurated, and coronated their symbolic rulers.[22] White citizens condoned and often cooperated in the misrule ritual, even allowing themselves to be taxed for the day to fund a party for the slave community. The atmosphere was clearly festive. One report, from Newport, Rhode Island, after the election of a new black governor in 1756, had it:

[T]he vanquished and victors united in innocent and amusing fun and frolic – every voice upon its highest key, in all the various languages of Africa, mixed with broken and ludicrous English, filled the air, accompanied with the music of the fiddle, tambourine, the banjo, drum, etc. The whole body moved in the train of the Governor-elect, to his master's house, where, on their arrival a treat was given. . . .[23]

The Dutch slaveowners of the Hudson Valley in the eighteenth century annually helped crown a black king on Pinkster (or Pentecost) Day.

The hour of ten having now arrived, and the assembled multitude being considered most complete, a deputation was then selected to wait upon their venerable sovereign king, "Charley of the Pinkster hill," with the intelligence that his respectful subjects were congregated. He was tall, thin and athletic; and although the frost of seventy winters had settled on his brow, its chilling

influence had not yet extended to his bosom. . . . His costume on this memo-
rable occasion was graphic and unique to the greatest degree, being that worn
by a British brigadier of the olden time. Ample broadcloth scarlet coat, with
wide flaps almost reaching to his heels, and gayly ornamented everywhere
with broad tracings of bright golden lace; his small clothes were of yellow
buckskin, fresh and new, with stockings blue, and burnished silver buckles to
all his well-blacked shoe; when we add to these the tricornered cocked hat
trimmed also with lace of gold, and which so gracefully set upon his noble
globular pate, we nearly complete the rude sketch of the Pinkster king.[24]

This account is characteristic of many in its gentle (albeit paternalistic)
accommodation, but other voices were active in opposition. White citizens of Salem, Massachusetts, petitioned the authorities "as great disorder usually exists here on [black] Election days by negroes assembling
together, beating drums, using powder and having guns and swords,
[and] a bye-law may be made to prevent these things."[25] Salem in 1758
outlawed black elections, a code that would be uniform throughout
New England by the turn into the nineteenth century, containing, if
not banishing, the black Lord of Misrule in the North.

   Among Southern slaves, many are the joyous accounts of Christmas
Day festivities. Most plantation owners allowed their slaves extra rest,
additional calories, and encouraged their entertainment and recreation.
Homes were opened for the annual punch, the slaveowner and his family might share a banquet together with his chattel, and subjects often
received gifts from the white masters and mistresses. The safety-valve
intention was evident, but co-option was implicit: To agree to celebrate
with "ole massa" was to agree to the system, in precisely the same way
that the feudal lords had maintained their positions for centuries.

   In many parts of North Carolina and Virginia, and perhaps in other
regions of the South, Christmas Day among the slaves involved a special kind of seasonal theatrical ritual.[26] This description was published
by George Higby Throop, a schoolteacher from the North, of a tradition he witnessed in 1849.

The negroes have a custom here of dressing one of their number at Christmas
in as many rags as he can well carry. He wears a mask, too, and sometimes a
stuffed coon-skin above it, so arranged as to give him the appearance of being
some seven or eight feet high. He goes through a variety of pranks, . . . and
he is accompanied by a crowd of negroes, who make all the noise and music
for his worship the John Kooner. . . . Breakfast was announced, and we had

barely left the table when a loud shout betokened the arrival of the hero of the Christmas frolic. We hastened to the door. As the negroes approached, one of the number was singing a quaint song, the only words of which that I could distinguish were those belonging to the chorus, "Blow dat horn ag'in!" One of them carried a rude deal box, over which a dried sheep-skin had been drawn and nailed, and on this, as if his salvation depended on it, the man was thumping with ear-splitting din. Beside him was another, who kept up a fierce rattle of castanets; another beat a jaw-bone of some horse departed this life; and still another had a clevis [shackle], which he beat with an iron bolt, thereby making a very tolerable substitute for a triangle. . . . John Kooner kept up, in the meantime, all conceivable distortions of body and limbs, while his followers pretended to provoke his ire by thrusting sticks between his legs. . . . They approached the piazza, knelt on the ground, and continued to sing, one of them improvising the words while the rest sang in chorus, "O! dear maussa! O! dear missus! Wish ye merry Christmas!" The expected dram was given them. A few pieces of silver were thrown from the piazza, and they left us, singing a roisterly song, . . .[27]

Harriet Jacobs, a slave from North Carolina, included a similar scene in her *Incidents in the Life of a Slave Girl*.[28] Other accounts of the John Kooners noted that the troupe was of ten to twenty men, and that some dressed like women.[29] The origin for this Christmas ritual in North Carolina might well have been imported in the imaginations of slaves brought from the West Indies, from which area the majority of American slaves came.[30] In the West Indies, festivals much like the Kooner can be traced back into the seventeenth century. The accounts are many and show us a widely and richly developed inversion ritual called John Canoe (or Jonkonnu). Slaves would select among themselves their John Canoe, who would then dress distinctively, sometimes in a European grand style, sometimes in animal skins with an animal's head mask. If the John Canoe affected European clothing, his headpiece might be fantastical, often stylistically suggesting a boat of some sort.

The John-Canoe is a Merry-Andrew dressed in a striped doublet, and bearing upon his head a kind of pasteboard houseboat, filled with puppets, representing, some sailors, others soldiers, others again slaves at work on a plantation, etc.[31]

He and most of his accompanying retinue would wear whiteface masks, more often of a rosy pink color, clearly intended to represent Caucasian skin tones.[32] There might be eight or more characters, including mu-

sicians, dancers, and other dramatis personae, at least one of whom
would be a comic character. Quite commonly, one of the members of
the troupe, which was all male, would dress as a woman, perhaps in fine
array.

Music, of a special sort, always enveloped the John Canoers:

> The confusion occasioned by the rattling of chains and slings from the
> wharves, the mock-driving of hoops by the coopers, winding the postmen's
> horns, beating militia and negro drums, the sound of the pipe and tabor, ne-
> groe flutes, gombas and jaw-bones, scraping on the violin, and singing of men,
> women, and children, with other incidental noises, make Kingston at this time
> a very disagreeable residence.[33]

> This day was the first of the Negro Carnival or Christmas Holidays, and at
> the distance of two miles from Kingston the sound of the negro drums and
> horns, the barbarous music and yelling of the different African tribes, and the
> more mellow singing of the Set Girls, came off upon the breeze loud and
> strong.[34]

> [T]hey again assembled on the lawn before the house with their gombays,
> bonjaws, and an ebo drum, made of a hollow tree, with a piece of sheepskin
> stretched over it. Some [of] the women carried small calabashes with pebbles
> in them, stuck on short sticks, which they rattled in time to the songs, . . .[35]

John Canoe, with his subjects in tow, would parade down the way, announcing his coming by bellowing, "John Canoe, John Canoe." The
troupe would visit a house or houses, present the "play," and expect to
be rewarded in kind. If no reward was offered, or if the revelers were
made unwelcome, this constituted provocation enough for resultant
rude or destructive behavior. It was at this point, as in callithumpian
parades, carnivals, and other such rituals cut from similar cloth, that
violence might erupt from its barely contained vessel. Anthropologist
Robert Dirks has shown that not only was the Christmas season in the
preemancipation West Indies a period of high caloric intake (and thus
available excess energy) by the slaves and the time of rituals of conflict,
but it was also by far the period during which a full range of black violence (murder, riot, rebellion) erupted against the white masters.[36] The
planters too realized this and ensured that counterforce was at hand.
Scott noted "the Kingston regiment marching down to the Court-house
in the lower part of the town, to mount the Christmas guards, which is
always carefully attended to, in case any of the John Canoes should take
a small fancy to burn or pillage the town, or to rise and cut the throats
of their masters, or any little innocent recreation of the kind, . . ."[37]

The term John Canoe itself suggests that much of the ritual was African in origin. Linguist Frederic Gomes Cassidy has offered the most convincing etymology of the phrase, by noticing that an Ewe-speaking witch doctor would have called himself (phonetically) *john ki-nu,* strikingly similar to John Canoe's hailing call. Additionally, the Papaws, who spoke Ewe, were the largest group of Africans imported into Jamaica in the eighteenth century.[38] It is clearly the case, however, that many aspects of John Canoe rituals are European, including important formal considerations. When the John Canoers were said to have ended their plays in the following manner (as they apparently often did in Jamaica),[39] European sources are manifestly at play: "[P]art of the representation had evidently some reference to the play of *Richard the Third;* for the man in the white mask exclaimed, 'A horse, a horse, my kingdom for a horse!'"[40] Perhaps even more significant are contemporaneous observations like this: "Then there was a party of actors. – Then a little child was introduced, supposed to be a king, who stabbed all the rest. . . . After the tragedy, they all began dancing with the greatest glee."[41] This description suggests that the John Canoe festivals were in part descended from European mumming plays of olden time, seasonal rituals of inversion themselves. Structurally, in fact, John Canoe and mumming plays are the same: Both consist of young men in masquerade who approach a dwelling noisily, threaten the inhabitants in various "playful" ways, and are bought off with gifts, money, food, or drink. The transmission of mumming plays into the West Indies has received some scholarly attention, and Roger Abrahams believes that

[the slaves] may have been taught by the overseer who was often of rural British origin, and was the member of the white segment of the plantation community with whom the slaves had the greatest contact. Or [the European rituals] may have been introduced by the European peasant groups with whom the negroes have lived and worked, such as the French fisherfolk, the British "White Bajan" or the Madeira Portuguese. No matter from whom these traditions were learned, pressures to deculturate brought about a volatile culture situation for the slaves. What emerged was a folklore tradition which had traits of both peasant Europe and aboriginal Africa and a feeling which is more identifiably West Indian as time passes.[42]

Whatever the source, the tradition continues. Pia Manadi Christmas masquerades in Jamaica and Belize today are among the last vibrant remnants of European mumming plays, although much changed by time and enculturation.[43]

Folklorists have divided mumming plays, which are typically performed from Christmas Eve through New Year's, into three types: sword-dance plays, wooing ceremonies, and hero-combat plays, although in practice their borders are seldom sharply drawn. It is possible to track these folk theatricals into the sixteenth century, when Rabelais, among others, mentioned mummers. Earlier than this the trail becomes somewhat overgrown, with only bits and pieces and hints showing up, among them the word itself in 1377.[44] Allusions to mumming crop up so far back in recorded history that some scholars think the tradition might predate the introduction of Christianity into Europe, or even that it derives from the ancient Greek comedies.[45] Clearly, mumming plays were once spread all over Europe, and they have been collected widely in the nineteenth and twentieth centuries, most systematically in the British Isles.

The most common extant mumming play is of the hero–combat sort. Again, there are as many plot deviations and character configurations as there are versions, but the following is a general outline melded to my belief that the songs and dances are as critical to performances of these plays as are words and stories.[46]

> *The Presentation.* A leader knocks on the door of a private home and seeks admittance for himself and his mummers, who are costumed, masked, unmarried males. He begs indulgence, creates a performance area, often in the kitchen, by "sweeping" a circle with a broom, and promises a good performance. One by one the characters enter and introduce themselves in rhymed and metered verse. Although the cast is fluid, there is almost always a demon or devil figure, a bizarre creature carrying a club and/ or a frying/dripping pan, a fool of some sort, a Father Christmas, and a man dressed as a woman (although these characters might overlap, e.g., the devil might also be the wildman).
>
> *The Combat.* At some point in the parade of characters, an important historical or religious figure (such as Saint George, King George, or Saint Patrick) is called a liar by

another character. A sword fight ensues, and the hero is killed.

The Cure. A doctor is summoned, and he enters in top hat, with medicine bag. Comic banter over the corpse follows while a price is negotiated to resurrect the dead hero. The doctor typically rambles on comically about his powers and accomplishment, produces a nostrum of some sort, and speaks a magic incantation over the body of the hero, who then miraculously returns to life.

Music and Dance. Songs and dances by the mummers follow, to the accompaniment of costumed musicians, and often involve the audience.

The Collection. A character enters who collects money from those present. There might be a session in which the audience tries to guess the real identities of the actors. At the last, an invitation is issued to the audience to attend a party or dance financed by the collections.

The mummers then move down the lane to the next house and present their Christmas play and their collection tray again. Often, in addition to money, food and drink are offered and consumed.

Folklorists disagree about why these plays came about and what they meant; but some of the best arguments remember that mumming plays are solstice celebrations. In fact, at the winter solstice, science and common sense both tell us that light begins its slow triumph over dark, a matter of great significance to high-latitude agrarian societies without artificial light, where "dark" had a palpability difficult for us, in our electrified age, even to imagine. Light truly meant life, and that its "triumph" occurred at a season of harvest, meat, fresh drink, and general plenty (hence, energy) only confirmed the importance of the "defeat" of darkness.[47] Functionally, purposes are sometimes more straightforward. Mumming plays ensured the circulation of marriageable males into the homes of nubile females, and committed each to a subsequent, unmasked, festive event, usually a dance. Henry Glassie, somewhat apologetically, offers a convincing Freudian interpretation of the cast in a typical Northern Irish mumming play, which begins with a jolly old man bearing "a great club as well as a suggestively feminine dripping pan" and concludes with Miss Funny, who carries a leather bag, and collects the money for the big party;[48] the intentions here are pretty clear. Additionally there are political aspects of mumming: The mummers visited all houses in the community, and once inside the homes of the wealthy and powerful often proffered a brand of social criticism. On occasion, they were even more explicitly political, as in the Luddite riots in England between 1811 and 1816, when rioting and mumming were thoroughly melded by blackfaced young working-class men.[49]

Mumming plays were brought to the New World in steerage with immigrants from England, Ireland, Germany, and other points in Europe, and they subsequently show up both in American cities and in deep country.[50] Philadelphia's court records for 1702 contain an indictment served on one John Smith for "being maskt or disguised in women's apparel; stalking openly through the streets of this city from house to house on or about the 26th of the 10 month [the day after Christmas]. . . ."[51] Bostonian Samuel Breck remembered mummers in his city from "as late as 1782."[52] Mumming plays have been collected in the mountains of Kentucky and West Virginia. There is copious newspaper documentation of mumming in nineteenth-century Pennsylvania,[53] and a Philadelphia newspaper of 1913 claimed that mummers practiced "right on up to twenty years ago."[54] Mumming plays developed characteristics specific to the American history and situation, as might be expected. American heroes replaced those of England and Ireland: Instead of Saint George and Saint Patrick there was George Washington.[55] Still, mumming plays have not been found in the United States in anything like the numbers found in Europe. Whether it is because American culture is folkloristically undercollected (arguably the case) or because it is too little based on the ideal that gave rise to mumming in the first place – the centrality of community – is still open to debate.

If one widens the lens to take in all ritual theatricals, one finds that early- and mid-nineteenth-century white Americans, from laborers through the middling classes, likely had a more extensive knowledge of them than we might think. Forms of carnival were not only known in this country, they were vital in many areas from New England to the Gulf Coast. An informant of Pennsylvania belsnickeling demonstrated his extensive knowledge of seasonal rituals when he explained:

I have often heard it said that [belsnickeling] was following out a custom established in the south when slaves would appear before their masters on Christmas Eve and there dance and sing and play the banjo for the master and guests' entertainment and after each number the slaves would be treated to the best in the house, the one occasion of the year.[56]

Even John Canoe was likely familiar to many Americans. Interest in life in the West Indies was great, as shown by the manifold first-person travelogues published and consumed during the time. "White man's burden" and active British abolitionism drove many of these works, which nearly always treated the lives and customs of slaves, including their seasonal theatricals.[57] Of mumming, the word and the performance were in unqualified usage in America, suggesting a tradition still near the forefront of the culture's memory. Schoolmaster Throop's 1849 account identified the custom of the John Kooner with mumming.[58] The *Philadelphia Sunday Dispatch* wrote of the traditional Christmas Eve roistering:

[T]hese calathumpian doings, rowdy as they are, come in direct descent from the freaks of those Christmas observers of Queen Elizabeth's time, who had their "Lords of Misrule," their "Christmas Princes," and their "Abbots of Unreason" and who kept up the frolic from Christmas even until the grand culminating point of the festival at "Twelfth Night."[59]

And, some years later:

The Mummers exist among us in degenerated forms as "Fantasticals" or "Calithumpians" – men who render the night hideous by their yelling, drumbeatings, and horn-toutings, and the day disgusting by their outrageous masking and foul disguises.[60]

When the callithumpians were sanctioned by civil authority in 1900 as the Mummers Parade, a cultural memory was manifest that knew the present spoke with the past.[61]

Outside of seasonal rituals, charivari – by name and by function – was known to many. It did, however, sometimes take forms and names different from those practiced and uttered in the Old World. Callithumpians, for example, often escaped from their role at New Year's and assumed the functions of charivari: At the College of William and Mary in 1847 students greeted an unpopular professor with a "callithimpian band of tin pans and horns and all non-musical instruments, till he must be deaf."[62] Moreover, there are hundreds (thousands?) of recorded instances of tarring and feathering, a variant of the charivari. This practice was usually followed by the dishonored person being forced to "ride the rail," related directly to "riding the stang," or the "hobbyhorse" in English rough music; again there are manifold examples.[63] "Lynching parties" and other vigilante actions were more malicious extensions of the charivari in America. Even the Ku Klux Klan seems to be derived from a tradition of "whitecapping," and was intended to enforce community mores, and some of its early-twentieth-century incarnations might have been substantial forces for ensuring the community's health.[64]

To pause for summary, important characteristics bond the various genres of folk theatricals introduced here.

> Young males, generally unmarried, are largely responsible for them.
>
> Masking of some sort is important.
>
> Violence is always barely contained, and it is possible for it to boil over.
>
> Each has music or sounds that approach what nonperformers would call noise.
>
> Although the surface is jovial, easy scratching reveals a dynamic of protest against social structures.
>
> Theatricals distort reality, thereby unsettling social norms, which allows for the possibility of reordering.
>
> The community obtains a mechanism to express its displeasure with some social condition, perhaps even remedy it.
>
> Each is great fun for the participants, and generally entertaining to viewers.

✷✷✷✷✷

IN SPITE OF THE LENGTHS to which I have gone to frame the family tree of Western ritual theatricals and abstract its characteristics, my primary interest here is to understand early blackface minstrelsy. Even on the surface, it appears that there were adequate numbers of Americans who knew enough about the ritual family, in whatever part and depth and corner of their collective imaginations, to support awarding folk theatricals partial responsibility for engendering a new form of

American popular theatre. The hard evidence for this actually having
happened is not easy to come by. I have yet to find irrefutable evidence
that T. D. Rice heard a John Canoe sing a song that he then introduced as "Jump Jim Crow," or that Dan Emmett had once been a
blackfaced callithumpian banging away on a noisy banjo, although there
are tantalizing suggestions of both. I have read minstrel endpieces and
farces that might be distant relatives of a mumming play, but not one
that *is* a mumming play. However, this is really not surprising. Plebeian
cultures, from which have come most of the audiences for folk theatricals, have until recently preserved their histories mainly in slippery oral
and collective memories. Further, "the folk" seldom expressed their
histories linearly and causally; their myths are elliptical, even recursive,
returning near a point and starting over again with no intention of
reaching the same conclusion. In the place of empiricism there is evidence once or twice reflected, dimmed by time and circumstance, and
brightened by the imagination; but still, I believe, vivid and full of significance.[65]

Some of the evidence follows from association, real enough to participants and audiences, but suspect to the scholar. A callithumpian procession in Philadelphia on New Year's Day 1834 comprised "Indians,
hunters, Falstaffs, Jim Crows and nondescripts,"[66] this only two years
after Jim Crow was first danced on the boards in Philadelphia. In Boston a "Calathumpian nigger" named "Jack of Spades" offered "to
dance, upon a wager, with any white imitator of negro extravaganzas."[67]
The cover of the *Kickapoo Whoop*, a minstrel songster from the late
1830s, whose title refers vaguely to Indians and Davy Crockett–like tall
tales, has a rough woodcut of Jim Crow featured prominently, and is
written, so the cover claims, by Santa Claus[68] (Figure 4). The minstrel
song "Settin' on a Rail" (1836) was widely understood to refer to "riding a rail."[69] The tune to the popular "Sich a Gettin' Upstairs" (ca.
1834) is perhaps modeled after "Getting Upstairs," an English morris
dance tune.[70]

One song in particular, "Clare de Kitchen," bears uncanny resem-
blance to certain aspects of mumming. As mentioned earlier, mumming
plays typically began with an entrance into the kitchen by a Captain,
who was sometimes in blackface and often carried a broom. Once in the
kitchen, the Captain then recited a verse something like this one from
Philadelphia in 1844:

Figure 4. De Kickapoo Whoop; or, Pee Wee Warbler, by Santaclaus. New York: Elton & Harrison, ca. 1840. Courtesy, American Antiquarian Society.

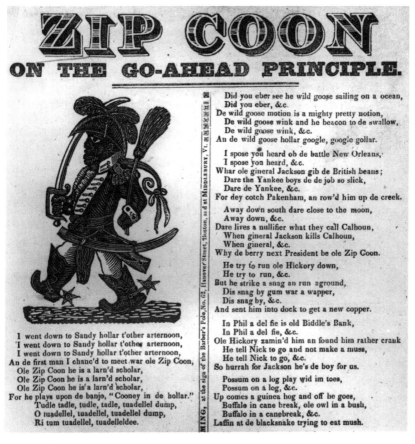

Figure 5. "Zip Coon on the Go-Ahead Principle." Broadside, published by Leonard Deming (Boston), ca. 1832–7. Courtesy, American Antiquarian Society.

Room, room, brave gallants, give us room to sport.
For in this room we wish for to resort.

With his broom or stick he cleared and defined the performance space, usually a circle. (There are as many variations as there are mumming plays.[71]) Compare this to the opening verse of "Clare de Kitchen," a highly popular song that was being performed by both T. D. Rice and George Washington Dixon as early as 1832 (and cf. Figure 5):

In old Kentuck in de arternoon,
We sweep de floor wid a bran new broom,
And dis de song dat we do sing,
Oh! Clare de kitchen old folks young folks
Clare de kitchen old folks young folks
Old Virginny never tire.

The images are slippery – they always are – but function in "Clare de Kitchen" much as they did in the mumming plays. The Captain proclaimed the kitchen to be a temporary extension of the mummers's domain – the street or lane – thus converting a private space into a public one. Theatres were equally ambiguous in the 1830s, for a ticketholder was welcomed from the street into a space that suggested the public, but was in fact semiprivate. (With the notion of privacy assuming greater importance yearly, the New Theatre, which opened in New Orleans in 1841, featured a lock and key to every box.[72]) "Clare de Kitchen" used the Captain's prop to sweep a symbolic space for public performance, an image that would not have been lost on the audience; nor on the prostitutes at "Long Wharf – Boston" who, we remember, did the same thing.[73]

✳✳✳✳✳

THERE ARE AT LEAST THREE primary features of early blackface minstrelsy that closely resemble attributes of festive folk theatricals: blackface masking, dramatic characterization, and the music itself. I shall discuss the first two here and reserve the third for treatment in subsequent chapters.

Blackface Masking

Important early evidence of mumming plays shows up in two paintings by Brueghel: His *A Kirmess in the Netherlands* features both a Sword Dance and a Saint George (hero-combat) play; the other instance was mentioned earlier, *The Quarrel between Carnival and Lent* (see Figure 3). In the Carnival section of this latter work, almost unnoticed in the center of the upper left quadrant of the painting, are five characters in a group before a half-door. One appears as royalty of some kind, with a sword; another might be carrying a scythe; a man has a club over his shoulder; another in white is turned away but might be carrying a broom (!) and appears to be receiving something from those in the house; and the last, walking toward the viewer, looks like a strawhatted woman hidden behind a white mask. All of the characters are archetypal to the genre, which leads to the conclusion that the "woman" is actually a cross-dressed male. Most interestingly, the Beelzebub (with the club) is seemingly in blackface. This form of masking fits nicely with conventional interpretations of mumming that equate blackness with the grotesque and night, both attributes of Carnival; it is further consistent with the hero-combat plays in which we see that the symbol of light/tranquility/sun triumphs over dark/turmoil/night.

Brueghel's mummer is no exception. The use of blackface is extremely common in mumming plays throughout its recorded history, in all times and places. The wildman, Little Devil Doubt, Cooney Cracker, and any number of other mumming characters could be and have been played in blackface. Beelzebub, or another form of the demon/devil, would typically be in blackface.[74] Chambers's listing of collected English hero-combat plays, mainly from the nineteenth century, includes several with blackface characters, and at least three in which all the characters are in blackface! Folklorist Alex Helm also points to the blackface character in one of the earliest collected hero-combat folk theatricals, published in chapbook form as early as 1771. Not just a black-faced Beelzebub, his name was Sambo.[75]

Scholars have noticed the relationship between mumming and morris dancing, another seasonal theatrical usually but not always associated with May Day. Morris dancers, like mummers, assumed personae through the use of masks and disguises; characters like Robin Hood, Maid Marian, the hobbyhorse, and the fool appeared and danced out the content of the folk drama.[76] Morris dancing, which might be as old as mumming, and perhaps even more widely spread throughout Europe, seems related to the Spanish "moresca," from the root word "Moor." Etymology helps explains why at least one morris dancer, and often all of them, characteristically performed in blackface, from the early record to the near present.[77] It also suggests origins for morris dancing during the period when European soldiers were pitted against the Moors, for the English a three-hundred-year span from 1152 to 1451.

Morris dancing in the United States enjoyed something of a vogue
during the formative years of blackface minstrelsy. In New York the
Courier and Enquirer of 3 January 1834 advertised a "Grand Fancy Dress
Ball, Masonic Hall, ... By particular desire the much admired Comic Morris Dance, by ten gentlemen." Ostensibly the same cast made
appearances at dances in New York "by particular desire" in February
and April that year.[78] The next year, for a "Grand Fancy Dress Ball"
in New York's Tammany Hall, there was featured "the celebrated
comic Morris Dance, by fourteen young Gentlemen, pupils of Mr.
Parker."[79] Barely more than a week later at the Bowery Theatre a
"Company of Morice Dancers" were billed, "who will go through an
entire new Comic Laughable Extravaganza."[80] Moreover, at Christmas-
time in 1839, the Broadway Circus in New York featured blackfaced
minstrels James Sanford and Joel Sweeney (to both of whose music the
Boston whores later danced) in "Novel Duetts, Songs, &c," a melodrama (*The Dying Moor's Defence of His Flag*, obviously with blackface
characters), and a "Comic Morris Dance by the whole company," virtually a full evening of holiday blackface entertainment.[81]

Although the whole notion of blackface masquerade among the
common peoples of northern Europe might have first followed from direct contact with dark-skinned Moors (but probably did not), the facts
seem to be that the rituals using chimney soot soon lost much if not
all of the racial association, and blackface masking became a means of
expressing removal from time and place through disguise. Even today,
morris dancers are not generally thought to be representing people of
African descent. Nonracial folk blackface masking was common in nineteenth-century America too, and strove to achieve similar ends. One
such telling example is that of the belsnickel. The *Philadelphia Pennsylvania Gazette* of 29 December 1827 – almost two years before George
Washington Dixon first sang the minstrel song "Coal Black Rose" –
wrote of Christmas festivities:

Our readers are perhaps aware this Mr. Bellschniggle is a visible personage –
Ebony in appearance, but Topaz in spirit. He is the precursor of the jolly old
elf "Christ-kindle," or "St. Nicholas," and makes his personal appearance,
dressed in skins or old clothes, his face black, a bell, a whip, and a pocket full
of cakes or nuts; and either the cakes or the whip are bestowed upon those
around, as may seem meet to his sable majesty.[82]

The belsnickel's traits, including blackface, held throughout the century.[83] The chronicle suggests, moreover, that from the belsnickel, callithumpians and Philadelphia Mummers learned to black up.

It is often difficult to construct an understanding that places race at the center of folk blackface; sometimes, as in the case of the belsnickel, it is impossible. In fact, it appears that in the culture of common people, masking in blackface was making a statement more about what you were not than about race. Belsnickels, callithumpians, mummers, and morris dancers were manifestly not trying to represent persons of African heritage. To black up was a way of assuming "the Other," in the cant of this day, a central aspect of the inversion ritual. Some of the most compelling evidence that this is in fact what happened comes from eighteenth- and nineteenth-century Caribbean John Canoe rituals, where slaves generally put on ritual *whiteface* theatricals, personifying *their* Other.[84] In the all-telling twist, there are accounts of early nineteenth-century *white* Jamaicans, before the full development of blackface minstrelsy in the United States, putting on their own John Canoe festivals, but in *blackface,* completing the full circle of inversion.[85]

Of course, on one important level blackface minstrelsy took as its signature characteristic the representation of black people, but in the ritual background loomed more profoundly Otherness, the accumulation of centuries of metaphorical use. Masquerade in folk theatricals allowed participants to act in ways generally unacceptable to official authority, to speak the unspeakable, and to connect the mask "with the joy of change and reincarnation, with gay relativity and with the merry negation of uniformity and similarity," for "[i]t rejects conformity to oneself."[86] However, to laugh at or even ridicule the mask is, curiously and somewhat ironically, an especially powerful form of acknowledging, or even engaging, Otherness. Perhaps it is much more: a way of actually incorporating the Other into Self, being coopted by it. Max Gluckman's analysis of saturnalias holds that opposition (or rebellion) does not necessarily follow from underclass engagement in a ritual of Misrule; rather, it more often implicitly affirms the Lord of Rule. Grotesque mimicry is affirmation; existing social structures are confirmed.[87] However, the Lord of Misrule ritual also demands that those in superior positions willingly take on the role of servants. On the face of things, the high becoming low presents us with a contradiction to Gluckman's

axiom, for, seemingly, structures *are* inverted, hence thrown into question – hardly a form of affirmation. We are thus left with a paradox,
where Lord of Misrule rites both necessarily affirm and destabilize. The
answer to the dilemma *is* the paradox, for generally the status quo is
maintained, with the power still invested in the powerful; but there are
exceptions enough, shown most convincingly in Dirks's work with re-
volts and rebellions in the West Indies during periods of ritual misrule,[88] to prove (the endurance of) the rule. From the perspective of
the powerful a static paradox was the best they could hope to maintain.

To anticipate somewhat evidence that is gathered in later pages:
When the institution of American slavery required a national dialogue,
blackface minstrelsy might have been one of the most effective of all
the forms it took, for it was, like the folk theatricals, implicitly paradoxical and dynamic.

Dramatic Characterization

Definition through an aesthetic of opposition was part of blackface minstrelsy from the early years. Two character stereotypes generally prevailed: the slave (of whom the ragamuffin Jim Crow would be the most
popular example) and the dandy (Zip Coon, Jim Brown, Dandy Jim,
and host of others). Similar images, often predating minstrelsy, can be
found throughout the folk theatrical family tree. Zip Coon was around,
at least sartorially, when the Pinkster King in New York wore a British
brigadier's jacket of scarlet, a tricornered cocked hat, and yellow buck-
skins.[89] So too was he, in dress and in grotesquely bad taste, in 1788
when Marsden reported on the Christmas festivities among Jamaican
slaves, closing with language and observations that resonate with those
of "highbrow" Jacksonian theatre reviewers.

The prime negroes and mulattoes pay a visit to the white people during the
festivity, and are treated with punch; one of them attends with a fiddle, and
the men dress in the English mode, with cocked hats, cloth coats, silk stockings, white waistcoats, Holland shirts, and pumps. They dance minuets with
the mulattoes and other brown women, imitating the motion and the steps of
the English but with a degree of affectation that renders the whole truly laughable and ridiculous.[90]

An anonymous resident of Jamaica in 1797 wrote of the John Canoers and how they "claim attention" with the "fantastic modern cut of their clothes, often of silk and sometimes enriched with lace; a quantity of hair on the head as preposterously dressed as some European beaux."[91] Cynric Williams, commenting on a John Canoe in Jamaica in 1823, reported that "[t]hey were all dressed in their best; some of the men in long-tailed coats, one of the gombayers in old regimentals."[92]

As for Jim Crow, we recollect the John Kooners in North Carolina who had "a custom here of dressing one of their number at Christmas in as many rags as he can well carry."[93] Early-nineteenth-century belsnickels were "dressed in skins or old clothes," with an "uncouth appearance – made up of cast-off garments made parti-colored with patches."[94] Callithumpians were similarly accoutered. Newfoundland mummers reported that "sometimes you'd dress in fine clothes, sometimes you'd dress in rags, you know."[95]

The Zip–Crow type of character opposition is found throughout the literature on folk theatricals, so commonly a feature that few folk plays do not employ it. Any John Canoe (of whom Zip is a parallel genre) had his foil, a Jim Crow type; Saint George needed his Beelzebub, and George Washington (the mumming character) his Cooney Cracker (who "chawed tobacker").[96] The "pairing" device in blackface minstrelsy is enriched by a sort of doubleness, for, lest we forget, these were white men playing at blackness. In the same persona, the blackface minstrel "Lord" was simultaneously white man and Beelzebub. From such a basic formulation, there follows the double wildman (*"Jump* Jim Crow"), or the wildman who "is a larn'd skolar" and "our President shall be" (Old Zip Coon) – both doubly preposterous and hilarious personae.

A similar double dynamic is at play in the character opposition between white male-as-black male and white male-as-black male-as-black female. No mumming play is without a female impersonator. Frequently during my period of study, and ubiquitously after 1843, minstrelsy featured the "nigger wench," a white man in black drag.[97] There is no question but that the prototype for minstrelsy's need to give slanderous image to the name of woman (white or black) could have come from the legitimate stage; but at least as likely, given early minstrelsy's male, generally common-class constitution,[98] is that the prompt for cross-dressing characters came from the traditions of ritual playacting much closer to the culture of the folk.

$$* * * * *$$

BY NOTING CONCURRENCES and resonances, I suggest here that early blackface minstrelsy was deeply rooted in a long line of folk theatricals, as the audience for and performers of minstrelsy were only recently removed from their accepted place in a longstanding, rural, often feudal, European culture. Accepting this relationship explains some perplexing problems about early minstrelsy. For one, there is the question of the incredible vitality of the genre from the moment of its "mythical" birth in 1829 when Dixon sang his "Coal Black Rose." The sense of "novelty" (a concept implicitly in opposition to the normative) might account for some of the early popularity, but would mitigate against minstrelsy's staying power. Something else is at work here. Could it be that audiences already possessed cultural knowledge of the tropes, even some of the structures and manners of expression? A zephyr from Great Britain, which succumbed to American minstrelsy after 1836, suggests that there might be some truth to this supposition, for English audiences were in a special position to appreciate minstrelsy: In many ways it simply brought images, symbols, and forms back home.[99]

Beyond these easy, but telling, observations there are contexts and landscapes in which folk theatricals and blackface minstrelsy both lived that may be even more significant. To see them together, as members of the same family, allows for new and different perspectives on how minstrelsy came to be in the first place and on what it meant to its time, and means to ours.

Any interpretive study of artistic genres must deal with the audience. Scholars seem in agreement that the house for blackface minstrelsy, especially in its first fifteen years or so, was generally male and drawn from the urban working class.[100] Given this, it is somewhat surprising that the dramaturgical wellsprings for minstrelsy have generally been assumed to be located in legitimate theatre, which, as Chapter 1 demonstrated, confirmed more elite tastes and values than those of the common people. Reasonably, a better site for audience definition would be that whence the audience had just come, or folk theatricals. We should have been led in this direction by noting similar ways in which folk dramas and minstrelsy manipulate characters and subjects. It is no fresh observation that the simple use of blackface signals to the audience that what follows is not to be taken at (white)face value, but at burlesque value, whether the audience be in a kitchen, on a street, or in the Bowery Theatre.[101] From this, it is no great leap to imagining that the use of blackface on the stage proper signaled parody of the legitimate "official" stage, in the same way that blackfaced "fantasticals" burlesqued the military.[102] Can Daddy Rice jumping Jim Crow onstage do anything but transform the stage (and all that implies) into a distortion of itself? By supporting antitheatre, common Americans delegitimized highbrow "Theatre" and turned the institution toward the audiences' need for expressive, common, lowbrow "theater."

The evidence is that they succeeded admirably. Common people controlled what happened on the minstrel stage in ways they never had in the legitimate theatre. The reasons for this happening when, where, and how it did have most fundamentally to do with social situations. I shall use the example here of mumming plays in a new social context, but any other folk theatrical would serve equally well.

Mumming thrives in rural plebeian societies. Thomas Hardy's extended treatment of mumming in *The Return of the Native* sets the scene nicely, if in a somewhat romanticized way. People depend heavily on each other for their collective and individual survival. Christmas mummers in Glassie's Northern Ireland typically visited every house in their area, and extended a welcome to all to attend the party they threw on Miss Funny's proceeds.[103] They served to bond a community through imagination, wonder, and laughter, and to define the things that threatened it, which might range from winter and sun-shorted days and famine to Oliver Cromwell and the English Protestants. Generally, the United States neither provided nor encouraged the social and physical environment in which mumming had traditionally flourished. In fact, in North America only coastal, isolated communities in Newfoundland established anything like the relationship to the land that held in England and Ireland, with their "openfield villages in which people lived closely together and worked cooperatively";[104] and it was only in Newfoundland that a vital mumming tradition was established and lived, almost up to the present. However, although it is true that mummers and their audience left Europe in steerage bound for the New World, and that often upon arrival they set about sculpting the individual out of the American frontier, in many other instances they set roots in New York's notorious fifth ward or in Irish Boston or Philadelphia's Moyamensing district. The plebeian urban American community is the analogue to the plebeian rural British community. In the United States the impulse toward mumming remained, but it was blunted by the cosmic difference between the Old World and old epoch and the new. Inevitably, once acclimated to their new place and time, these people created their own theatricals – ones we today brand "popular theatre."

Of course this new urban culture of the common was not nearly as homogeneous as the old, as persons of different social and cultural backgrounds were thrown together. Many tried to maintain some degree of ritualistic identity, unique to their own communities, but such was a rearguard action. The cities were a machine for acculturation, and the popular theatre both invested in the enterprise and benefited from it. New rituals issued from the wedding of old ones, as cultural manners came to know and like each other: Pure blood lines mixed with the stuff of the Other, procreating the new.

Minstrelsy was obviously startling in its immediacy. Reports of audience behavior confirm that the house felt fully in its right to respond spontaneously, forcefully, and vocally to events on the stage. More than perhaps any other form of American theatre in the period, minstrelsy involved the audience. The most successful actors were those who could sense the needs and moods of the audience, and play to them; as a result, it was generally necessary to be a good improviser of both line and action, a gift attributed to Rice on many occasions.[105] Something quite similar happened with folk theatricals. Glassie recorded the memories of old-time Irish mummers:

[The] audience did not sit quietly. Their laughter was great and loud. They felt free and nearly obligated to comment on the happenings, goodmanning each performer. One woman is remembered for her comical wish that her doctor were half so good as the one who rushed to the dead man's side. . . .

The distance between the mummers and their audience began to decrease with Captain Mummer's rap. It further diminished through the requests and subscriptions, and was lost in the guessing tussle – a happy merging of audience and performer in a single act.[106]

Good mumming performances must have been electric. A woman reportedly became hysterical when Beelzebub was killed by Prince

George in her kitchen.[107] On the cusp of the twenty-first century, in an age replete with social mechanisms for ensuring distance, it is difficult to imagine the pleasurable jolt provided by unmediated sound/noise/color/flash/action directly in your face. Likewise, to define blackface minstrelsy as only a case of ritual inversion is to ignore its performance aspect, a unit of the moment that does not lend itself easily to definitional oppositions and inversions. That moment, known to all humans, is both static and dynamic, and seeks to reconcile style and meaning. We might have better audience data on carnivals and mumming plays than we do on minstrel shows, and overwhelmingly informants speak not about symbolic oppositions or qualities or politic intentions, but about the whole great thing, and of how it makes one feel good, or even great. Samuel Kinser's *Carnival, American Style* confronts this problem, one of scholarly method and ethnographic experience, and solves it by quilting a book, with black-and-white patches of expert scholarly analysis set off by colorful swatches of Kinser's own visceral joy at the moment of Mardi Gras.

A similar kind of understanding of the motley experience of minstrelsy is a job for the imagination, and one worth being about.

To turn to the manifest crux of blackface, race: Starting from some understanding of the intensity of experience that surrounds, for example, a mumming play, one might be able, theoretically, to imagine that early blackface minstrelsy was about race without being necessarily racist. The theatrical imagination set up a dynamic between people of different races that provides also a means for incorporation.[108] That is, in parallel with the tradition of grotesque humor among the folk, could minstrelsy too be filled with "the positive regenerating power of laughter?"[109] Didn't slaveowners hope that the John Canoers felt better toward them after the exhilaration of Christmas Day? To borrow from Eric Lott's happy formulation, was minstrelsy about racial thievery, but also love and the pleasure we take in it? As scholar Samuel Kinser noted in a moment of self-revelation:

Some people use the codes to construct ceremoniously, others to construct grotesquely. But since the constructions are only part of Carnival, and tend to change their significance afterwards, what indeed do these dreams mean? Maybe the best thing to do, you know, even if – just a minute, let me check, I think, yes, it seems so – even though it's now Ash Wednesday, is to laugh about it.[110]

A view of the total minstrel performance, mediated through laughter, shifts the locus of meaning. Historians have typically interpreted the minstrel show through its texts: examining song lyrics, looking at minstrel plays, conundrums, and stump speeches, viewing extant images, reading reviews and biographies. These often, in unambiguous tones of black-and-white print, proclaim virulent racism. To imagine a performance of a minstrel show, however, is to envision something else. On the very surface of it, working-class white men paid scarce specie – perhaps a third of their day's wages[111] – to watch the antics of "black" men. This alone is an astonishing acknowledgement of presence. These were not the early century voyeurs who peeped in on real black people at Congo Square in New Orleans, but people up close to an issue that had shades of gray, an ambiguity developed in subsequent chapters.

The most useful models available to us from folk theatricals are those in which there is a downward role inversion from social power: where whites put on blackface, where men dress as women, where the fool is played. There is no question that derision is intended; but so too is incorporation of the Other. The power of subsequent laughter, a form of truth, joins rather than divides. Performance suggests time and again that early blackface minstrelsy was as much about healing as about wounding, as the ancestral theatricals also taught understanding.

Paradoxically, however, all festive theatricals are joyous, healing, and entertaining, yet also potentially violent. All of them have been banned repeatedly by the Lords of Rule for becoming kinetic.[112] One wonders if the relationship between the acting and the action is a singular one, where performance becomes violence and violence is performance. Clearly, the callithumpians enjoyed the ruckus, as they enjoyed the acting; other ritual actors held similar views. This point might be difficult to comprehend today, for much has changed since the time of the callithumpians. By the 1840s, theatre managers were intentionally removing us, the audience, from the visceral and essentially performative aspect of theatre and encouraging an approach from the realm of the intellectual.[113] Theatres got darker, quieter, more secure, and more private. Against this picture, imagine a scene involving conflict and swordplay brought directly into your kitchen, not five feet from where you sit or stand. Such imagining helps one understand how John Canoe was frightening;[114] or how the Irish mummers caused children to become upset, or an adult woman to believe that a man had been killed in her kitchen;[115] or why Newfoundland mummers, typically not in blackface, were called "the Dark Ones."[116] Even the belsnickel, the progenitor of the mythically jolly Santa Claus, would visit Christmas Eve and

[the children] could hear his coming which was terrible in heinous noises, rattling of chains, etc. His appearance was still more frightful, wrapped in furs or skins like a huge animal. No wonder the children hid and sometimes fell into fits when they saw him.[117]

Then imagine a system, slavery, that functioned only because of the threat of violence, with but a single ritual release day, one on which slaves can visit symbolic violence on the masters, and it is easy to understand how life spilled over into art.

What does an understanding of folk blackface tell us about early minstrelsy's meaning to its audience? Again, let us not underplay the manifest fact that early minstrelsy is a "delineation" of African Americans, for at the most obvious level, this is clearly what is going on. Moreover, sometimes the burlesques are nothing more than crudely comic degradations of a class of less fortunate people for the purposes of group aggrandizement. However, we must not forget Raymond Williams's axiom that any historical moment for those outside the circle of power is a cultural mixture of the residual and the emergent, the result of ebbing and flowing of the past and the present.[118] We must then set ourselves the quixotic task of capturing the tide.

3

Jim Crow

Oh, Thomas Hamblin is arrived, who all New York does know
To be better than the best in Hamlet and Othello –
Oh his Wirginius is fuss chop – his Brutus isn't slow;
But if he makes you weep too much, come back to see Jim Crow.
    Jump about, wheel about, and Jump Jim Crow &c.

I have given you this gem of poetry entire, that you may perceive how
well founded is my assertion, that tinsel melo-drama and fustian farce
have drove their Juggernaut car over the old worship of the drama, and
enthroned folly paramount upon the fall of reason.[1]

THE CAREER OF Thomas Dartmouth Rice (1808–60) is well discussed, if not well documented. As a young man Rice was a carpenter apprentice in his native New York City. He also appeared occasionally in New York theatres in supernumerary roles in the mid- and late 1820s. By 1828 Rice had turned to the theatre full-time and gone to train in the southern troupe of Noah Ludlow, where he was "to do any thing on the stage, and to assist the 'property-man.'"[2] During this time he also performed with the western troupe managed by Sol Smith, generally in the towns and cities of the Ohio River valley. James Gordon Bennett, the influential editor of the *New York Herald*, came to be on close terms with Rice and wrote biographically of him in 1837 that he was based in Kentucky during the late 1820s and stayed there for three years, a period consistent with what is known of

Rice's movements. While there, so Bennett claimed, he played small parts, usually comic, for which he showed an early flare; he also likely used the opportunity to study "the negro character in all its varieties. He eat [*sic*], drank and slept with them, went to their frolics, and made himself the best white black man in existence."[3]

The myth that quickly grew up around Rice maintains that on some occasion during 1828–31 he observed an old black stablehand (sometimes said to have been crippled), who sang a funny kind of song and danced a peculiar hopping, unjointed dance. Rice then outfitted himself like "Jim Crow" and took to the stage (in Louisville, Cincinnati, or Pittsburgh, depending upon the telling) with his blackface interpretation of the song and dance, to instant and wild applause.

A careful comparison of sources makes it possible to offer a somewhat clearer and more accurate picture of the first performance of "Jim Crow." Joe Cowell, English comic actor, noted in his autobiography that he was in Cincinnati at the end of 1829 performing with the company managed by Samuel Drake, which stayed in Cincinnati through January 1830.[4] There he reacquainted himself with "a tall, scrambling-looking man with a sepulchral falsetto voice," whom he had known from some time before at the Park Theatre. Cowell deepened his friendship with young Rice, and claimed to have exposed him to blackface songs in early 1830. Sam Cowell, Joe Cowell's son, who was only about seven years old, specialized during this time in singing "African Melodies" (including, apparently, "Coal Black Rose"[5]), for which he "made a prodigious hit[;] from ten to twenty dollars, and sometimes much more, would be thrown on the stage."[6] By so doing, Master Cowell was following the lead of Thomas Blakeley and George Washington Dixon, both of whom were then singing "Coal Black Rose" in eastern theatres. Joe Cowell, with a paternal and a professional interest in blackface song and performance, did not make notice that Rice too was singing blackface; in fact he found Rice "a very unassuming, modest young man, little dreaming then that he was destined to astonish the Duchess of St. Alban's, or anybody else [with 'Jim Crow']."[7] This implies that Rice developed his act after the Cowells departed in early 1830. (Cowell's account also raises the intriguing prospect that the man was taught here by the child.)

Sol Smith's *Theatrical Management in the West and South for Thirty Years* next catches up to Rice in the summer of 1830:

Previous to going South we accepted an offer from Mr. Parsons, acting manager for Mr. Drake, to perform twenty nights in Louisville, receiving for our services the sum of $220. Mr. T. D. Rice was a member of the company here, and was busily engaged in composing and arranging his *Jim Crow* songs, . . .[8]

Ludlow, in his highly detailed autobiography, undoubtedly based on notes and journals, confirmed Smith's recollection. He reminisced that Rice had been with Drake's company for the "year or so previous [i.e., in mid–late 1830]" and that "during which time he had been . . . singing the negro song of 'Jump, Jim Crow.'"[9] Newspapers show that Rice was in Louisville in the late summer of 1830: The *Louisville Public Advertiser* claims that a letter for "Thomas D. Rice" was being held in the post office on 2 September 1830; and when Drake's company opened its season on the 18th, Rice was on the bill, acting both in *Town and Country* and in *The Rendezvous*.[10] Reminiscences thus suggest that Rice first performed his song in mid-1830.

This date is consistent with the first record of performance known to me: The playbill for 22 September 1830 in Louisville, Kentucky, included "'JIM CROW' by MR. RICE."[11] Rice quite probably first jumped "Jim Crow" sometime in 1830 between late spring and 22 September, most likely in Louisville on the latter date. That there is a significant kernel of truth to the myth is suggested by the outlines of the legend of the birth of "Jim Crow" already being in place by 1837 (in Bennett's account) – therefore easily within the living memory of those who might have been there – and by the story being broadcast so widely for so long, yet never disputed but in the minutiae.

Nonetheless, the myth was not without its measure of fabrication. For example, there is nothing to indicate that "Jim Crow" swept all before it. The song is not listed in any others of Drake's detailed Louisville advertisements – hard to believe if the song were such a big draw. One week after the first documented performance, a review of the theatre season in Louisville by "Lope Tochio" devotes a long, highly laudatory paragraph to Rice. "This gentleman's *Wormwood* [in *The Lottery Ticket*], is equal to any I have ever seen, and is well calculated to bring the risible faculties of an audience into action." Nothing, however, but for an obscure criticism of Rice's propensity to introduce "local sayings and bye words, in order to create a laugh," could be remotely construed to refer to any performances by Rice of "Jim Crow," a fact most curious given the myth of the instant hit.[12]

By 1831, though, Rice's reputation throughout the West was growing, based largely upon his performances of "Jim Crow." During 1832
he brought his extravaganza to the East, where audiences were already
hearing word of its novelty.[13] He enjoyed increasingly successful en-
gagements in Philadelphia, Baltimore, and Washington in the late
summer–early fall of 1832, and then headed for New York City, no
longer a supporting character but a headliner. News went before: "Mr.
RICE whose celebrated Song of JIM CROW has drawn crowded houses
in Baltimore, Philadelphia, &c is daily expected, and will make his first
appearance here immediately on his arrival."[14] His tumultuous reception at the Bowery Theatre on 12 November 1832 was the stuff of legend building. From this moment, Rice's career accelerated at an unprecedented rate.

JIM CROW. – "*Oh rare Jim Crow!*" – Thy manly notes piercing th' affright-
ened ear of night still, still linger on my brain. – Thy graceful figure still
floats upon my fancy – and when thou "jump" on thy light fantastic toe, "*sic
transit gloria mundi*" – Vestris' occupation gone – no longer "*dieu de la danse.*"
Thy godlike energies eclipse his fame and Terpsichore herself seeing thy "visage in thy mind," adopts thee for her own! Happy Kentucky that gave thee
birth. Happier [New] York that brought thee forth. Still happier man that
found thy worth, *viz:* the Manager of the Bowery Theatre. The fame thou fre-
quents is hallowed to the Muses, and laughing millions own thy sway. Mazeppa capers to affright – Jim capers to delight – fear follows *his* steps – fun
frolics round – thine humor laughs in thine eye – a cupid cushions on thy lip
– wit sparkles from thy tongue, and when at length thou shuffle off thy mor-
tal coil, thoer'lt share with the rarest wit, the rarest epitaph, "OH RARE JIM
CROW."[15]

Over the next four years Rice toured incessantly, playing in all major
American cities, East, West, and South, to warm receptions and boun-
tiful receipts.[16] On 7 June 1836 he boarded a packet ship for Liverpool,
and a yearlong tour of England, Scotland, and Ireland, with a short side
trip to Paris.[17] He proved to be the smash hit of the season over there
as well, apparently outdrawing a whole raft of popular American stars
then trying the English waters: Hackett, Forrest, and Hamblin, among
others.

In London, Jim Crow is even more popular than in New York. It is heard in
every circle, from the soirées of the nobility, to the hovels of the street sweep-

ers. 'Tis Jim Crow here – Jim Crow there – Jim Crow every where. The ex-
clusives of Almacks, and the chimney sweeps of St. Giles –

> "Wheel about, and turn about,
> And jump Jim Crow."[18]

The *Spirit of the Times* stated that

Nothing since the days of Garrick or Kean has equalled the popularity of this
"Virginia Nigger." He is, by all accounts, coining money, and by no means
among the loafers of the metropolis: Dukes and Duchesses, Lord Lieutenants
and Fields Marshals, and we shall not be surprised if the youthful Queen [Vic-
toria] herself should send an invitation to Rice to jump Jim Crow for her at
the Palace.[19]

The *Boston Post* made it official: "The two most popular characters in
the world at the present time are Victoria and Jim Crow."[20]
    While in England and in the prime of his glory, Rice met, courted,
and wed Charlotte B. Gladstone, the daughter of the proprietor of the
Adelphi Theatre, a venue Rice favored while in London.[21] The nup-
tials were announced in many American newspapers, suggesting further
the dimensions of Rice's popularity: "Important, if True" headlined the
Boston Semi-Weekly Courier.[22] There were rumors that he would eventually settle in England,[23] but he returned to the United States with his
bride at the end of August 1837, a vastly wealthier man; he was said to
have made "money like water."[24] Rice made the crossing on at least two
other occasions, opening at the Adelphi in February 1839[25] and again in
December 1842.[26] After each trip he returned to touring in the United
States, his popularity as high as ever. The constant was the basis of his
favor: the perennial audience delight, "Jim Crow."[27]

*****

MY PRIMARY CONCERN, though, is not with the biography of T. D.
Rice, although some of it is necessary. I am rather about unearthing the
Jacksonian "worlds" that gave "Jim Crow" fit, the song's audience, the
social contexts, and the understandings that followed.
    The theatrical audience for "Jim Crow" is perhaps the easiest of my
intentions to fix, for many newspapers of the time loved to point at it
in disgust, leaving a historical record. We have seen already how the
patrician William T. Porter disdained the hoi-polloi as they swirled

around Richard III on the stage of the Bowery in late 1832, at which time he reported too that they forced Rice to repeat "Jim Crow" twenty times. A strikingly similar scene is described at Rice's Chatham Theatre benefit in October 1840:

Long before the curtain rose, they were obliged to refuse selling tickets for the pit, and every part of the theatre was crammed to suffocation. After the first piece, the pit took possession of the stage, and for a time it seemed doubtful whether a sufficient space could be cleared for the performances to proceed. – The boys were in full feather, and the police officers were entirely unequal to the emergency. Bitten apples and pennies were thrown upon the stage, and the ragged little rascals who had taken possession, were in paradise – chasing one another across the stage, picking up the apples and hurling them back into the pit, roaring and yelling, and enjoying the frolic immeasurably.[28]

These "rascals" seemed too to have concerned an aristocratic critic from Richmond, who insisted that Virginia had nothing whatsoever to do with the provenance of "buffo negro songs which have attracted so much attention at the North and in England." To attribute them (he was talking mainly about "Jim Crow") to Virginia was, in his view, "a libel upon the good taste and intelligence of our people – nay, upon us as civilized community." He outlined an audience, both for and against this music:

But we scarcely believe a respectable audience would patronize or encourage negro buffo songs here. We hope they would not. – It is a duty society owes to itself to discountenance everything which tends to vitiate public taste. Virtue has her strongest support and defence in a refined and intellectual disposition of the public mind, upon which public amusements and entertainments exert a mighty influence. It is of the greatest importance, therefore, that such exhibitions should be chaste and intellectual. The public should place their severest reprehension upon every species of amusement not bearing that character.[29]

The *New York Herald* was more explicit: "Jim Crow Rice first started into favor under the fostering care of the Bowery boys, and how well he retains their patronage the audiences of the Chatham are proof."[30] Even Rice himself noted in a letter to James Gordon Bennett that his American supporters were, well, "unsophisticated."[31]

Rice, apparently, appealed to a wider audience in Great Britain than in the United States. Too many times do the papers note the attendance of the Duke

of Devonshire (one example among many) at Rice's performances for some of
that rank not to have been enchanted. American newspaper readers marvelled
that the Duchess of St. Albans sent up, from Brighton to London, her carriage and four greys to take Jim Crow down to her great marine fête on the
sea shore. Jim jumps into the carriage – is attended by two liveried footmen –
arrives in Brighton – creates a prodigious sensation. He is shown over all her
grounds. In the evening he sings "Jim Crow" – receives fifty pounds as a mark
of the Duchess's love – and is sent back to London as he was carried off.[32]

That the upper crust was in the audience during his 1836–7 British season is indisputable. The data are not complete, but it appears that there
was a gradual "lowering" of the social status of the audience in subsequent tours. However, from the first, as well as at the end, there were
the common sorts. The English critic for the *Figaro in London* noticed
that Rice was "imperfect," and then sniffed that there was

an urbane community of gin bottles, which spoke strongly in favor of the social attributes of the company. The musical powers of the audience were ex-
erted on this occasion with considerable effect, and the manner in which they
took up the burden of "We won't go home till morning" was particularly re-
freshing.[33]

The *London Satirist* patronized those "who can discover anything irre-
sistibly amusing in the nigger character" by recommending Rice's performance – from the context an allusion to the lower classes. A different number of the same paper revealed social perspective when the
reporter noted that "a Jim Crow mania has seized on all classes of the
community," then seemed not to see the contradiction as he continued:
"Jim Crow may do for America, but for England such trash is value-
less."[34]

As for gender, there is no evidence known to me countering the
scholarly wisdom that young and middle-aged men typically made up
the audience, with women in attendance primarily in the notorious
third tier. Evidence by implication is the rule here. When the *Spirit of
the Times* reviewed a gala benefit evening at the Park (with no blackface) and noticed that "[b]oth in the pit and boxes the ladies (God bless
them!) outnumbered the men,"[35] it is noteworthy because it was obviously unusual. A reviewer of the circus at New York's Bowery Amphitheatre in 1839 was excited about the audience: "so respectable in
appearance, so cheerful, and yet so quiet . . . no noise, no row, no

whistling, no cat-calling nor caterwauling . . ." The reason for this exceptional behavior: the audience, "nearly half of the gentler sex, . . ."[36] A Boston reviewer observed, extraordinarily, that "the ladies far outnumber[ed] the gentlemen" at the circus.[37] The trial of William R. Pelby, son of the manager of the National Theatre in Boston (where Rice often performed), for beating William B. English with a stick turned on the "respectability" of his father's house, and a prosecution witness observed: "excepting a few benefits, we never saw twenty ladies in the boxes."[38] In short, audiences for Rice's brand of blackface theatre tended to be male, youngish, and lower class. That the mass-oriented daily press (of which Bennett's *New York Herald* is the exemplar) generally approved of him suggests that their readers did as well. A profile of Rice's audience thus extends to include those who supported the *Herald:* males of the petite bourgeoisie and of the middle class. That the men (probably unmarried) among these overlapping groups were the same types who enacted Jacksonian street rituals is more than coincidence.[39]

Thomas D. Rice, like his audience and many of his blackface colleagues met with in this book, lived, as a young man at least, on the periphery of "respectable," family-oriented, middle-class life. Perhaps born in poverty, he apprenticed in a trade that would have accorded him some solid respectability, but (at twenty or so) opted for a life among the socially suspect of the theatrical world, moreover as a member of a troupe on the western theatre circuit, virtually on the wild frontier. Further evidence of his social marginalization can be found in the activities of his family and near family, as captured in the records of the Police Court. Rice had a brother, George, who also made a (minor) career of dancing "Jim Crow" in 1837–41. The Police Court books of New York City show him to be in frequent trouble with the law during the mid-1830s. The *New York Transcript* reported: "George Rice, (a brother of Jim Crow), was charged by Sparks, the officer, with creating a disturbance at the Bowery Theatre."[40] He could not secure a bail of $200 and was thus imprisoned. George Rice was brought to trial on 10 July 1835 along with George W. Thomas, said to have been a keeper of a porter and gambling house at 55 Bowery, and others for "an atrocious assault and battery upon James McAnnal"; Rice was judged to be guilty.[41] The next year, on the 5th of April, the same paper reported:

George Rice was put upon his trial for assaulting and beating, on the 12th of November last, Mrs. Mary Connally of No. 8 Ludlow street. The Jury found him guilty, and the Court, in the plenitude of its mercy sentenced him to pay a fine of 6 cents only, and to be immediately afterwards discharged.[42]

T. D. Rice's brother was like thousands of other young men who show up in the court indices, brought in for fighting, rowdyism, "disorder in the streets," or any number of other social activities that were unacceptable to those who operated the court system, yet were part of the culture of common-class life.

T. D. Rice, who does not show up in the court records, apparently had a paramour who did, however.

A scene of no ordinary character was exhibited in the police office on Saturday [21 December 1833], growing out of a complaint preferred by Mr. Gale, generally known as the "Mazeppa" of the Bowery Theatre, against a female member of the family of Mr. Rice, the celebrated "Jim Crow" of the same establishment. Mr. Weyman, the magistrate presiding on the occasion, had his hands full at the hearing which [had] a serio-ludi-*crow* character from beginning to end – the end of which was, that Mazeppa and Madame Jim Crow, who unfortunately rented apartments in the same dwelling, were recommended to live more neighbourly for the future, and in expectation that this good advice would not be rejected, all the parties were dismissed.[43]

"Madame Crow" is only one of the thousands of lower-class women indicted during this period for various forms of "disorder," including, frequently, violent conduct.

In summary, there was considerable overlap between Rice and his audience. He can be tied (sometimes obliquely, to be sure) to a culture of fisticuffs, riotous drinking, gambling, general rowdiness, and (perhaps) cohabitation without need or benefit of legal or religious sanction. His world, like that of so many covered in this book, was of the moment and the body – not at all like that of the middle or elite classes, with their cerebral fixation on delayed gratification, restraint, and disciplined resolve.

*****

THE BEST PROOF of Rice's world exists in his signature song. First of all, his was a world of considerable fluidity and ambiguity, just as there is no collection of verses that give special definition to "Jim Crow." Practically, there are far too many verses for there to be a single, definitive set. A "penny ballad," published by Leonard Deming of Boston and likely hawked by street vendors, contains sixty-six verses.[44] Another was titled boldly: "50 Verses: The only Correct Copy of the Extravaganza of Jim Crow."[45] Sheet music published by E. Riley in New York in January 1833 had forty-four quatrains.[46] Many of these verses (and those in the song versions not detailed here) are unique. The song was so popular (and itself about burlesque) that it invited parody; thus time and again editors, singers, and street poets added their own verses, only necessarily ending with the couplet, "Weel about and turn about and do jis so, / Ebery time I weel about, I jump Jim Crow."

There are some generalizations that can be drawn from the study of hundreds of verses. First, the song is "about" the American Southwest (at that time the region west and south of the Appalachian Mountains). No version of the song known to me fails to base Jim Crow in the Southwest at some point, often by reference to the Mississippi River, to New Orleans, and to "ole Kentucky,"[47] whence he hails. Jim Crow typically claims to be out of the Southwest "roaring" or "whooping" tradition, personified by the exaggerated exploits of the legendary riverboatman Mike Fink and the frontiersman Davy Crockett. Roarers boasted that they could outfight, outeat, outdance, outcuss, outlie, and outsex anyone, and set about proving it through evocative language, clearly based on a rich oral tradition.[48] By comparison, Jim Crow could "whip [his] weight in wild cats, eat an alligator,"[49] or, even more impressively, "wip de lion ob de west, I eat de Allegator."[50] Of fighting mere mortals:

> When I got out I hit a man,
> His name I now forgot,
> But dere was nothing left
> 'Sept a little grease spot.[51]

and

> So I knocked down dis Sambo,
> And shut up his light,
> For I'm jist about as sassy,
> As if I was half white.
> But, he soon jumped up again,

> An 'gan for me to feel,
> Says I go away you niggar,
> Or I'll skin you like an eel.[52]

Jim Crow was also something of a womanizer:

> I went down to de riber,
> I didn't mean to stay,
> But dere I see so many galls,
> I couldn't get away.[53]

and

> I'm for union to a gal,
> An dis is a stubborn fact,
> But if I marry an dont like it,
> I'll nullify de act.[54]

He was always single and more than available for any sexual dalliance. In brief, he was a child of the West and an aspect of its imagery, one that appealed powerfully to urban, eastern, common men.

Perhaps more than anything, however, Jim Crow was a political creature, as the allusion to the raging nullification issue in the verse above suggests. In Atwill's edition of the song, Jim Crow goes to Washington, deals with the bank question (he's antibank), takes on Tristam Burges (an anti-Jacksonian congressman from Rhode Island), U.S. Bank President Nicholas Biddle (whom he calls "Ole Nick," a term also used during the period to refer to the devil), and controversial New York newspaper editor James Watson Webb (*Courier and Enquirer*), and then offers advice to President Jackson himself. If these and other verses reflect the views of the audience (and surely they did to some extent), they confirm what Alexander Saxton has written about Jim Crow's fans: that they were passionately political, Democrats, supporters of Jackson, and antibank.[55]

> But Jackson he's de President,
> As ebry body knows;
> He always goes de hole Hog,
> An puts on de wee-toes [vetos].
> Old hick'ry, never mind de boys,
> But hold up your head;
> For people never turn to clay
> 'Till arter dey be dead.[56]

Jim Crow would lend his name to political agendas for the rest of the century. A journal of 1843 titled *The Political Jim Crow* had as its object "to satirize [President] John Tyler and his hopeful sons."[57] In this light it is not surprising that a whole raft of vicious legislative actions governing racial matters would later appropriate Jim Crow's name, and cast it thus into infamy.

Once it is clear that "Jim Crow" is at base a political song, we are closer to the heart of the matter, with a sharpened understanding of why the song shows up in so many socially fraught, highly politicized moments. I will give example to only three of them here.

The first concerns the burning of the Ursuline convent in Charlestown, Massachusetts (outside Boston), one night in August 1834. That evening some "one hundred and fifty to two hundred [rioters gathered], disguised in various fantastic dresses, and with painted faces, [and] immediately commenced breaking open the doors and windows of the Convent, . . ."[58] As in most callithumpian demonstrations, which this surely was, care was taken by the "midnight leaders of misrule"[59] to ensure that human life was not endangered. Accordingly, inhabitants of the building were escorted out. Once this was accomplished, however, torches came out, piles of combustibles appeared, and the convent – a symbol both of middle-class values (at least twelve expensive musical instruments, dozens of music books, and hundreds of pieces of sheet music would be destroyed[60]) and of Catholicism (as such a victim of the tensions between "native" and "Irish" in the Boston area) – began its rapid burn into the annals of American history.

Arson was a capital offense at that time, punishable by death. Trials, highly visible and widely reported, followed from the torching. The most notable of these was that of John Buzzell, a brickmason who lived immediately across from the convent, accused by the authorities of being the ringleader. His trial, the first and the most enthusiastically prosecuted, was widely covered in the period's media. Toward the end of defense testimony, Asa B. Barker took the stand.

I am a member of the fire-department of Charlestown. I have seen the prisoner before the fire, but was not particularly acquainted with him. When the first alarm was given, I went with engine No. 4; we stopped opposite Kelley's house [where Buzzell lived]. When No. 13, of Boston, came along, ours was seized hold of by others, and pulled up to the Convent. The faces of these persons were smutted, and they had on tarpaulin hats. A man with a speaking trumpet called up to No. 13, to stop; there was a tall man, weighing 200 to 210, with false whiskers apparently. . . . The engine was then carried as far as Kelley's, and there we continued. Buzzell came up and leaned on the brake; they asked him to sing "Jim Crow"; he said he had a cold, and was hoarse. While the prisoner was standing by the engine, the large man and a short one came along with smut on the face; the short man said, "he set on fire the small building twice, and the damn'd fool of a Charlestown engineer ordered it put out, and did not succeed after all. . . ."[61]

The prosecution's summary featured centrally Barker's testimony and attempted to turn it against Buzzell.

We have now traced the prisoner up to the time of the burning of the tar barrels. Where was he after that? He was seen by no one. . . . Where was he? And this is a circumstance that strikes me with great force. This man who could be seen by every one before, is not seen while the Convent is in the possession of the mob. When the Convent is in flames, he must then come out; and then Templeton sees him where he would naturally be; Barker too at that time sees him by the engine; and then he was asked to sing Jim Crow, the *Io Triumphe* of the rioters. . . . When this Convent was in flames, he is requested to sing the *Io Paean* of triumph, and excuses himself as having a cold; and this, at a time, when the heart of every honest man must have sunk within him.[62]

Buzzell (and all the others, save one) were acquitted of arson charges; but the indictment of "Jim Crow," the "*Io Triumphe*" and "*Io Paean*" of rioters, stands yet unchallenged.[63]

The second exemplary moment occurred three years later and a fair distance from Charlestown, in Belleville, Ontario. There a crowd attacked Mr. Benjamin, editor of the *Belleville Weekly Intelligencer,* and burned him in effigy (a form of the charivari). Motivated by political animosity, the crowd accused Benjamin (wrongly) of being Jewish. A report published shortly after the incident claimed that while the effigy burned the mob sang:

> Last Friday night some wicked boys
> Thought they would something do:
> So they turned out, and wheel'd about,
> And hung the Belleville Jew.
> Jew Benjie then to get revenge
> Did raise a cry and hue
> Of Maw-worm snarling hypocrite,
> Oh! Saintly Belleville Jew.[64]

The tune implied – both by "wheel'd about" and, as we shall see, by the meter – is obviously that of "Jim Crow." Whether or not Benjamin's persecutors were capable of making up such verses on the spot is immaterial; mediated representation expressed what "Jim Crow" signified broadly.

My third example shows that the spirit of burlesque, political action, charivari, and carnival found in the first two was apparently part of "Jim Crow" from the outset. Molly Ramshaw in her study of T. D. Rice claims that a year or two before Rice came to the East, right when he was starting to develop his act, "there was a man in [a Cincinnati] prison, under sentence of death, who used to write from twenty to thirty 'Jim Crow' verses daily, parodying local social and political matters, and sen[d] them to Rice to sing at night."[65]

Why is "Jim Crow" sounded out at these and other such supercharged, ritualized social moments? Part of the answer surely is that the song was embedded from the first in a powerful form of social and political discourse, early blackface minstrelsy; but I would suggest too that "Jim Crow" was especially appropriate for such a role because of its rhetorical nature and its theatrical and musical qualities.

In its early years, blackface minstrelsy was much more about theatre and dance than about music. "Coal Black Rose" – believed by those who lived then to be the first minstrel song – outlined a dramatic situation and was easily converted into a playlet (as, in fact, it was by George Washington Dixon as early as 24 September 1829, renamed *Love in a Cloud*). "Jim Crow" follows from that beginning. Its theatrical essence was obvious to many. Ireland's *Cork Herald* observed of the song:

["Jim Crow"] has a feature that belongs to few songs – it is mostly made up of dancing. Half of each verse is chorus, and then all the chorus is motion – so that it is of a compound and really complex character. Mr. Crow's agility in describing the evolutions that the words enjoin – for he addresses himself in the imperative mood "Jump Jim Crow," – is truly magnificent. He has all the velocity of a dancing master, with the quaint capers of a cleave-boy – the bewitching grace of Douvernay, in partnership with the sylph-like movement of Taglioni. He varies his jumpings to an infinite extent, starting with different steps, and terminating with different positions in each verse. Then there are eight verses to the song, and it is encored six times; which draws deeply upon Mr. Crow's ingenuity to vary the pantomime, and re-model the extrav-

agance of this grotesque transaction. And so he does; for each bound he gives
is other than the last, which proves that motion is commensurate with space,
and of course illimitable.[66]

Y. S. Nathanson said of "Jim Crow" that it was "a dramatic song, depending for its success, perhaps more than any play ever written for the
stage, upon the action and mimetic powers of the performer."[67] T. D.
Rice himself came from the theatre and always remained a part of it,
never becoming a member of a minstrel show, which form I argue in
Chapter 5 is much more about musicmaking than about "showing."
During the early years Rice would perform in the minstrel piece and
then act a part in legitimate theatre. (He made something of a speciality of Mawworm in *The Hypocrite*, for example.) All descriptions of his
art (as the above) suggest that he was especially sensitive to the visual
and theatrical aspects of blackface: the costumes, the ways in which the
body, movement, gesture, and physical disposition gave meaning, even
the black mask itself – a quintessentially theatrical statement.[68]

As for the music to "Jim Crow" (Musical Example 2), it might itself be from the tradition of carnival and misrule. The song has suggested to many origins in some oral tradition, although no one has ever
found a source. An assessment of Rice as performer, published near the
premiere of "Jim Crow," might offer a clue, although it is admitted-
ly oblique. Two weeks after the first recorded performance of "Jim
Crow," Rice sang and played the part of Mungo the slave in Bickerstaffe's *The Padlock*,[69] which was reviewed by "Lope Tochio": "Our
friend Rice in Mungo, was all that could be wished, though, notwithstanding our former remarks relative to localities, he entered, singing a
Kentucky corn song."[70] Ludlow, in his account of the birth of Jim Crow,
suggested that Rice had first sung it in the character of "a *Kentucky
corn-field negro*."[71] Could it be that "Jim Crow" is a corn song, a song
like those sung by African Americans at corn huskings, big parties at
which two groups of shuckers enthusiastically (and sometimes violent-
ly) competed to be the first to finish their half of the corn, which entitled them to first shot at the fine food and drink set out by the farmer?
Huskings and Christmas were the two times of the year when the master ritually served the slave, a period of misrule.[72] George Tucker in
1824 described the songs of the season:

Musical Example 2. "Jim Crow" (New York: Atwill's, ca. 1833).

[T]he corn songs of these humble creatures would please you . . . for some of them have a small smack of poetry, and are natural at expressions of kind and amiable feelings – such as, praise of their master, gratitude for his kindness, thanks for his goodness, praise of one another, and, now and then, a *little humorous satire.*[73]

Tucker spoke further of how "(t)he airs of these songs has not much variety or melody, . . ."[74] Of "Jim Crow," too, one notices that there is not much to be heard. It is a simple little ditty of only eight measures and few notes. Harmonies are simple and of a supporting nature (that is, unnecessary if all one has is, for example, a fiddle or a voice). Rhythmically, the extended use of dotted figures provides propulsion but is not deeply interesting by itself. The *Cork Herald* said of it "brief and pretty," if "paltry."[75] Charles Hamm has observed that it is "in no way remarkable," that it is, in fact, "quite clumsy, sounding almost like a patchwork of several different melodies."[76] The *London Satirist* was less circumspect: "America has sent us a filthy abortion of a song, with neither talent nor humor."[77] Philip Hone called it a "balderdash song."[78] With these evaluations in mind, imagine twenty-one verses (Atwill's edition) or forty-four (Riley's); or even (more likely) only an appropriate selection but multiplied by the five, six, ten, or twenty encores that were commonly demanded. To understate, the implied length of production merits the descriptive term "extravaganza," but the experience of the music must have been something that we might today call "minimalist," "recursive," or – depending upon perspective, judgmental nature, and patience – "antimusic" or even, somewhat more technically, "noise."

"Jim Crow" thus functions much like sound in almost all ritual theatricals, all of which flaunted their antimusical quality. The "music" of the rough-music (happy term!) rituals was as raucous as the visages were frightening. Roisterers would beat on pots and pans, play proper instruments improperly, thump homemade drums, shout and scream – "the very cats were dumbfounded by it."[79] "Gangs of boys and young men howled and shouted as if possessed by the demon of disorder."[80] "Troops of young men, in fantastic dresses and masks, marched through the streets ringing bells, blowing tin horns, squeaking upon six-penny trumpets, clattering upon tin kettles and making just as much noise and discord as possible."[81] A New York troupe in 1843 "with tin pans for bass drums, and tin horns for trumpets . . . began to discourse such music as was rarely heard by ears of mortals."[82]

[Belsnickels] infested the stores and played on antique musical instruments as a prelude to passing around the hat, and generally departed with a parting salute on their tin horns. Some were quite proficient as musicians and handled the violin, cornet, bones and tamborine in a lively manner, but the majority were simply frightful. Glee clubs, attired in quaint costumes, the singers with blackened faces, made the air hideous with their alleged warbling.[83]

Bands of masqueraders made night hideous, while horse fiddlers added their atrocious discord to the general din. . . . Troops of youngsters and oldsters, with tin horns, made satanic music all along Eighth and Chestnut streets, while others lacking the horns, yelled "Gideon's band" in a style that

> Cracked the voice of melody
> And broke the legs of time!

To induce infants to slumber must have required paregoric by the bottle full.[84]

The shivaree in *Oklahoma!* is a pale, dull imitation in comparison to the caterwauling imaginings of the real thing.

Related theatricals featured similar sounds. Mummers approached houses making a hellish racket. Benjamin Latrobe spoke of the music at black carnival in New Orleans in 1819 and called it "squalling," "uncouth," and "detestable."[85] Pinkster Day brought music that was "singular in the extreme."[86] Christmas Day in the Caribbean heard "a great number of negroes, beating old canisters, or pieces of metal."[87] Williams, "grumbling in indignation at the incessant clamour of the cocks on the morning of Christmas-day" was "assailed with another sort of music [that of the John Canoe], not much more melodious," and he detested the "howls of the musicians."[88] To distill these rituals to a syllogistic essence: "strange," violent, comic human-demons perform "strange," noisy, rough music; they disrupt the status quo; thus cacophony functions to disorder a world by itself shocking "the very moon," implying reordering.

The sounds of ritual manifestly assaulted those who described them in studied, proper, and disapproving prose. To the active participants, though, these were immediate moments of play, of fun and carnival.

This kind of seeming contradiction is not unique to social rituals. The implicit dynamic between the ludic and the agonistic is richly documented in the literature on popular, working-class, American theatre in the first half of the nineteenth century, most auspiciously in the example of the Astor Place Riot in 1849, which left twenty-two dead.[89] To act before common audiences was generally to promise violence, but not necessarily to deliver. Blackface minstrels worked from this same premise. The lithograph of "the *fifty-seventh* night of Mr. T. D. RICE, of Kentucky" in "Jim Crow" at the Bowery Theatre (Figure 6) wonderfully juxtaposes blackface minstrelsy and violence. One could hardly construct a more powerful illustration of the paradox as the blackface figure of laughter grins out from a swirling stage of white male agonism.

Then there were the sounds themselves, in name and in description music that "made night hideous" and "murdered sleep." The cover of Jacques Attali's flaming book *Noise: The Political Economy of Music* features a reproduction of Brueghel's *The Quarrel between Carnival and Lent* (see Figure 3), and this painting serves as a touchstone throughout. Attali, a social economist, has fashioned a rich, multilayered thesis that finds its genesis in an understanding of the relationship between the "noise" and the "music" in Brueghel's work.

More than colors and forms, it is sounds and their arrangements that fashion societies. With noise is born disorder and its opposite: the world. With music is born power and its opposite: subversion. In noise can be read the codes of life, the relations among men. Clamor, Melody, Dissonance, Harmony; when it is fashioned by man with specific tools, when it invades man's time, when it becomes sound, noise is the source of purpose and power, of the dream – Music. It is at the heart of the progressive rationalization of aesthetics, and it is a refuge for residual irrationality; it is a means of power and a form of entertainment.[90]

"Music" is a metaphor for the official social code; "noise" is implicit violence, a challenge to law's authority, as Carnival is a challenge to Lent, as callithumpians were demons of disorder. Early minstrelsy's music (or, its noise) jangled the nerves of those who believed in music that was proper, respectable, polished, and harmonic, with recognizable melodies. "Jim Crow" was not at all the way music was supposed to be: It was music for the croaking voice and the wild fiddle; the tune is

Figure 6. "View of the Stage on the *fifty seventh* night of Mr. T. D. RICE, of Kentucky in his original and celebrated extravaganza of JIM CROW on which occasion every department of the house was thronged to an excess unprecedented in the records of theatrical attraction. New York 25th November 1833." Collection of the New-York Historical Society.

awkward, repetitive, and even boring; the texts are disjointed, generally nonnarrative, and unrealistic. This music assaulted sensibilities, challenged the roots of respectability, and promised subversion, a world
undone, and, concomitantly, a new set of codes.

Could it be that "Jim Crow" was not, then, a song about African
Americans so much as one that promised a new code, as the ritualized
"demons of disorder" (who often, of course, appeared too in blackface)
were not attempting to demean those of black skin, but were adopting
the visage of the Other in an effort to reconfigure a hard world? If so,
how does "Jim Crow" fit with a world in which real black people were
chattel, or were crammed into the stinking, filthy confines of New
York's Five Points?

In surprisingly ambiguous ways, in short. "Jim Crow" was clearly
many things to many people, of all ranks, races, and genders. At the
upper social end of the male coterie that supported minstrelsy, "Jim
Crow" was a song about racial inferiority. If one just reads the newspapers – written by the educated elite, if not also the social, political,
and economic elite (the same ones who believed that *Othello* was a play
about the dangers of miscegenation) – one finds exactly what one would
expect: "Jim Crow" is about a deservedly unfortunate "nigger," worthy
only of a novelty laugh or two. The evidence at this level of discourse
is uniform and unambiguous. It is in the streets, among the powerless,
that the racial features of a blackface Jim Crow are less clear, where issues of identity, representation, and race are more complicated and less
unequivocal.

For instruction, let me turn to the case of *Barbadoes* v. *Bolcolm*, Boston Justices' Court, as reported in the *Boston Post* on 30 March 1840.
The defendant, Bolcolm, a white man, was a laborer (a housepainter)
who lived in Southack Street. He was charged with having "malicious-
ly and mischievously" painted the clothing of Rebecca Barbadoes, a
"pretty little pickininy about six years old." Bolcolm acknowledged having soiled Rebecca's clothes, but disputed the damages claimed by the
suit: $20. The prosecution exhibited Rebecca's hand-me-downs – "bon-
net, silk neckerchief, fur cape, black dress, and pantellettes" – and each
was shown to be splattered with green paint. To explain how this might
have happened Bolcolm's brother was produced; he "mounted the
stand with a broad laugh, as if the taking of an oath was a capital joke."
From this witness, the court learned that a number of children had

gathered around the paint shop on the day of the alleged assault, drawn there "by the music of a fiddle, which was then playing in the building." The defendant was said to have tried to drive them away, but the children "in turn became very saucy, and gave him some lip." Bolcolm's counsel argued that the actions of the children ought to factor much into mitigation of any damages assessed. He further pointed out that "green is a very pretty color – soothing and grateful to the eye – the almost universal hue of vernal nature, filling the mind with happy and springlike thoughts"; that, in fact, Bolcolm was doing Rebecca the favor of adornment. Beyond that, the lawyer contended that the valuation placed on the garments were "immensely atrociously" inflated. He added, grotesquely, that

[h]e did not believe, that if the girl and her painted costume were put up together at auction, that they would fetch so much as had been demanded for the costume alone. Nay, he would go further, and aver, that if her ancestors were thrown into the bargain, not a man of common sense could be found who would give twenty dollars for the lot.

After the defense rested, the plaintiff's attorney called the star witness, Thomas Brown, a "very young child," perhaps black (although such is never stated), and a "very intelligent one, especially upon the subject of fiddling." Master Brown was asked simply to identify the tune to which Rebecca was compelled to attend and dance. He testified that the tune was "Jim Crow."

Prosecuting counsel then proceeded directly to his closing argument.

What do we find in the first place? Why, some idlers playing on a fiddle, and the tune "Jim Crow," in a street inhabited by people of color, and continually traversed by their children. What race possess such ears for music as the colored people, and what colored child can be expected to withstand the temptation of listening to "Jim Crow?" Yes, your Honor, if they will play "Jim Crow," the little boys and girls will "do jist so," as they have done. Therefore, the defendant is answerable for the collecting of the children round his paint shop. As to the question of damage, I can hardly trust myself to speak. It is generally admitted that people of color are human beings, and have the same feelings as white folks. They are equally sensitive, and even, perhaps, more proud; and I would ask, what must have been the feelings of Mr. Barbadoes, when he saw his child – the pretty little girl before – come home besmeared with paint; green paint, too – a color, which every man of taste – any artist – must know never looks well on a yellow ground; and, by close examination, your Honor will find that Rebecca's complexion is not black, but is even a shade lighter than the average of mulattos. – It is the insult which I would have your Honor look at – I put it upon the ground, that it is not the less an insult to spit upon a man's face, because it can be wiped out, as it is said the paint may be cleansed. – Having said thus much, I will not trouble your Honor with any further remarks, but leave the case, with a full confidence in your Honor's judgment, in the hands of the Court.[91]

Proceeding to judgment, the court ignored altogether the matter of Rebecca's skin color and its inappropriateness with green, but noted that she was surely tempted to the paint shop by the sounds of the fiddle, and acknowledged too that Bolcolm was justified in being irritated by the crowd. At this point, things were, in the words of the reporter, "about balanced." Thus, the only question was the one of damages, and the Judge awarded Rebecca $5.25 and charged Bolcolm court costs.

There is much to be learned from this story. For one, the actions and words of the attorneys (and the judge, to some extent) are emblematic of racial attitudes extant among their cohort. There is condescension, easy acceptance of slavery (manifest in this case most cruelly), and a whiff of white fear at "the insult" of miscegenation. Toward all common people, black and white, there is patronization at best and disgust at worst. In common-class Bolcolm and his brother we find a degree of racism, surely, but one less abstract than that of the legal establishment.

Music is identified here as central to life among common persons, both black and white, and accessible and meaningful to both. As for Rebecca and her friends, surely the first question has to do with why black children would even want to listen to a minstrel song, one generally considered to be for white consumption; yet they seemed to have accepted it as in part their own, a song to which they gave the endorsement of dancing. In this they were not alone, for African-American musicians could be heard to play and sing minstrel songs during this period, and there is some evidence that African Americans attended the theatres and heard minstrel songs performed there.[92] Could it be that "Jim Crow" and kindred songs functioned, during this period, for black people much as they did for common white people, as songs of subversion, about dancing and the body and laughter, and of how the performance of joy and pleasure can remake a less than perfect world?

Fascinating too about this story is the evidence of racial mingling on the streets near the paint shop. It appears that it was easy sometimes, uneasy at others, and sometimes both. Backgrounding my reconstruction of this scene is the axiom that race is the determining factor in how well persons of different color get along. I believe myself, in the final analysis, to be in error in this regard. The evidence of the matter suggests that race was not the most telling factor – at the level of the common person. Rather, people had character first and race second. Any reading of the daily newspapers of New York, Boston, or Philadelphia,[93] especially the "Police Court" column, will reveal a common world in which blacks and whites lived by, worked with, drank among, fought with (to be sure and not to be understated), and loved each other. Miscegenation was deeply distressing to the middle and elite classes in part because it was so common among the lower. In Massachusetts in the 1830s the only legal distinction between blacks and whites was that they could not marry with each other; yet apparently many did so, for the court reports are filled with mixed-race couples being brought into the halls of justice for the "unnatural" sin of amalgamation (the period's term for miscegenation). Of course the reporter, an agent of the paper's clientele, was always incredulous that a white man or a white woman could ever be attracted to someone of the other race.

To read between the lines, though, is to discover a world in which comradeship and love often had no eyes for color of skin, a world in which white women shrieked out in emotional pain because the courts condemned their black husbands to penitentiary for breaking the amalgamation laws.[94] Lucy Hemmingway, "a very fair complexioned white woman, . . . well dressed, and decidedly handsome, and of the imperial order of beauty," admitted in court to being married to John Cleaveland, "a negro lumper on the wharves," and to being "perfectly satisfied with him for a partner." John Alexander Marshall, "a venerable coal black swain of a white woman," was imprisoned for his union, released, then reimprisoned for returning to her.[95] Sexuality and love were not the only bonding agents, however. Sometimes there was criminality: Benjamin Underhill, black, and George Smith, white, were brought into police court for together stealing six water pails.[96] Sometimes there was just friendship: A "notorious ruffian" named John A. Rose, who "ran with [fire] engine company 36" in New York, was charged with a "Gross Outrage" – his dog had allegedly bitten another man! Rose's main witness was his friend and companion Jim Brown, "a negroe," who also ran with the same company and who believed that

Rose "ought to be let off."[97] We have here a common symbol of the
working-class male – the engine company – with "runners" (who accompanied the engines and the crews to the fire) both black and white,
and pals to boot.

Moreover, sometimes blacks and whites were together at their ease
in simply sharing the present. A sort of emblematic Rabelaisian scene
was uncovered by the New York police when they raided a gambling
house in 1840, and gives example to total and easy "amalgamation." Inside, the officers found about twenty persons "of all sizes and colors,"
being led by a "master of the ceremonies, an out-and-out darkey." At
a table in the corner, "a little black rascal of twelve years, assisted by
two little white ones of eleven or under, were roaring a love song,"
while in another corner, "a knot of little amalgamationists were ap-
plauding the exertions of a bit of a niggar, who was jumping 'Jim
Crow.'" As the police made their move, tables and chairs were tossed
about, "glasses and tumblers went crash, crash, crash, in all directions
– and to crown the whole, two feminine blocks of ebony and a little
Irish woman set up a pullaloo that was equal to the keen of a Munster
funeral."[98]

The evidence, in total, suggests that urban life during the Jacksonian period was most highly integrated racially among the lower classes.
It is conceivable that this time and place found the races living together as easily as any before and perhaps more so than any since.[99]

It is clear too that as life was creolized at the level of common urban
people, so too was music and dance. Rebecca Barbadoes had not seemed
to believe that "Jim Crow" belonged to whites alone. Julius Caesar, "a
dirty looking negro loafer," purported to find nothing wrong with re-
questing that Anglice, a traveling fiddler and "decent looking white
man," play "Jem-along-Josey" for his party.[100] What we today call "fiddle tunes" are usually associated with white culture and often presumed
to have derived from older Anglo-European melodies; but scholars have
looked largely in vain to find the precedents. The documentable history of fiddle dance tunes for the most part starts in the very period
under study in this book. Moreover, the evidence I have been able to
gather concerning urban musical culture suggests that it is impossible
to separate out independent white or black strains of musical culture.
"Fiddle tunes" like "Jim Crow," "Jim Along Josey," "Zip Coon," and
other minstrels standards of the time were sung, heard, danced to, and

loved by both blacks and whites, and were doubtlessly made together as well.

Of dancing, several steps in minstrelsy might once have been part of black dancing practice – most important, the shuffle steps, both the single and the double. Charles Dickens capped his description of an 1842 visit to the Cow Bay, a notorious Five Points tavern/brothel, with the dancing of Juba, a black man.

> [S]uddenly the lively hero dashes in to the rescue. Instantly the fiddler grins, and goes at it tooth and nail; there is new energy in the tambourine; new laughter in the dancers; new smiles in the landlady; new confidence in the landlord; new brightness in the very candles. Single shuffle, double shuffle, cut and cross-cut; snapping his fingers, rolling his eyes, turning in his knees, presenting the backs of his legs in front, spinning about on his toes and heels like nothing but the man's fingers on the tambourine; dancing with two left legs, two right legs, two wooden legs, two wire legs, two spring legs – all sorts of legs and no legs – what is this to him?[101]

When T. D. Rice jumped "Jim Crow," he was doing a variation of the shuffle, "in which the feet remain close to the ground and upper-body movements predominate."[102] Lest one think that these dances were for professional black or blackface performers only, many, many accounts from the period find white, common (and, sometimes, not so common) people in the friendly circle of a tavern, dancehall, or brothel dancing the shuffle or some other ostensibly "black" dance. A witness in the trial of Owen Malone, a white man charged with "being a common fiddler," observed that "(t)hey go the double shuffle there [to Malone's music] in great style, till they get all snarled up in one general heap of a fight."[103] Luke Cavanagh, "a very pretty little boy about seven years of age," obviously white, was brought in by the watch for "figuring in negro dances, at some of the low public houses in Centre street."[104] New York's *Evening Tattler,* after attending an 1840 "Fireman's Ball," reported that "Alderman Phenix cut the 'pigeon wing' with a degree of excellence that was the admiration of every one"; it then added that "we decidedly think that Alderman Bailis took the shine out of him at the pushing step, and the shuffle."[104] In short, shuffles were danced by blacks, whites, and minstrels all.

Then there are the nominally "white" dances, principally the breakdown – not a step at all but a generically fast, energetic dance. Very early on this dance is associated with minstrelsy: In October 1833 Rice concluded his performance at the Baltimore Theatre with "A Virginia Break Down."[106] John Diamond, Dick Pelham, Frank Brower, and other minstrels made the energy of a breakdown central to their reputation. When Master Miles, the butcher boy, accepted the challenge for a match with John Diamond (for fifty dollars) he danced a breakdown.[107] However, breakdowns were also claimed and danced by blacks, and one authority has maintained that any "dance in Negro style was called a 'breakdown.'"[108] In 1840 when Lewis Davis, "alias Master Juber [Juba], a gentleman ob color" was arrested for theft, he was identified as "at present engaged in travelling through the states, dancing negro extravaganzas, breakdowns, &c";[109] and Dickens was quite specific in naming the dance he saw Juba dance at the Cow Bay, "a regular break-down." However, these are black performers perhaps trying to appeal to white pocketbooks by dancing white dances; yet if that is the case, what are we to make of the robbery of James Davis, a white man invited by a black man to attend a "regular 'breakdown'" nearby, obviously organized by and largely for African Americans.[110]

Black Americans performed minstrel songs and whites sang songs that were some part of American black culture. African Americans danced "white" dances, and whites danced "black" ones. Who owned these songs? Who owned this music? Who owned this culture?

The multiracial world I describe helps explicate one of the most curious features of "Jim Crow" and many other minstrel songs of the period: the sympathetic, even respectful, expression of what it was to be black in a country of slavery.[111] In truth, nearly all minstrel songs from this time characteristically open with a framing chorus or two that establish the spirit of burlesque (and carnival) by mocking the safest of targets – blacks; yet one must not stop there. A version of "Jim Crow" published in 1834 set a scene, characteristic of inversion rituals.

> At de Five Points
> De niggers had a hop,
> I went a little while,
> Didn't mean to stop.
> The house was topsy turvy,
> All turned upside down,
> And de niggers had de dance,
> Ten foot under ground.
> De white folks got a barrel of flour

And knocked de head in,
And den de way dey cried fire,
I'm sure it was a sin.
De niggers rush'd out,
As if it was a shower,
And when dey got up stair,
Dey let 'em hab de flour.

Mockery and denigration, in this case, though, are strawmen, for there is a moral purpose to the story.

Such a nasty set of niggers,
I'm sure was nebber seen,
And such fun in wite folk,
I tink was berry mean.[112]

Some verses to "Jim Crow" are even staunchly antislavery. Verse thirty-six in the widely distributed sheet music published by E. Riley sets the scene: imminent civil war over the nullification issue of 1832. The next three verses discuss how blacks might fare in such a time.

Should dey get to fighting,
Perhaps de blacks will rise,
For deir wish for freedom,
Is shining in deir eyes.
And if de blacks should get free,
I guess dey'll fee [see?] some bigger,
An I shall concider it,
A bold stroke for de niggar.
I'm for freedom,
An for Union altogether,
Aldough I'm a black man,
De white is call'd my broder.[113]

The meaning of "Jim Crow" is thus slippery – all contestation and ambiguity. The song is, in this respect, much like a carnival, for it is of the common people (and not), of social criticism (and centers of power), of hope (and control), noise (and music), the public sphere (and the private), the body (and the mind), the obvious (and the subtle), all mingling, smudging, transgressing, fun, and blackface – all paradox and meaning, if you'll allow me my carnival moment.

*****

THE CASE OF EDWARD SHALES neatly glosses many of the images and their paradoxical meanings. When Shales – a serious English actor who fashioned a (riotous and popular) following for his (horrendously bad, thus comic) playing of Shakespeare ("We suppose Shakspeare must die – be murdered – that Mr. Shales may live"[114]) – came to Boston in 1840 for his farewell tour, the theatre was packed. The actor apparently never understood why a small knot of men jumped upon the stage while he was in the midst of *Richard III* and whitened him with flour.[115] His audience knew, of course – including the poet "Cheeks," whose satire is titled:

> To Edward Shales, Esq.
> The Great Native Tragedian.
> "Hung be the heavens with black!" alas!

After setting the scene, Cheeks moves to the denouement:

> So I must cease – and yet a word –
> In Bosworth's bloody field,
> What thunders of applause did greet
> Your entrance with that shield.
> "But why," you ask with modesty,
> "True talents ornament –
> "Those dread torpedoes at me hurled –
> "With fell precision sent?"
> "And why the screech – the laughter loud –
> "The whoop – the bark – the yell –
> "The cat-calls – and those dreadful sounds
> "As if from fiends of hell?"

For Shales had grabbed his shield and rushed on "eager for the prey," unaware that some black rogue had replaced Richard's coat-of-arms with the inscription – "Shales for this night only!" – heralded under a jesting image of Jumpin' Jim Crow.[116]

*****

THERE WAS NO CHARACTER like Jim Crow for that time. The only remote equivalent was Col. David Crockett, roarer, braggart, fighter, dancer, fiddler, frontiersman, orator, politician, part myth, part man. In 1835, according to the *Boston Post*, Davy Crockett ("a Congressional Merry Andrew" and his party's "most successful clown") and Jim Crow teamed up and toured together.[117] In league they jumped and whooped, lied and satirized, exaggerated and trivialized, and loved and fought, thus blurring the boundaries between the real and the representational. Between them they gave joint definition to some of the central mythical beliefs of common people, white and black, of the East and West, North and South, all caught up together in an epoch of change out of their control.

4

Zip Coon

Negro Dancer and Buffalo Singer;
A wretch, a reprobate, a sordid slave,
Compound of bully, liar, fool and knave;
A shameless hypocrite, a common cheat,
A being only born to stink and eat.
But why on such a creature's vices dwell?
Quick; take him, Devil – he's too long from hell.[1]

I went down to Sandy hollar t'other arternoon,
An de first man I chanc'd to meet war ole Zip Coon,
Ole Zip Coon he is a larn'd scholar.
For he plays upon de banjo, "Cooney in de hollar."
Cooney in de hollar an racoon up a stump.
And all dose 'tickler tunes Zip use to jump.
Oh de Buffo Dixon he beat Tom Rice,
And he walk into Jim Crow a little too nice.[2]

W HILE, ON THE SURFACE, "Jim Crow" is a song about and
by an impoverished Southern slave, "Zip Coon" occupies
the other pole, as a delineation of a Northern black dandy.
In at least as many ways as it is different, though, "Zip Coon" is like
"Jim Crow." For one, the text to this song of 1833 follows a similar pattern.[3] The first few verses of almost all versions frame the "blackness"
of the character with demeaning representations of African Americans
– much like "Jim Crow." One hears of 'possums, 'coons, chicken feet

("widout any butter"), a blue-skinned girlfriend named "Suky," and exaggerated pretensions (Zip as "a larned skoler"). Then the verses generally move on to the heart of the song – the body politic – sometimes replete with anticipation of the Crow–Crockett alliance of 1835:

> I tell you what will happin den, now bery soon,
> De Nited States Bank will be blone to de moon;
> Dare General Jackson, will him lampoon,
> An de bery nex President, will be Zip Coon.
> An wen Zip Coon our President shall be,
> He make all de little Coons sing posum up a tree;
> O how de little Coons, will dance an sing,
> Wen he tie dare tails togedder, cross de lim dey swing.
> Now mind wat you arter, you tarnel kritter Crocket,
> You shant go head widout old Zip, he is de boy to block it
> Zip shall be President, Crocket shall be vice,
> An den dey two togedder, will hab de tings nice.[4]

Zip Coon as president! Almost as ridiculous as Davy Crockett in Congress (Tennessee–Democrat, 1829–31; Tennessee–Whig, 1833–5), or, apparently, General Jackson as president. The song is a burlesque on middle-class social and political pretensions. As such, "Zip Coon" is part of a tradition that extends back before minstrelsy. A print from 1829 in the series "Life in Philadelphia" by Edward Williams Clay makes this clear. It is entitled, "How you like de Waltz, Mr. Lorenzo?" These words are spoken by an elegantly dressed black woman and addressed to a black dandy. The response by Mr. Lorenzo – "Pon de honour of a gentleman I tink it vastly indelicate. Only fit for de common people!!" – confirms the atmosphere of pretension. A good belly laugh in response was a victory for the common people.

An issue addressed in this song – perhaps *the* issue – is that of honor, how it is achieved and maintained, and by whom. There is no doubt there really were dandies of color during the Jacksonian period; the newspapers were full of disdainful reports. Why were they so threatening that an entire song was devoted to this phenomenon? These were times in which modes of achieving and maintaining honor, both personal and that of the community, were specific to class. An "affair of honor" among important powerful men was the occasion for a duel, and during the period at least one congressman was killed and an important New York newspaper editor (Webb, of the *Courier and Enquirer*) was

seriously injured. An affair of honor usually involved written (not ver-
bal) insult and the appearance of cool detachment from the consequences, which were planned for a remote time and place. On the other hand, among the common people an insult led to a fight, on the spot,
and perhaps one that was "no holts barred," "rough-and-tumble." The
fighting was ferocious, and eyeballs, fingers, or testicles might be lost,
but typically not life (unlike in a duel with pistols).[5] "Zip Coon," in his
sartorial remoteness from the day to day, in his aspirations to be "a
larned skoler," and in his mien and bearing was the antithesis of the
way common people – and especially, of course, black people – should
act. The genius of the song, from the perspective of the white working-class audience, was its ability to ridicule both up and down the social ladder simultaneously, making a funny song a double treat, and to
give expression to white common-person feelings of being bracketed
out of the day's sociopolitical dialogue. Zip (a name dressed up from
the common African-American name "Scipio") gives character to the
reason why blacks cannot possess the "honorable" status accorded
whites and, at the same time, expression to the abstract, distant, unnatural, and, finally, unworkable pretensions of the powerful.[6]

     The biggest joke of all is in the music, the very thing that has given
"Zip Coon" currency to this day (as opposed to the tune "Jim Crow,"
which has gone almost completely from the collective memory of
American musical culture). First of all, "Zip Coon" is what we would
today call a fiddle tune, although in its day it might more likely have
been termed a jig. In any case, this is music for dancing, and as such
the song belonged to all the participants, not just the singer or instru-
mentalist. There is nothing here like the melancholic quality of some
of the turns in "Jim Crow"; instead, the music's infectious melody and
sharply accented rhythms bespeak motion, dancing, perhaps sex, and a
"good time" generally (Musical Example 3). There are good reasons for
this, for it might have been that "Zip Coon" was associated with brothel life from the first. G. P. Knauff, arranger and compiler of the *Virginia Reels* (1839), included a somewhat dressed-up version of "Zip Coon,"
titled "Natchez on the Hill."[7] One wonders if definition by opposition
is not implied here, for the phrase "Natchez *on* the Hill" alludes to the
big, grand houses on the bluff; "Natchez *under* the Hill," by which title this tune was and is much more often known, refers to "a place of
resort, in fact, a home, for prostitutes, thieves, robbers, and scoundrels

Zip Coon

Musical Example 3. "Zip Coon" [tune only] (New York: Atwill's, 1834).

of every description," where the "fiddle screaks jargon from these *faucibus orci*."[8] Zip might, in fact, sing his song of pseudolearning and class to a bawdy song.

*****

T. D. RICE NEVER REALLY *was* Jim Crow; he was always an actor
playing a part. The same is not true of George Washington Dixon, the
only blackface performer of the period mentioned by his contempora-
ries in the same breath with Rice and the one whose name was most
often linked to "Zip Coon." Dixon, in all the complex contradictory
ways by which meaning follows from the song, actually lived out its
themes. His life, thus, becomes the glass by which we can magnify "Zip
Coon."

Dixon was born in Richmond, Virginia, probably in 1801.[9] It appears
that he was of humble birth, perhaps the son of a barber and a washer-
woman. He might have received his education at a charity school. One
source claimed that at age fifteen "his voice attracted the notice of old
West, who attached him forthwith to his itinerant circus company,
in the capacity of ostler and errand boy."[10] There is no question that
he apprenticed in the traveling circuses. In early February 1824 he appeared with Joe Cowell's Circus in Charleston, South Carolina,[11] and
in 1825 we find him in Salem, Massachusetts;[12] but by July 1827 Dixon
was knocking on fame's door when he made his New York debut.[13]
The next month Dixon was back on the road, in Buffalo with Blanchard's Family Circus, singing "Barney, Leave the Girls By" and re-
citing "Frenchman's Flea Powder."[14] In late April 1828 he was billed
with the Albany Circus Company, with whom he then toured through
at least August of that year.[15] Early the next year he was back in his
native state, in Alexandria, with Harrington's Circus, and for the first
recorded time being hailed as "The American Buffo Singer."[16] Dixon's
stardom came in 1829 when, during a three-day, late-July span, he appeared at the Bowery Theatre, the Chatham Garden Theatre, and the
Park Theatre and at all three sang in blackface "Coal Black Rose," performing for "crowded galleries and scantily filled boxes," a solid indication of the heart of his audience.[17] On 24 September of that year at
the Bowery Theatre, Dixon presented what appears to be the first
blackface farce, titled *Love in a Cloud,* the narrative of which was tak-
en from "Coal Black Rose."[18] He was now a star, a headliner, right in
the middle of the public eye; at his benefit night at the Albany Theatre
(14 December 1829) the gate was $155.87, the largest for the season out-
side of the opening night.[19]

The years 1830–2 were good ones for Dixon.[20] He continued to perform widely and frequently, and was often billed in one or the other of
the New York theatres. He also began to make political statements

through his songs, a direction, as we shall see, that he continued to follow. He sang, for example, at a 25 November 1830 Washington, D.C., demonstration in support of that year's republican revolution in France, before a crowd estimated at 120,000 persons.[21] So wide was Dixon's renown by this time that his name was featured on a songster first published late in 1830 (and in print for many years), a small book-length collection of song texts consisting mainly of the songs by which he was then known. *Dixon's Oddities* began with the song he had sung for the masses at Washington, "A National Song," which praised liberty, freedom, and republicanism. Also collected there are skits, comic songs, a version of "Coal Black Rose," and "The New-York Fireman," in which Dixon compares firefighters to the revolutionary forefathers, in so doing extending honor and prestige to the working-class, clublike organizations whose public responsibility was dousing fires, but whose social function was often community definition.[22]

Evidence of his growing fame, professional standing, and acting and singing skills are to be found in many places. One of the most compelling is a playbill for Baltimore's Front Street Theatre dated 9 November 1832.

First Night of Mr. Dixon as "Splash,"
in the Beautiful Comedy of *A Lesson to Lovers,*
First Night this Season of *Down East; Or, The Militia Training.*
Major Joe Bunker, Mr. Dixon.
Last Night of the Celebrated Songs of Jim Crow,
and Clar de Kitchen!
Six New Comic Songs.
The Popular Medley, Introducing Twenty Different Airs; among
which are: I.O.F. Star Spangle Banner, March to the Battle Field,
Ye Sons of Columbia, Derry Down, Over the Hills, Goddess of
Liberty, All Hail LaFayette, Farewell Land of the Brave.
During the Evening, Mr. Dixon will Sing: Analization:
Or, What are Baltimoreans, Philadelphians, Virginians,
Washingtonians, Bostonians, New Yorkers,
Ladies, Dandies made of?
Also – *The Fashions of Baltimore, Major Longbow in Baltimore, The Lion of
the West, The Royal Lady Ann, or a Trip to Washington.*
And, for the last time, with Additions,
Jim Crow, and Clar de Kitchen.
To which will be added, Mr. Dixon's Highly Popular Lecture
As given by him in *The Hypocrite.*[23]

This extraordinarily ambitious performance found Dixon singing both
in whiteface and in blackface (including both "Clare de Kitchen" and
"Jim Crow" before Rice sang them in New York), playing in a staged
"fantastical," and acting a part from *The Hypocrite*, among other bits –
a performance worthy of a benefit, indeed! Dixon's fame and oratorical
skills were such at this time that the Front Street Theatre advertised:

President's Message. – In consequence of the great anxiety to know the subject of the President's Message, an arrangement has been made with Mr.
G. W. Dixon to obtain a copy of the above interesting document, which will
be received by express, and will be delivered at the Front street Theatre This
Evening, immediately after the first piece, which will give many an opportunity to hear the contents thereof. . . . After which Mr. G. W. Dixon will read
the President's Message. Mr. G. W. Dixon, the distinguished Comic Vocalist, will [also] appear in his extravaganza of "Jim Crow."[24]

After this wealth of performance activity, the record gets short on
the details of Dixon's career in 1833.[25] It might well be that he embarked
on another career this year, one that he would maintain to be his true
calling until the day of his death: newspaper editor.[26]

[T]he Devil or his evil angel inspired him with the idea that he was a literary
genius and he resolved to publish a newspaper. . . . [H]e commenced the publication of the "Stonington [Connecticut] Cannon," which obstinately refused
to go off; because why? – he charged it to the muzzle with lead, without any
powder.[27]

No issues of the *Cannon* seem to be extant, suggesting, indeed, a
misfire.

In a pattern that will become familiar, Dixon went back to the theatre circuit after the failure of his media enterprise. Harrisburg, Pennsylvania, was abuzz in January 1834 with his presence "in company with
several artists." The local *Telegraph* copied a notice from the *Bedford
Enquirer* regarding the special talents of Dixon:

Few Melodists have gained more celebrity or been so universally admired,
. . . The many effusions from the pen of this gentleman independent of his
vocal powers, is sufficient proof of his being a man of considerable talent and
originality – you should hear him sing his national air "on wing that beamed
in glory" [and it would be] unnecessary for us to enlarge on his merits as a
vocalist – for his Melodies, display a feeling of Patriotism which attracts the
attention of every beholder.[28]

In Harrisburg Dixon also appealed for subscriptions to his weeklies, the *National Register* – "devoted to Science, Literature and General Information and [which] contains the most interesting documents" – and the *Ladies Musical Magazine,* which published "American Literature, Music, and Selections from the most celebrated European periodicals, . . . [and] the words and music of the most fashionable new songs, elegantly arranged for the Piano Forte."[29] Subscriptions must have been few, for no record exists today of the journals. Dixon also performed in nearby Gettysburg, where an account in the local *Star* helps us sketch in another part of his character.

G. W. Dixon had the pleasure of singing, &c. &c. for the citizens of this borough, during the past week. It was rumored yesterday that he, or his partner, went off on Sunday last, not *on* 'wings of glory,' but with his wing *in* somebody's *new* coat.[30]

There would be plenty of such episodes over the next several years, enough to suggest a person lacking in certain socially desirable attributes. One of the Philadelphia newspapers around this time called Dixon "the greatest locomotive humbug in christendom."[31]

In 1834, Dixon first began to sing the song on which his renown came finally to rest. "Zip Coon" was not likely of his composition: Robert Farrell, a circus clown who had toured with Joe Cowell in 1832,[32] was probably singing it by 1833 in the Washington and Baltimore theatres,[33] and a Mr. Palmer sang "a Negro Song, in character, called 'Zip Coon,'" at the Richmond Hill Theatre in New York on 4 March 1834.[34] Only later that month is there record of Dixon singing it.[35]

To give example to the complex ways in which blackface worked during the period, Dixon featured "Zip Coon" in June at the Philadelphia benefit for Andrew J. Allen, one of the period's most extraordinary personalities – and a black man.[36] Complicating understanding even further were the events of July 1834 in New York City. Beginning on 7 July, at the height of a record-breaking heat wave, mobs of young men rampaged through the city, attacking businesses, institutions, and homes associated with the abolitionists, and the homes, churches, and persons of African Americans associated with the abolitionists;[37] but, as often happened during riots, the theatre became involved as well.[38] On the night of the 9th, mobs assaulted the home of abolitionist Lewis Tappan, made their way into a black church on Chatham Square, and then moved on to the Bowery Theatre. According to the *New York Commercial Advertiser:*

A Mr. [George P.] Farren, the stage manager, an Englishman, and whose benefit night it was, had been accused of using language disrespectful to the Americans. Hand bills to that effect had been posted up through the city during the day. An immense crowd surrounded the Theatre, and soon effected an entrance. They then took entire possession of the house; and notwithstanding the apologies and entreaties of Messrs. Hamblin and [actor Edwin] Forrest, they succeeded in putting an end to *Metamora*, without waiting the tragic conclusion to which he was destined by the author. By the interference of the municipal authorities, the Theatre was at length cleared and comparative order restored.[39]

The *Commercial Advertiser* was a newspaper supported largely by New York's business interests, and one that had a generally dim view of the goings-on among the lower sorts. The *New York Sun*, the first small-sheet "penny press," was more a paper of the common people; significantly, it put a substantially different spin on the theatre riot, under the title "A Small Muse [*sic*]." The report went that the crowd rushed into the Bowery, that Hamblin would not be heard by the crowd, and that Forrest, the heroic tragedian and a great favorite at the Bowery, was then heard, but to little effect. Then:

Mr. Dixon, the singer (an American,) now made his appearance. "Let us have Zip Coon," exclaimed a thousand voices. The singer gave them their favorite song, amidst peals of laughter, – and his Honor the Mayor, who as the old woman said of her husband, is a "good-natured, easy fellow," made his appearance, delivered a short speech, made a low bow, and went out. Dixon, who had produced such amazing good nature with his "Zip Coon," next addressed them – and they soon quietly dispersed.[40]

There is much ripe here for comment, but let me direct special attention to the image presented – that of the Mayor coming onstage and giving perfect example to the burlesque that is "Zip Coon," and probably being blithely unaware that he and his ilk were the ultimate targets of the song's barbs.

   If "Zip Coon" in fact is about the unjust denial of honor to common white people, accomplished by the symbolic elevation of those on the very bottom, there is a parallel with the attacks of the mob on black Americans – scapegoats for the absent abolitionists. The song and the riot were both about who would control public discourse and community values, with class at base the issue.[41] Community traditions were also at contest; the reported response of some rioters was to procure a hogshead of indelible (black!) ink into which they intended to immerse the (white!) abolitionist leaders were they to capture them.[42] (The transliteration here is critical – from tar, the stuff of manual labor, to ink, the medium of the word – and is developed later in this chapter.) Take special note, though, that a working-class organ (the *Sun*) emphasized the importance of "Zip Coon" in defining and assuaging the grievances of the rioters, and the role that Dixon played in performing for and addressing them. There are many important markers here for understanding Dixon and the function of blackface minstrelsy generally.

After more touring (during which he had introduced a new skill – ventriloquism[43]) Dixon relocated to Lowell, Massachusetts, a then-burgeoning city recently born of the American industrial revolution. By April 1835 he was once again editing a newspaper. *Dixon's Daily Review*, with its motto "Knowledge – Liberty – Utility – Representation – Responsibility," was first of all a Whig paper, and politically supportive of Daniel Webster, a vignette of whom was featured in the masthead.[44] Dixon's politics were thus Whiggish, not Democratic like those of Rice.

It is implanted in us even to revolt at *discords* of every description. *Harmony* has long been our study and our delight – and so long as the voice given to us with our other physical powers shall remain, so long shall it be raised in the maintenance and dissemination of sound Whig principles – and in uttering *notes* of warning to our fellow countrymen again the – you know who.[45]

His politics, though, were not of the elite sort personified during that time by Henry Clay, but owed a great deal to the principles of radical republicanism that supported so many of the era's working-class, urban, political movements. Like radical republicans, Dixon (who long advertised himself as "The National Melodist") was ever ready to hoist the standard of patriotism and republicanism, as his "New National Song" of 1830, dedicated to the French Revolution and sung to the "Marseillaise," made clear:

The lordly Eagle's pinions ply
With uncaged pride behind.
Death, death to all the base-born knaves
Her mighty course would stay, . . .[46]

The *Daily Review* was more, though; it claimed, significantly, to be an "advocate of sound morals." Dixon exulted in his second number:

We are aware of the vast responsibility incurred – and which is too often but little realized – on entering upon the momentous vocation which we now assume. The conductor of a public press takes upon himself not only cares, and perplexities, and hazards, in regard to his condition, but obligations of a higher and nobler character come upon him, as the dispenser of good or of evil, to the minds of thousands perchance, that receive his productions as their moral and political aliment.[47]

He was particularly interested in the role of woman in the era's social construction. "Enchanted woman! thou balm of life! soother of sorrow! solace of the soul! how dost thou lessen the load of human misery, and lead the wretched into the valley of delight!" There is more, much of it affirming Dixon's manifest belief that woman should subordinate herself to paternalistic shelter.

But if the white hand of a fascinating female be twined around his arm, how joyous, how lightly doth he trip along the path! . . . On the errors of women let us look with the allowance and humanity of men. Without thee, how heavily would man drag through a dreary world![48]

By 1835 the template had been milled by which we might understand some of the more extraordinary aspects of Dixon's life to come, and something too of common-class white male attitudes toward women, to which he gave example.[49]

Within the month, Dixon came into conflict with an important element of Lowell society. He was reported to have "flogged one of the editors of the *Lowell Castigator,* and was hunting after the other."[50] Again we have first inkling of a pattern, where issues of honor and insult are settled on the street, "man to man." In this regard, it is significant that Dixon never seems to have dueled, although there were breaches of honor enough, but settled his accounts after the manners of the common people. It was also at this time that the *Boston Post* intimated that Dixon was charivaried, and ridden on a rail "free, gratis, for nothing."[51]

Dixon's Daily Review did not make its way. By the first of July 1835 news was that Dixon had "sold out his *Daily* at Lowell," and that the new publishers wanted it made clear that he no longer had anything to do with it.[52] However, by August claims were published that he had started a new paper, the *News Letter,* to be issued both in Lowell and Boston.[53] No copies seem to have survived, though, to tell us the nature of the enterprise; or whether it even made it to the streets at all.

Again, thus, a mere "melodist," Dixon took to the circuit hustings. He made several successful appearances in Boston in February 1836, to "immense applause"[54] (Figure 7). He seems also to have acted in a play at the Tremont Theatre.[55] His audience remained as before; the highbrow *New York Times* pinched its nose and reported the following.

Tremont Theatre. At this classical establishment, Mr Dixon, "the American Buffo singer," is at present the star. His *third* night is announced! Will some of the enlightened citizens of the emporium favor us with their opinion of his performance? Is his Zip Coon as thrilling as Mr Wood's "Still so gently o'er me stealing?"[56]

Mr. Wood was the day's reigning opera star, giving basis once more to judge that opera and blackface occupied different poles and engaged discrete audiences. In this light, it is especially interesting to note the song Dixon first introduced at his "Grand Musical Soirée" in Boston's Masonic Temple on 16 April 1836, and repeated at another on 30 April. The program announced "the 'Fireman's Call,' adapted to the celebrated air, 'When the Tramp of Fame,' sung by Mr. Wood, in the *Maid of Judah.*"[57] It is easy enough to understand this song's dedication ("to the Officers and Members of the Fire Department of Boston"[58]) and the text, both of which affirm the social utility of and honor due volunteer fire companies, for those who made up and ran with the fire engines were Dixon's constituency; but why would Dixon set such a sentiment to a sensuous Italianate melody from Rossini's *Maid of Judah,* which had, in fact, been performed in New York by Wood within the month?[59] Moreover, why feature so prominently in the bills "Mr. Robinson, of the Academy of Music, London," who would "preside at the Piano," an instrument already strongly associated with middle-class, family values? Didn't Dixon know that by such actions he was sure to alienate those of the pit and the galleries who had long stood with him? Another word Dixon employs is "Concert," a term that might seem innocent enough today, but one then highly fraught and revealing of his grander strategy. Concerts at this time were coming much into favor, in implied opposition to "Theatre." The latter already had a long history aligning it with the sybaritic, the overwhelming of reason with emotion, the visceral, the body, the third tier, the popular, blackface, and more – all things anathema to developing family-based systems of value. Concerts were, instead, cerebral, exclusive, and a European tradition; they might also be construed to be uplifting, even moral, especially if some didactic song by someone like Henry Russell was included. Musical styles were based on European models and spoke of traditional and hierarchical structures, both social and musical. This was also where the money lay, for the very ones who patronized concerts were the ones building the American industrial machine. Quite simply, Dixon, ever the opportunist, saw an open purse and made a grab for it. He hoped to remold himself into an idol of the white middle class by espousing their values and respecting their traditions (new and fluid as they often were).[60] The next several years will present one ludicrous scene after another as Dixon/Zip Coon tries to leave his blackface behind him (and all that suggests) and show his fresh white face to fresh, white paying audiences. Dixon came to answer to his own burlesque.

The aftermath of the last grand, musical soirée concert presents an illuminating instance of how Dixon could never be other than he was. Of the concert's ticket revenue, Dixon was to receive one-third; but as his printer held a financial encumbrance against him, he agreed to leave the proceeds in trust, to be called for by the concert's orchestra conductor, John Friedheim. However, before the affair could be resolved to everyone's mutual satisfaction, Dixon and the printer appeared before the trustee with a forged order.

> Boston, May 23d, 1836.
> Mr. Martin pay to Mr. Dixon the money you have on hand received at the Concert in the Temple on the 30th of April.
> J. L. Friedheim

Once the money was delivered, Dixon turned it over to the printer. The forgery was discovered and, for paying a debt from his rightful part of the proceeds, $23.50,[61] Dixon was marched off to jail. "*George Washington Dixon*, now cormorant of Boston jail, and ex-publisher, ex-editor, ex-broker, ex-melodist, &c., is quite out of tune," wrote one New York newspaper.[62] At the trial in mid June, several character witnesses were called, some of whom noted that he was "a harmless, inoffensive man, but destitute of business capacity." Another, quite forthrightly, "in reply to a question whether Dixon was *non compos mentis*,

Figure 7. George Washington Dixon, the American Melodist. "Pendleton has published a very correct likeness of Geo. Washington Dixon, the 'American Melodist,' who has gained a high reputation as 'a buffo singer'" (*Boston Post,* 8 February 1836). Courtesy, American Antiquarian Society.

said: – 'I consider him as being on the frontier line – sometimes on one side, and sometimes on the other, just as the breeze of fortune happens to blow.'" The prosecution was never able to prove that Dixon knew the draft was a forgery, at least beyond a doubt, and the jury returned a verdict of not guilty.[63] Once exonerated, Dixon addressed "a rowdy rabble outside, from the steps of the courthouse, and had the consolation of their 'most sweet voices.'"[64]

Dixon felt that his honor has been sullied by these proceedings and set about trying to shore it up in the public eye; but the guardians of the press, who had generally turned against him (perhaps for good reason), cut him no quarter. Porter's *Spirit of the Times* was especially ferocious:

We have received a long rigmarole address to the public, printed on a half sheet of whitey-brown paper, and signed *George Washington Dixon*, in which the writer endeavors to exculpate . . . [himself] from the charge of having been acquitted by a Boston Jury of the crime of Forgery on the ground of being deemed *non compos mentis*.

Now in the first place, the said Field Marshal, Cap*ting*, Orator, Buffosinger, Zip Coon Dixon never wrote a word of the address to which his name is attached, and in the second, so far from clearing Dixon of the charge of being "wanting in his upper story," the writer has satisfactorily demonstrated that he himself has "a spacious upper loft untenanted." . . . Mister Zip Coon is at his old tricks again. So far from possessing the ability to write a letter Miss Nancy-Coal-Black-Rose Dixon cannot begin to write ten consecutive words of the English language, and he must have encountered "the Schoolmaster abroad" in the Athenian city that teaches "penmanship in six lessons," and that lately too if he can sign his name.[65]

Porter, the patrician, is beating the upstart Dixon with two sticks: the one of blackness, the other of learning. Dixon is cast to be crazy and degenerate enough that he might really be black – pedigreed back to the "King of Congo." If actually black, learning is moot, for everyone knows that Zip Coon really *isn't* a "larned skoler." To aspire to rise from blackness to the light shed by print is a journey too fraught for the imaginings of mere common people. Porter struck only the first chord on this particular lyre.

Dixon went back to giving concerts, clearing in late July 1836 a reported $527.50 in Boston money, if true an extraordinary take for the day. The *Lowell Journal* intoned: "We hope, George, you have taken enough at this pull, to enable you to fork over. We're short."[66] By the end of the year, he had moved to Boston and started up yet another paper, the *Bostonian; or, Dixon's Saturday Night Express.* He was immediately again in hot water. Other papers accused Dixon of inventing an "elopement story," and a reporter in the *Boston Herald* called him a knave.[67] Dixon countered that his story was really about "mores in high places in Boston," and included a line of warning:

Beware! ye guardians of public morals! We know your faults, and if ever we should engage an artist to paint them in their true colors, you'll start back affrighted at your own pictures!

As for being a knave ("which appellation we care very little for"), Dixon lashed back at Henry F. Harrington, "Little Harry, [editor] of the *Penny Herald,*" and claimed that the charge came from "the milk and water brain of a Fool." He added graphic punch with a woodcut of "Little Harry the Great Unbeliever," portrayed as a monkey. Whether fabricated or not, stories about elopements, mores, and the illicit doings of high society would shortly become a Dixon stock-in-trade.

Number 5 of the *Express* (24 December 1836) carries on its inside pages further guardianship of public mores; but in many ways, the editorial features on the front page (hereafter sampled) reveal more about Dixon, and by extension, blackface minstrelsy. Near the head, a poem entitled "The Sabbath" intones religious piety: "Forget the earth – and learn to think of heaven." Further down, a plug is given for the Boston Phrenological Society, devoted to the pseudoscience of cranial dimensions, bumps, proportions, and properties. On the economy, Dixon expressed a hope that soon we will see "all the laboring classes, not only well employed, but promptly and liberally paid." Another article, more surprisingly, rejoiced that more than eight hundred persons had recently attended the Female Anti-Slavery Fair. Most extraordinary of all was the article "Slavery in Cuba":

By the most authentic accounts, it appears that as many slaves are now smuggled into Cuba as were ever imported, when the trade was nominally legal; another instance of the futility of laws against the sentiments of a large majority of the people, and showing that the good and wise of every country must combine and declare with effectual energy that the rights of the feeble shall be protected, and those who still insist upon living by piracy be outlawed from the race. It is said that seventy slave ships are owned at Havana, and that some of them are navigated by Americans! This we can hardly believe.

Could it be that George Washington Dixon – the Zip Coon – was not only of the working class, but also antislavery, a paragon of the large number of labor abolitionists?[68]

The new year, 1837, brought much of the same and much new. The *Boston Post* accurately assayed Dixon's worth and his capability for self-inflicted damage.

If there is a difficulty any where to be found, George is sure to fall into it, and he finds it impossible to make head-way long in one track. The real truth appears to be, that, with the best disposition in the world, he is deficient in that species of cunning, artifice and petty selfishness, which is generally supposed to be requisite to command success in this heartless world; but this, however, is the common luck of men of genius. No man has ever endeavored to get along in life more than George has, but he cannot accommodate his independent spirit to the caprices of the day and "crook the pregnant hinges of his knee," for any man's favor. Goldsmith's celebrated lines upon the illustrious Burke may, without the least impropriety, be applied to George: –

> Though equal to all things, for all things unfit;
> Too nice for a statesman – too proud for a wit;
> For a patriot too cool – for a drudge disobedient,
> And too fond of the *right* to pursue the *expedient*!!!

. . . One great cause of George's failures, accidents and indiscretions, is, that in all his enterprises he takes hold of the hot end of the poker, and thereby his business transactions occasionally appear rather equivocal, at least. A distinguished Philosopher and clean shaving Barber in Brattle street, thus briefly, but correctly, describes him – "Dixon is like a cow that occasionally gives a good pail of milk, and then kicks it right over."[69]

The occasion for the *Post*'s lament was another legal entanglement. Early that year, Harrington, editor of the *Herald*, sought to extract a measure of revenge against Dixon by charging him with stealing a half ream of pink paper from, extraordinarily enough, the *Herald*'s chief competitor, the *Post*! The *Lowell Courier* had the most apt and colorful description of the proceedings, which I quote at length for its tone and color as well as information.

The first day of February will not hereafter be used in the almanacs as a dead blank – a dull, monotonous nothing. It will arise and claim its place along with its kindred Fourth of July and Eighth of January, and the hundred and one other days sacred to the memory of great events. It was on this veritable day

in the year of our Lord one thousand eight hundred and thirty seven, new
style, at ten minutes and twenty three seconds past three o'clock in the after-
noon, wind S.S.E., that *George Washington Dixon,* the American Melodist –
the great Buffo Singer – the immortal original Zip Coon himself – was brought
before the Police Court, charged by his brother editor Henry F. Harrington
(Esquire) with stealing half a ream of letter-paper from the office of the
Morning Post. – We are thus particular about dates, that future chronologers
and historians may be under no misapprehension relative to the positive commencement of this new era; an era that will be held in remembrances by the
"sons of song" long after their great master spirit has gone off in a double
shuffle to a place where all is "discord, harmony, not understood." (Pope.) We
were present in Court at the time he was brought in: and of course we are
unable to say what was going on without. But we are informed there was a
strange conflict in the musical elements. All the "discord of sweet sounds" that
ever rent the air, seemed now to have put on their most unearthly cadence.
The wind howled as wind never howled before. A large bazoon that had lain
for years with other broken trumpery in a garret, leaped out and "whistled itself" into the tune of "Still so gently o'er me stealing." A large yellow dog ran
down State street with his tail between his legs, barking a double bass, followed by a score of puppies, discoursing in their tenor, treble and alto pipes.
Half a score of cats, who had not had a regular night concert for a week, now
came forward in broad daylight, to complete the concatenation of events, and
to add horror to the catastrophe by their categorial notes. A flock of wild geese,
whom the peculiar fatuity of the times had led to wend their way towards

"The chilling regions of the frozen north."

before their time; tacked short and went back, to the south with such croak-
ings as never geese wild or tame, ever uttered before. In short, it seemed as
though all the unwritten, unread, unsung, and unearthly music, that ever beat
upon the tympanum of the human ear, now joined melodious to swell the
air, and to echo back, so far that it might not return again, the "music of the
spheres."[70]

The court, that august arbiter which (sometimes!) metes out blind and
objective justice, is here represented to be on the brink of surreal burlesque, near a point where Dixon lived habitually, and which he shared
with the callithumpian hordes that had seemingly invaded his trial.

Harrington himself presented a vigorous prosecution case, "in the
presence of the densest crowd that ever sweltered in the Court Room,"
an indication of Dixon's following. The judge termed the case a "difficult one," but affirmed the defense argument that the identity of the

pink paper had never been established beyond doubt, although it was "almost morally certain, that the larceny had been committed." Legally, however, he felt bound to discharge Dixon, and did so. As had happened before, Dixon strode to the steps of the courthouse and delivered a speech upon his unjust persecution at the hands of fellow editors, to "an immense collection of people. He is certainly a *rara avis* – a regular 'Non Such' – and of unrivaled eccentricity!"[71]

Dixon immediately adjourned to the stage, hoping to cash in on his enhanced notoriety, and held another "Grand Musical Soirée" on 4 February 1837, at which Professor Nolcini presided at the piano and "Signor Perez . . . introduce[d] several brilliant pieces on the Guitar."[72] However, before he could reap the bounty he had sown, Dixon was back before the court, barely ten days after his exoneration, this time charged with forging signatures to a bail bond secured after being sued for debt in July 1835. He was taken back to Lowell, the scene of the alleged crime, and imprisoned there. Predictably, responses to his arraignment were extreme, from all sides. The *Lowell Advertiser* smirked that "George has been a great eulogist, the defender of the Constitution! But he cannot defend himself."[73] After a hearing on 15 February, Dixon had his bond set at one thousand dollars, an extraordinary sum for the time, and after being unable to procure security was imprisoned in Concord, Massachusetts.[74] Newspapers crowed in anticipation of his conviction. The *Dedham Patriot* punned that "'the American Melodist' should be sent to Sing Sing, instead of Charlestown."[75] The *Lowell Patriot* was most fulsome, choosing to print a long, satirical poem about Dixon by one "Iron-Filer," replete with puns on blackness ("a *black* flood of venom") and concluding verses that feature images from the charivari, turned on Dixon:

> Or if you should for time to come,
> Conclude to keep your cranium,
> Tie on an ass' ears, then glory
> In symmetry of upper story;
> Screw on a tail, that all may see
> A real monkey, cap-a-pie.
> When such-like decorations find
> Your body pattern'd like your mind,
> Put on that grin of face and lip,
> That far out – "Coons" the real "Zip";

Mount on your hobby horse, and che [?]
At others for deformity.
The honors of *this* world's creating,
Are not the *only* ones in waiting –
You're *nominated* to be *run*
*Gall-Spitte*r for "the wrath to come."
I would advise you, though 'tis plain
All efforts to reclaim are vain.
Go chew a bible leaf, once more
That truth be where 'twas ne'er before;
'T would be but justice to your sconce
To let it taste some truth for *once*.[76]

After more than a month in jail, Dixon's case was brought up before
the Court of Common Pleas on 16 March 1837. This time he was convicted, but immediately an appeal was filed with the Massachusetts Supreme Court.[77] Following the pattern, Dixon's trial here on 17 April
was something of a circus. The prosecution relied upon circumstantial
evidence to prove that Dixon had caused the signatures to be forged,
the fact of forgery agreed to by the defense. Dixon's counsel countered
with a conspiracy theory that tried to implicate two disgruntled former
employees of the editor. Before judgment was turned over to the jury,
the judge instructed it to pay particular attention to the sufficiency of
the evidence, and left the impression that he felt there was a lack of
proof. The jury was unable to arrive at a decision and the charges were
subsequently dropped.

Before leaving the Court, Dixon requested permission to address the people
in it, which was very much crowded during the whole trial, but as Judge
Wilde would not consent to listen to his sweet voice, he retired, and harangued
the multitude below. He remarked, that he would rather suffer another imprisonment, than not have had an opportunity to clear his fame before the people,
and "show the world he was a gentleman." He [spoke] in ecstasies of the lux-
uries he enjoyed in Concord Jail – the smiles of the ladies, and the delectable
pic-nics they supplied him.

This reporter for the *Post* acknowledged that "I begin to think that the
Melodist bears a charmed life – and as was often said to be done in old-
en time, has made a bargain with the Being of Darkness for a certain
term of years, during which he may defy the majesty of the law, and
the wrath of his enemies."[78]

As before, Dixon took immediately to the stage in the city of his trial, appearing before a Lowell audience on 27 April in a concert dedicated "to the Ladies of Concord." Dixon sang his best-known songs, including "Zip Coon," and presented "Sketches of Col. Crockett," in
honor of the recently martyred hero of the Alamo.[79] If there is a smack
of opportunism in all this, in fact a reporter did claim to hear Dixon
say after his last trial, "this will make my fortune."[80] He continued to
give concerts throughout New England that summer and fall, including a swing through Maine. During this tour he often whipped up the
audience by singing a new song, "The Brave Sons of Maine," followed
by the introduction of Mr. Greeley, an American citizen who had been
imprisoned by the British in Canada, a region that the audience (and
Dixon too) believed was American soil "guaranteed to us by the treaty
of '83."[81] Dixon reported to the editor of the *Portsmouth Journal* that
his "success in Portland has been quite brilliant."[82] It was at this time
too that the *Spirit of the Times* editorialized: "Dixon, the American *Buffalo* singer, is tuning his pipes at 'Bangher,' down east. George is a genius, he is, and we should not be surprised if he left town in character
– that is, 'settin' on a rail.'"[83] Porter thus lays claim here to being the
first to parody the European "buffo" with the wildness and strangeness
of the American "buffalo." It was a counterburlesque that fit and one
that would stick.

That fall Dixon appears to have toyed with the idea of touring with
James Salisbury, a black "split-birch bark" player who typically performed on Ann Street, Boston's most notorious. Salisbury was something of a virtuoso who could play waltzes, jigs, and reels equally well.[84]
To have shared the stage with a black performer would then have been
nearly unprecedented in the annals of American popular culture, as well
as indicative of Dixon's egalitarian politics; but Dixon chose rather to
try and embrace the other pole of musical culture. His 6 December 1837
Boston concert was to be held at the Opera Saloon, which had been fit-
ted up "after the manner of the Operatic Saloon in Paris." Further, the
concert would feature selections from the operas *Massaniello, Cinderel-
la, La Sonnambula,* and *Maid of Judah.*

> Ladies are respectfully informed that this will be a "Dress Concert."
> To prevent confusion, carriages will set down their company, horses heads
> turned towards Milk street.
> Tickets $1 – each ticket to admit one gentleman and two ladies; single tick-
> ets, 50 cents.[85]

Dixon's clear intention here is to appeal to an audience significantly more upscale than that which had supported him in the past. He now pursued those who had the leisure and work schedule appropriate to concerts starting at 8 o'clock (as this one did) instead of the more plebeian 7 or 7:30.[86] One suspects that such was a manifestation of what appears to be congenital insecurity about his place in the world. (This, of course, is why he was so successful impersonating Zip Coon, who suffered from the same malady.)

More positively, Dixon was boldly proclaiming himself to be what no entertainer from the popular stage had been before: a musician! Not an actor, like Rice, but one who could conquer the almost aseptic environment of the concert hall with the sheer power of music; and, unlike almost any other performer of his time, he had the credentials and the capabilities. As much as the newspapers loved to impugn Dixon's character, not once did they bestow anything but praise upon his musicianship: "his voice seems formed of music itself – '*it thrills* it animates' . . .";[87] "a voice which *all* unite in pronouncing to be of remarkable richness and compass."[88] Some of the music he sang required considerable technique, skill, and vocal range ("The Fireman's Call" among them). He felt qualified enough as a musician to advertise himself as a "Professor of Music" in Lowell.[89] It had always been his calling – Dixon was a musician! – but the path to success for singers in the popular vein was virtually untraveled; Henry Russell was practically inventing the notion at this very time. As usual, Dixon knew better where he wanted to go than how to get there. He would always prove a more proficient scout than general.

It was also in December that a political group wishing to prevent the election of Mayor Samuel A. Eliot to another term tried to split his vote by putting forward a flock of candidates with special constituencies. The technique was to plaster the city with election handbills. There was, for example, a "Day and Martin" ticket composed of "colored waiters and boot blacks," a "Pauper" ticket to gather the poor vote, and a handbill for the "Liberal" ticket, which was topped by the eminent George Washington Dixon! Burlesque here has invaded electoral politics – even better, blackface burlesque – for what would it say if Zip Coon were elected Mayor of the "Literary Emporium," as Boston so often and so pretentiously liked to proclaim itself?

Notwithstanding, the drafted candidate issued the following statement:

My name having been used without my authority, as a candidate for the
Mayoralty, by some of my fellow citizens, I beg leave to inform the public
that I do not desire the office, and shall not accept of it if elected.

Yrs, &c.,

Geo. W. Dixon[90]

Instead, Dixon urged the reelection of his fellow Whig, Mayor Eliot.
The *Boston Post,* which supported the Democrats, wrote: "We admire
Mr. D's fidelity, but disapprove of his taste. His preference can only
be reconciled upon the principle of sympathy which is known to exist
between great minds of similar attributes – Mr. Eliot's admiration of
music is only equalled by the love the American Melodist bears the
Art Divine."[91] One wonders about the seriousness of this positioning
and politicking. Did Dixon ever seriously entertain notions of running
for office? (It would have been in character to have done so, and failed.)
In fact, myth, a form of popular cultural truth, took his "campaign"
quite seriously. Dixon's obituary in a Baton Rouge newspaper claimed
that "(s)o great was his popularity in Boston at one time, that, when
put forward in jest, by a few convivial politicians, he only lost the election to the civic chair by one vote."[92] Another account had him within eight votes of Mayor's office.[93] Alas for the myth, though, the facts
tell quite another story. The official tally found that Eliot had been re-
elected with 3,475 votes; "Geo. W. Dixon" received but nine.[94]

Early in 1838 word circulated that Dixon was to leave Boston for
Washington, where he planned to edit a Whig newspaper.[95] He stayed
a while longer though, and threw himself into a concert for charity, to
"alleviate the sufferings of the indigent,"[96] at which he continued to offer music from the operatic repertory. (A somewhat unreliable source
claimed that the receipts "were literally so applied [toward the indi-
gent], for he pouched them himself, . . ."[97]) At a Boston concert on 26
February one of his songs was said to have been encored four times.[98]
This concert was moreover the last for the year, according to my record. Dixon clearly was aiming for something other than a musician's
career, and his vision led him to move on that spring, not to Washington, but to New York City.

There, naturally, he ventured a new newspaper, the *Polyanthos and
Fire Department Album,*[99] which turned out to be the most successful
and influential of all his publishing enterprises. Early numbers seem not

to have survived, but their effects are recorded. It is clear that Dixon from the first intended a paper for the working class (as signaled by the second part of the title) and one that would expose upper-class "libertines," especially those with a taste for the seduction and deception of lower-class women – a fuller development of the "elopement story" of a few years before. Toward an end of "moral reform," Dixon, perhaps in his very first issue of the *Polyanthos,* published an exposé on the (likely) relationship that Thomas Hamblin, the noted womanizer and manager of the Bowery Theatre, was having with one of his brightest young stars, who also happened to be well short of twenty. Long frail, Miss Missouri was dead within ten days of the article, precipitating a nasty scandal. A coroner's jury found that she died as a result of "inflammation of the brain caused by great mental excitement, induced jointly by the violent conduct of Miss Missouri's mother [who apparently ran a brothel] and the publication of an abusive article in *The Polyanthos.*"[100]

Most of those in a position to know believed Hamblin guilty of adultery with the fragile young woman.[101] The truth aside, Hamblin seems to have considered Dixon's behavior to be a breach of honor. It is not surprising, given Hamblin's history of violent response to insult,[102] that newspapers reported

George Washington Buffalo Dixon has this day [28 July 1838] . . . received a most tremendous quilting, at the hands of Thos. S. Hamblin. I have heard no particulars, except that Buff, as editor of *The Polyanthos,* was severely beaten by Arbaces. It is the only way in which his feelings can be reached.[103]

Dixon took steps that such would not happen again, and the *Baltimore Sun* noted this in August that year.

We take it that Mr. George Washington Dixon, erst the American melodist, now editor of a scurrilous print in New York, gets more kicks than coppers in his new vocation. On Friday he was assailed by a man named Johnson, who undertook to castigate him with a cowhide. The melodist drew a pistol and shot him in the leg, somewhat impairing the gentleman's *understanding.* The wounded man, however, nothing daunted, again renewed the attack, when Dixon aimed a second pistol at Mr. Johnson's seat of honor, and gave him such an argument *a posteriori,* as tore open his unmentionables, and ploughed a passage through the flesh, tracking its way with blood.[104]

Whatever his failings, Dixon was no coward – "He is brave to reckless-
ness"[105] – and his press attacks on Hamblin and other such "philander-
ers" continued full force (Figure 8).

In the *Polyanthos* of 8 December 1838 he reported that Rowland R.
Minturn, a middle-aged, unmarried merchant from one of New York's
most powerful commercial families, was enjoying a dalliance with the
wife of Mr. James H. Roome, shipmaster.[106] On 20 December Minturn
leapt from the roof of his house, killing himself "while in a state of
mental depression."[107] Dixon also during this time charged the Rever-
end Francis L. Hawks, Episcopalian Rector of St. Thomas Church in
New York City, with sexual adventure, and provided the illicit details.[108] The outcome of this revelation (assuming it was such) would
shape Dixon's 1839, and perhaps Hawks's as well; for on the last day of
1838 Dixon was back in court, charged with criminal libel against "the
People," but specifically against Hawks.[109] Delivered up to competing
newspapers was a New Year's carnival feast.

A miserable looking, loaferized, hermophrodite specimen of the half-breed
negro, was brought up, charged with publishing a filthy and scurrilous libel
on the Rev. F. L. Hawkes [*sic*], the rector of St. Thomas Church. The com-
plainant having sworn to the falsity of the publication, Mr. Justice Lowndes
ordered the accused to find bail in the sum of $2,000, and as he was not pre-
pared with that amount, he was committed to close custody.[110]

Widespread knowledge of and interest in this case, and its defendant,
are evident from the fact that the *New York Herald* never once seemed
to believe it necessary to mention Dixon's name. Anonymity also made
appear more feasible the charge that the defendant was a mulatto. Here
the *Herald* tried to blacken Dixon the blackface with blackness, the sur-
est way for editor Bennett – a man of strongly held opinions on African Americans ("Niggers and thick lips from Timbuctoo cannot expect
to compete long with the pure Anglo-Saxon blood"[111]) – to damn eter-
nally the singer-editor.[112]

   After nearly a week in jail Dixon procured his bail and was free; but
before he had time even to leave the building he was arrested once
again for libel. In an unusual application of the criminal libel laws, the
court upheld three related motions charging Dixon with libel against
the late Minturn, on behalf of Thomas R. and Edward Minturn, brothers of the deceased. The former swore that Dixon's article "he verily

Figure 8. Engraving of Thomas B. Hamblin as "Il Jattattore; or, the Evil Eye," in "Gallery of Rascalities and Notorieties – No. 8," from *The Flash,* 31 October 1841. Courtesy, American Antiquarian Society.

believes to have been, in its effects upon his mind, the immediate cause
of his brother's sickness and subsequent death – and that the matters
contained therein are utterly false and untrue."[113] Dixon was held to
bail in the amount of $3,000 for each one of the three charges, or
$9,000, the largest bail amount known to me from this time. To Dixon
(and many others, apparently) the bail figure was set so that he would
have to endure lengthy jail time preliminary to the trial; it thus served,
not incidentally, to suppress the *Polyanthos* as well. Dixon's counsel
asked that it be reduced, but the district attorney opposed his request.
His arguments are worth recording, for they show the courts, the district attorney's office, and the mass press to be in league against the ilk
of Dixon.

Your honor, as counsel for the people of this city, I must oppose any reduc-
tion of the bail in this case. The publication alluded to has been the indirect
cause of the premature death of three persons, and it is time that some stop
should be put to print that is not only a disgrace to the city, but a scandal on
the periodical press. The accused is a *criminal of the blackest dye,* and by his
infamous publication is morally guilty of no less than three murders, and I
hope this court will not diminish the amount of bail one iota![114]

The bench concurred, and bail remained at $9,000. Astonishingly (in
manifold ways), a person came forward to provide surety for the full
amount, claiming to be worth $100,000. She was Adeline Miller, one
of the most famous of New York's madams. Thus, not for the last time
by any means, is Dixon linked with the world of prostitution, a big
and prosperous business in New York at that time.[115] For reasons that
are not clear, Miller surrendered Dixon back to the court one month
later.[116] At that point Dixon, charged with a total of seven libels (four
against Hawks, three against the Minturns), was sent to "the Tombs"
to await his trials, docketed more than two months later.

The Minturn trial came first, on 15 April, and lasted three full days.
It was the biggest news of the day; the *New York Express,* just by way
of example, printed more than seventy column-inches of proceedings.
Opening statements by the defense centered on the socially offensive
nature of the *Polyanthos,* arguing that that fact alone established guilt.
Dixon himself provided much of his opening defense, although (significantly) we have his arguments not unalloyed but rather colored through
prose like: "a rhodomontade oration, in which he made frequent use of

the terms 'stone walls,' 'conflict,' 'rescue,' 'female honor,' and 'sacred liberty.'"[117] The prosecution then opened its case and spent the whole first day examining the husband of Mrs. Roome and trying to prove that his wife was, in fact, "a common prostitute," and thus a service at Minturn's discretion. To establish this would be to claim that community mores and honor were not at stake, and that Dixon's actions were then reprehensible, insulting, and libelous. The defense wished only to prove that the allegations in the story were substantially true, and could thus not be construed as libelous. To this end a Mr. John Bowman was called to the stand and described a scene in which he saw Mrs. Roome and Minturn naked and in bed together. No detail was spared.

DEFENSE: . . . Now, Mr. Bowman, pray where could Mr. Minturn have lain?

WITNESS: . . . Right on top of her.

Bowman testified further to "seeing *the act*" (emphases original). Summations dealt with issues of press freedom. Dixon's counsel read from the state constitution on the liberty of the press. The prosecution "detailed the injuries which must result to society in the liberty of the press, if the law of the land did not step in to stay the plague which was raging among us." The judge instructed the jury that it was to establish "if the publication *was true,* and then if made from good motives and justifiable ends." The jury, after hours of deliberation, returned to the packed courtroom and acknowledged that they had been unable to agree upon a verdict. Ultimately, the prosecution chose not to retry Dixon, and charges were dropped.

Nevertheless, at the moment of perhaps his greatest legal victory, Dixon languished still in jail. Yet unresolved was the matter of bail for the Hawks indictments, now reduced to three in number. On the 20th, to little ado, the judge lowered bail from $9,000, which was argued widely to be entirely justifiable before the trial, to $900, suggesting a kind of tacit (and, one hopes, embarrassed) acknowledgment of pretrial judicial complicity. This amount was quickly procured, and Dixon was free.[118]

Not surprisingly, an unleashed, even triumphant, Dixon was sure to antagonize many in the press establishment, and some bore down upon him.

George Washington Dixon: To those who know the true character, and something of the personal history of this imbecile vagrant, the exuberance of indignation with which he is pursued, appears truly ridiculous. That he is disgusting, a nuisance, and a bore, we know – and so is a spider. Nobody would dream, however, of extinguishing the latter insect with a park of artillery; though all the city seem to have fancied that George Washington Dixon could be conquered with no less. The truth of him is, that he is a most unmitigated fool; and as to his pursuing any person with malice, he is not capable of any sentiment requiring the appreciation of real or fancied injury. If he were kicked down stairs, he could not decide, until told by some one else, whether the kick was the result of accident or design, and if of design, whether it was intended as a compliment or as an insult.[119]

Dixon responded to this sort of treatment in the pages of the *Polyanthos*, which he had started up again days after his release: "A portion of the press . . . have told you that I was one of the most dangerous of men . . . [that I induced to] mob violence, and that my attacks were so successful, that they drove some of the unhappy victims to madness, despair and suicide." Dixon insisted that he was but out to protect the sanctity of marriage from a group of wealthy, rapacious adulters. "As we aim the shafts of our satire at sin and iniquity, we also are foes to those who wantonly endeavor to destroy the peace of a domestic fireside, . . ." In verse, Dixon played on the image of his masthead, which meant "many flowers."

> As the warm suns of summer opes the sweet flow'r
> *The Polyanthos* shall bloom in the fair ladies bow'r
> The symbol of Truth, the libertines dread,
> Who dares to tramp o'er it as it blooms in its bed,
> The pride of the virtuous, who cherish its birth,
> And value it only for intrinsic worth.
> It cares not for sect, or party, or power,
> For these cannot poison the unsullied flower,
> That blooms for the people, the great and the small,
> Expending its fragrance on each and on all.
> It will live to behold the just and the right,
> Raise the standard of virtue in the sun's brightest light.[120]

Dixon did, in fact, score important points, and right along the line he intended. As a result, some others of the press softened a bit toward him. During his trial he had presented a spirited, intelligent, and effective defense, one that turned on ferreting out the facts. Even the *Herald*, which had refused even to print Dixon's name at the time of indictment, confessed as much:

The trial of George Washington Dixon, . . . has created, throughout the city, and in almost every class of society, a greater sensation and a more marked curiosity, than any trial that has taken place, since . . . [the Helen Jewett murder trial in 1836]. This interest has been produced by the extraordinary disclosures made by the witnesses – the glimpses which the evidence affords us of the morals of certain classes of society – and the connection and bearing which the administration of the laws has with the moral principles which regulate certain orders of society and begin already to affect the permanency of our republican institutions.

The *Herald* continued by framing the trial and suggesting that Dixon might actually be doing the common people of New York City a service by publicizing the current state of affairs and institutions, whereby the powerless are seemingly at the eternal mercy of the powerful:

These fashionable libertines, by their political connections with the courts, lawyers and juries, can at any moment stifle the voice of truth – and make black white, or white black, whenever it suits their purposes to conceal their wickedness, and to preserve the reputation of their friends from the consequences of their own acts.[121]

"Make black white, or white black!" How far the *Herald* seems to have come from the not-so-distant days of tarring Dixon with race.

The language employed by the *Herald* hints at what Dixon was about. He was, first of all, not alone, nor even the first; only the most notorious. The Presbyterian minister Rev. John McDowall in the early 1830s had set about trying to reform public mores by discussing them openly and in detail. One of his first steps had been to announce the publication of a monthly paper, for quite specific reasons.

Public evils can be removed only by the public. The evils must be shown to the public to interest them to remove the evils. The pulpit and the press are the only sources through which the public mind can be enlightened. I have tried the former to as great an extent as the Providence of God prepared the way for me, and failed to get before the people. *On the press, then, hangs my last hope.* The Providence of God urges me to seize on it, and to ask every man who loves the truth what he will do to circulate this Journal.[122]

McDowall's Journal (Figure 9) had then begun publishing information on seduction, the prevalence of prostitution, the names of brothels, of prostitutes, and of their clients. Featured more prominently, however, usually on the front page, had been reports from organizations like the New York Magdalen Society, the Society for the Promotion of Chastity and Moral Purity, and the American Society for Promoting the Observance of the Seventh Commandment, among others. In the beginning, the *Journal* had had the support of some of the leading figures in various reform movements. However, foreshadowing the events of 1839 (and after) a grand jury had brought an indictment against the *Journal* in 1834 "as a nuisance which calls loudly for the interference of the civil authorities."

Under the pretext of cautioning the young of both sexes against the temptations to criminal intercourse, it presents such odious and revolting details as are offensive to taste, injurious to morals, and degrading to the character of our city. We believe the representations therein made . . . inflame the passions of the young, and increase the evil which they profess to discourage.[123]

The indictment was upheld and *McDowall's Journal* was, almost paradoxically, shut down for being a obscene press.

Dixon was a disciple of McDowall, although distant, to be sure.[124] He was first among the second wave, a group of reformers who tried to improve prevailing social behavior by turning the press into a kind of mediated charivari – from tar to indelible ink – a public exposing and ridiculing of the morally offensive, especially those that threatened the sanctity of the community. The editors of New York's the *Flash* (an immediate descendant of the *Polyanthos*) – William Joseph Snelling, George Wilkes, and George B. Wooldridge (all once and some future friends of Dixon) – claimed to "walk invisible and intangible; yet . . . stick to their enemies like tar and [be] as impalpable to . . . attacks as feathers."[125] As those who effect charivaris are masked and anonymous, so were the editors of the *Flash,* who identified themselves publicly only as "Scorpion, Startle & Sly"; likewise, their intention was to shape through entertainment – a carnivalistic engagement with the humanly compelling. Thaddeus W. Meighan of the *New York Sporting Whip* (motto: "Place in every honest hand a WHIP – To Lash the Rascals Naked through the World") in 1843 used the editorial "we" emphatically: "[W]e conceive it our duty to 'go ahead,' *a la* Davy Crocket [*sic*], and break up the dens ourselves." That he did so in league "with a fine-

Figure 9. Masthead to *McDowall's Journal*, March 1834, showing his printing press shedding its illuminating rays over the world. Courtesy, American Antiquarian Society.

looking, talented vocalist" (Dixon!) is more than incidental.[126] Throughout the issues of "low" newspapers like the *Polyanthos,* the *Sporting
Whip,* the *Flash,* the *True Flash* (Wooldridge and Dixon, editors), the
Libertine (Wooldridge, editor), the *Rake* (Meighan, editor), the *Satirist
of New York and Brooklyn* (Wooldridge, editor), the *Whip* (Wooldridge,
editor), and – happy name! – the *Regulator* (Dixon, editor) overarching
social issues of the day were confronted.[127]

      None of these was more important than the relationship between
the private sphere (and actions in it) and that which belongs to and in
the public, traditionally a function of charivari. Resultant discourse
used this very language. The *Herald* reflected thoughtfully in the aftermath of Dixon's trial that

one of the most remarkable points in this case is the opinion given by the
Judge that because "the individuals were all private the public could have no
interest in their affairs, and, therefore, the publication was not made with a
good motive."

    We conceive that this opinion is only one way to fritter away by inference
the broad principle of the constitution, guaranteeing the liberty of the press.
The principle on which the institutions of a republic are founded, is a principle of morals in official as well as in private life. Every thing that affects this
great basis, is public, and of the most momentous public character too. The
judge supposes that nothing is public but that which may be called political –
either dirty whig or dirtier locofoco. Here lies his mistake in applying the law.
One man kills another, and because they are both private individuals, if the
press makes comments it may be construed into a libel. Another man seduces
his neighbor's wife – or at least meets her clandestinely and breaks up the
peace of a family, and because both the parties are not in official life, the motive of the press in commenting upon such acts, is to be considered unjusti-
fiable and therefore libellous – Oh! most lame and impotent conclusion!

The *Herald* concluded by wondering if "the miserable instigations of
miserable lawyers – or the narrow minds of narrow judges, [are] en-
deavoring to bend the broad basis of the constitution to suit special
purposes or to gratify libertine principles,"[128] thus at least temporarily
aligning Bennett with Dixon. The judiciary seemed always to have the
final word though. In late 1843 Mike Walsh – advocate of the working
man, Congressman-to-be, and editor of the *Subterranean* – faced a sentencing hearing after being convicted of libel. Judge Tallmadge used the
opportunity to lay out the legal issue, and the role of the courts:

In recent instances, . . . public journals have indulged in attacks not only upon public character, but had entered the private sanctuary of families, which they have assailed in a manner that calls loudly upon the public authorities to suppress. That the public press have the right to assail those in public station when actuated by good motives and justifiable ends none will deny, but when it attacks individuals and assails private character and relations without justification, its course is to be sincerely deprecated. When men are assailed, who are not in public life, and held up to contempt and ridicule without good cause, this court will exercise their power to suppress such wrong by the severest punishment within its jurisdiction.[129]

Although unquestionably Walsh, Dixon, and others of their editorial cohort had something about them of the rogue, the scoundrel, and the fool, one must be impressed by their consistent and persevering commitment to opposing Judge Talmadge's point of view. Dixon alone endured public beatings (on three documented occasions, while fending off at least two others), regular indictment (with, presumably, attendant legal expenses), months in jail, and unending ridicule. So likewise did Wooldridge, Snelling, Wilkes, Meighan, and Walsh. These were not men who did not know the business they were about.

Dixon's crusade, though, was ultimately doomed to failure. In part the times sealed his fate: The aftermath of the panic of 1837, the nation's worst depression to that date, was not a particularly propitious time for a new enterprise. His readership was never enough to ensure anything like material comfort, and he never appreciated fully the dangers of attacking the powerful and the wealthy. It was left to others – particularly Wilkes, who started the *Police Gazette* in 1845 – to entertain a large paying readership with the behavior and mores of the rich and famous and thus establish a journalistic genre, one still very much with us today.[130]

There was still, though, the matter of Rev. Hawks's charges against Dixon. Trial was set for mid-May 1839, and the press palpably licked its chops: "This will be one of the most piquant and interesting libel cases ever tried in this city."[131] However, there were some astonishing turns ahead, with an acute one occuring on 10 May: Dixon appeared before the Court of General Sessions, withdrew his plea of not guilty of publishing a libel against Rev. Hawks (a relatively minor charge), and changed it to guilty. He was in court again the next day and did likewise to the two remaining charges, including the major one by which he was accused of publishing false charges of fornication against the minister.[132] Dixon was back on 13 May for his sentencing. When asked if he had anything to say in mitigation, he responded (uncharacteristically), "Nothing." The judge stated that

> the court was disposed to make an example of him in order to show that citizens when they become editors did not cease to feel bound to perform the duties of citizens on that account, and that they would not be permitted to assail the characters of their fellows with impunity . . . [and] hoped the punishment inflicted would serve to intimidate others from the commission of like offences.[133]

Sentence was then served on Dixon: six months in the New York State Penitentiary at Blackwell's Island, breaking stones.

> The great event of passing sentence on Dixon, the African warbler and libeller, is over. He bore himself like a very Brutus on the occasion, and affected to be sustained by conscious rectitude. He was rather pert to the Recorder, and showed symptoms of a speech, which he had probably committed to writing, as he had a roll of white paper pompously displayed under his arm. When the Recorder announced six months imprisonment at Blackwell's Island, he inquired, in an impertinent tone, whether the punishment covered the three indictments against him, or only one, but received no satisfaction on that head. He became somewhat peremptory in his manner, and the officers were commanded to remove him. Then it was that he attempted to do the pathetic, and actually pumped out a few tears from his blue-white optics. He was at once hurried off to the steamboat, on board of which the thieves and vile women, convicted at the late term, were embarked. He begged and implored to be spared this degradation, and offered grandly for the privilege of an exclusive conveyance; but the authorities were inexorable, and he was compelled to go on board, and the moment he was fairly on the deck, he exclaimed, in a theatrical air – "*This is a pretty situation for an editor.*"[134]

What are we to make of this extraordinary scene? Why would Dixon, who had showed such tenacity at the Minturn trial, turn over and plead guilty, without even the benefit of the circus that would surely attend his trial, and lead to his greater notoriety? This does not sound like the entertainer he most certainly was at heart. It may be useful to view the impending trial from the perspective of Dr. Hawks. Dixon and his counsel had already shown themselves to be formidable opponents; they were sure to make accusations and sling mud, and Dr. Hawks "may explain and explain till doomsday – but these facts and their inferences [will] adhere."[135] There was no victory in pursuing such a course. Perhaps Hawks considered dropping the charges altogether, just to protect his honor; but to do so would have been widely interpreted as acknowledgment of his wrongdoing, so there was no option here for a man of the cloth. Perhaps, then, Dixon told the truth when he claimed later that Hawks had paid him $1,000 to take the fall and preserve the Reverend's honor.[136] To Dixon, always impecunious, $1,000 for six months of (hard, to be sure) work, room and board included, was not a bad return. The behaviors of leading figures at the proceedings support this supposition, such as Dixon passing up his chance to deliver a soliloquy before the court and his fans. Hawks apparently waved the palm of forgiveness over Dixon and proclaimed benevolence, that "dove-eyed mercy" might prevail[137] – a thoroughly appropriate gesture for a Christian minister of high virtues! However, shortly after Dixon began serving his sentence, Hawks was drummed out of his rectorship by his congregation, ostensibly for the failure of a church school he had established. He relocated to the then-frontier of Mississippi, from all appearances a sullied and guilty man in exile.[138]

Dixon was no victor either, though, for finally there was proof positive of his incontinent ways. Within days, the *New York Herald,* with perhaps the world's largest circulation, was copying the *Baltimore Chronicle,* without necessity for editorial comment.

Dixon is a mulatto, and was, not many years ago, employed in this city, in an oyster house to open oysters and empty the shells into the carts before they were carried away. He is an impudent scoundrel, aspires to every thing, and was fit to be any body's fool. Somebody used his name (such as he called himself, for negroes have, by right, no surnames) as the publisher of a newspaper, in which every body, almost, was libelled. He is now caged, and, we may hope, will, when he comes out of prison, go to opening oysters, or some other employment appropriate to his habits and color.[129]

✳✳✳✳✳

THE REST OF DIXON'S CAREER can be summarized more briefly. After six months in jail he returned to New York City, reestablished the *Polyanthos,* and continued to hammer away at the old villains. He also charged several new miscreants with tearing the social fabric, most notoriously Fanny Elssler, the dancer, whom he accused of all sorts of immoral sexual behavior. Dixon even incited and led a riot against her on 21 August 1840.[140] He, with typical want of modesty, copied his "Speech" that night into the pages of the *Polyanthos* for 6 March 1841. There he invoked the folk traditions that underlay the mob's actions when he closed his tirade with: "I apprehend that the music will be the good, old air of 'The Cherivarie.'"

Dixon's confidence in himself and his crusades was fully restored.

> The *Polyanthos* cannot die. The protecting Providence that watches over the safety of the just, and defeats the machinations of the wicked, will make it bloom. . . . We prophesy that the latest descendant of the youngest newsboy will animate his hearers with the desire to emulate the enviable fame of DIXON! Our name will be handed down to the end of time as one of the most independent men of the nineteenth century! Our *very hat* will become a relic.[141]

Dixon then fastened onto an issue that would occupy him for several years, yet another one of sexual politics: abortion. In any reading of the period's newspapers, one cannot help but notice the large number of big (hence, expensive) ads for the "Preventive Powders" or services of "Madame Restell" or "Madame Costello," or some other "Madame." Dixon fixed on Madame Restell as most significant of those who provided back-room, illegal abortions for a fee. He charged that she was responsible for several hundred such procedures and, in an editorial in the 16 February 1841 number of the *Polyanthos*, vowed to "Keep It Before the People." He railed against the whole idea of "preventive powders," because "abstinence, the laws of nature, instinct, the church, and the land all concurred in viewing the end of marriage as the procreation of children." In addition, the availability of abortion led inexorably to wanton behavior:

> Seaman, you are going to a three years voyage, and have this security for the good behaviour of your wife; certain acts have certain consequence. . . . Not at all – all this is at an end. Madame Restell shows your spouse how she may commit as many adulteries as there are hours in the year without the possibility of detection.
>
> Young man, you took to your bosom the image of purity, a thing upon which you think the stamp of God has been printed. . . . No so; Madame Restell's Preventive Powders have counterfeited the hand writing of Nature;

you have not a medal, fresh from the mint, of sure metal; but a base, lacquered counter, that has undergone the sweaty contamination of a hundred palms. . . .

Young woman, married or single, if you have sinned, it is of no consequence. Here is a mother confessor that will shrive and absolve you. . . .

Unmarried mother! there is a churching for you also. Go to Madame Restell. . . . She will tell you how to impose upon your husband or deceive your lover.[142]

By mid-March 1841 Dixon's campaign had produced its result: Restell was taken before the police, charged, and jailed. Dixon devoted several issues of his sheet to the story, often illustrating the news with a woodcut of a woman in a bonnet, embroidered upon which was the head of death, a skeleton hovering in the shadows.[143] When Restell was convicted in July Dixon rejoiced and published anonymously a damning account of her trial.[144]

Dixon enjoyed higher status than perhaps ever before. He was treated gently, warmly, and sympathetically by many of his colleagues when in September he was once again attacked in the street and "is now lying with his head split open, and his interesting locks all gory – the effects of a blow from an axe in the hand of a rowdy. . . ." According to this account, Dixon was, at the time of the attack, "standing near his new office – he has a new one every other day – concocting an article about virtue, morality, and genius, . . ."[145] The *Sunday Mercury* teased Dixon, who was "renowned for his genius, his championship of virtue and morality, his vocalism, and his splendid head of hair" and admitted to admiration of him.[146] The *Uncle Sam* acknowledged his "talent" as a writer and editor. In proof, it quoted a long section from the *Polyanthos,* for it was "bold, poetical and musically written." Just a portion to fix the command of language and the sentiment:

Where is the foundation of this affected contempt? Who feels it, and for what? Have we ever seduced virtue and betrayed innocence? Have we ever trampled upon a man's holiest rights, those guaranteed by Heaven, and surrounded with denunciations of eternal retribution? Have we ever wound our way into the affections of some happy heart, like Satan into Paradise, and left blighting desolation, where we found the roses of virtue distilling their fragrance?

The *Uncle Sam* then resumed its own voice:

Here Dixon rises above himself. Not in the palmiest days of his Ethiopian glory, when he introduced Coal Black Rose and Zip Coon upon the boards of the

Park, the Columbus in a career of renown, in which so many have since embarked, did he ever attain to the height of his present position. Genius will triumph over every obstacle, and in spite of the jealousy and opposition of the
combined New York press, must come off victorious. Read the following, and
hide your diminished heads.

By way of proof of beauty and power, the copy of the *Uncle Sam* in the
American Antiquarian Society shows – a cleanly cut rectangular hole!
Dixon's passage had been clipped by some admiring reader!! No high-
er compliment would he ever garner.

Go on martyr to virtue, go on and prosper! Go on getting out extras, and de-
fending the sacredness of the marriage institution. Go on, through malice, opposition, fiery trials, persecutions and assassinations – posterity will do thee
justice; and the next time you get a letter from an iceberg, let us know![147]

The city courts continued to demand Dixon's attention that fall, although he seems largely to have ignored them. The *Herald*, continuing
in its efforts to blacken Dixon, noted on 6 October that "George W.
Dixon, a nigger, . . . indicted for assault and battery," failed to appear
and forfeited his recognizance. Dixon did not show as well on 1 November, again losing his bail.[148] Nor did he report ten days later to respond to the charges of assault and battery upon Formal.[149]

A campaign was launched about this time by the district attorney
against the presses believed to be yellowing New York. Wooldridge,
Wilkes, and Snelling were charged for a libel and "for publishing an
obscene paper" (i.e., the *Flash*) on 22 October 1841.[150] Dixon was arrested on 19 November for publishing his obscene newspaper and indicted
on 13 January 1842; once again, though, the editor failed to appear, and
forfeited his recognizance.[151] A bench warrant for his arrest was issued
on 13 April, supposedly for his nonappearance; but Dixon had handed
the *Polyanthos* over to Louse Leah some months before, making further legal proceedings unpromising, and the indictment was accordingly dropped.[152] Snelling and Wilkes, two of the editors of the *Flash*,
were brought to trial on 14 January 1842, with Wooldridge, the third
editor, turning people's evidence;[153] he pled guilty on reduced charges
a few days later.[154]

Wooldridge had another turn later that year when he was brought to
trial in September for publishing the *Libertine* (in which he had printed "Dance on Long Wharf – Boston"), and it was judged to be an ob-

scene paper. The next day, the 15th, he pled guilty to publishing more obscenities in the *Whip* and the *Satirist of New York and Brooklyn,* for which he was fined six cents on each count. The former offense, however, led Wooldridge to serve a two-month penitentiary sentence.[155]

The cohort of editors dedicated to mediated charivari (the *Satirist* was modeled on an English newspaper of the same name but subtitled *The Charivari*)[156] was driven apart at about this time, and the courts manifested their various interpersonal difficulties. On 10 December 1841 Wooldridge sued Snelling and Wilkes, while Snelling obtained a warrant against Dixon. Dixon, not to be outdone, countersued Snelling.[157] Of the latter action, the now solitary (and ostensibly anonymous) editor of the *Flash* insisted that "(t)he fellow [Dixon] tried, but could not be believed on oath." He claimed that Snelling was arrested on the warrant of Wooldridge, "and was allowed to go at large on his parole."[158] The editor of the *Flash* was, of course, Snelling himself.

Snelling's animosity toward Dixon resulted in the 11 and 18 December 1841 numbers of the *Flash* being dedicated to attacks on him (Figure 10).

We know him for a greedy, sordid, unscrupulous knave, of old; . . . We are aware that men are judged by the company they keep and that we shall be blamed for having had anything to do with such as Dixon. Be it so. – We deserve rebuke, we have suffered for our folly and, if that is not enough, we are content to sit down in sackcloth and ashes; the meet attire of fools who trust to a person so vile that the English language cannot express his unmitigated baseness.[159]

In so doing, Snelling provided us with the most detailed picture of Dixon by any of those who knew him, but one that was also surely a purposeful distortion, even a vitriolic burlesque, one that must be finely scrutinized. He began with a recapitulation of Dixon's birth, rearing, and career up to the 1838 move to New York. Snelling was living in Boston during the time of Dixon's travails there and was friendly with him. The editor of the *Flash,* to his credit, did find some virtues in what was otherwise represented to be a mottled, unsubstantive life.

It would require a folio to recount all his achievements in the New England States alone, and a true account of them, if there were a possibility of ever getting the truth from his lips, would be the most amusing book ever written; but he never told it, from his cradle, when a lie would serve, or did one honest action, if he could help it, and never will, on this side the grave. Other men lie and cheat from a necessity, or at least, with a motive – with him, falsehood and fraud are instincts, which whips and chains cannot subdue or fire burn out. He alone, of all the men we ever knew, lies and swindles as Irishmen fight; for fun, and because he cannot help it. His vicious propensities are not, however, dangerous. His tongue and types are alike incapable of slander and he never takes more than enough for his present purposes. He is heartless and ungrateful; but no one expects anything else of him. – He is the incarnation of meanness and petty larceny; but has neither heart nor ability for villany on a large scale. He may plunder a till or pick a pocket, but he will never rob a bank or cut a throat.

Snelling believed what the evidence too suggests, that Dixon "might have done very well as a singer, in a small way; but his damning itch for notoriety and his unutterable conceit and presumption always blinded him to his true interest."

Snelling concluded one essay as follows: "We have known him long and there has been great loss of coin and reputation and small pleasure in the acquaintance. We regard his acquaintance as the greatest misfortune and disgrace and the most grievious error of our whole life." Nevertheless, the two men were cut from the same cloth. Snelling's biographer provided a fitting assessment of his life and work.

[Snelling] was sincere, fiery, and uncompromising, ever a champion of the oppressed and a passionate advocate of his own high ideals of "truth" and "freedom," but he dissipated his energies, neglected his education, and ruined his health in a series of mad quixotic adventures. His publications reveal a man of great talent, perhaps of genius, who found neither the leisure nor the opportunity to be a great writer.[160]

Resonantly, such too could have been said, verbatim, of George Washington Dixon.

A useful service rendered by Snelling in his hatchet job on Dixon was to impart some detail to the relationship between George B. Wooldridge and Dixon. In fact, Snelling confessed that in place of his two-part piece on Dixon he had originally intended to publish an exposé of a "keeper of a place of assignation, a pimp, a poltroon, a traitor, a state's evidence" – his way of avoiding Wooldridge's name. Snelling tried to blacken the "pallid" Wooldridge with Dixon, by reporting this night-time Broadway scene:

GALLERY OF RASCALITIES AND NOTERIETIES.

Figure 10. "Gallery of Rascalities and Noterieties [*sic*]." "The cut on our outside represents Coco La Cour [Dixon], as he first appeared in the character of Zip Coon at West's Circus. The dress is not peculiarly appropriate; but it was the best that West's wardrobe could supply, and he had neither cash nor credit to obtain another. The original rags were borrowed from one Mungo Caesar Napoleon Cuff, a retired woodsawyer." From *The Flash*, 18 December 1841. Courtesy, American Antiquarian Society.

One [Dixon] was a slight built, dark mulatto, five feet seven inches in height, dressed in a frock coat and glazed patent leather cap, and though of an ineffably vagabond appearance, was apparently much scandalized by the more unutterable blackguard upon whose arm he leaned. The latter vagrant was a tall, clumsy, ill jointed, ill favored, ruffian soaplock, whose hang dog look cried "gallows" louder than a trumpet, and in whose great, yellow and treacherous eyes, the Almighty had mercifully written "rogue," as a caution to his fellow creatures to beware.

His face was of a pallid hue, and half encircled by a huge pair of ragged, black whiskers, and his assassin-like eyes, rolled around, in a sea of discolored white, with a mixed expression of cowardice, treachery and villainy I never saw equalled. . . . Arm in arm these worthies staggered along, till they arrived at the "Elssler Saloon," when, as if by mutual consent, they gave each other a fraternal hug and dived together into the abyss.[161]

Fancy aside, less is known about Wooldridge's life than most others in his cohort, which is doubly unfortunate since he will later play a pivotal role in this study. He seems to have been a New Yorker, for both of his parents and other relatives also lived in there. His parents ran a tavern on Chambers Street in the mid-1830s, with "public rooms and bar."[162] City directories showed the family operating taverns at various Broadway addresses during 1838–40; in 1842, Lydia, "widow of George" (thus, likely the junior George's mother) took over the business. Snelling claimed that Wooldridge "had always been a source of sorrow to his father, as well as expense, in saving him from the consequences of his transgressions, which might have included robbery."[163] Thaddeus Meighan, editor of the *Weekly Rake*, dug into Wooldridge as "the dullest donkey that ever cropped a thistle, [and] as ignorant as he is stupid." In a charge that Dixon also faced, Meighan insisted that Wooldridge "could not write a line of sense or English."[164]

Apparently the first newspaper with which Wooldridge was associated was the *Flash*. Once infected, though, he edited, coedited, or wrote for a number of others. After the falling-out with Snelling and Wilkes, Wooldridge banded with Dixon to publish the *True Flash*, which seems to have failed after a few issues. In 1842 his enterprises grew into a small industry when be began editing and publishing the *Libertine*, the *Whip*, and the *Satirist of New York and Brooklyn*. Each one of these carried the scandalous news of the day and featured vignettes of New York's low life. The *Flash* included a regular column (likely written by Wooldridge) that, at base, rated New York's brothels for cleanliness, respectability, and beauty of the denizens. It might well be that Wooldridge had inside information. Snelling, backed independently by Meighan, insisted on several occasions that Wooldridge "had married a common prostitute, in a common brothel"; he added bigamy to his charge as well, for he did not believe that Wooldridge could produce papers of divorce, although the latter had since married again. In addition, he charged Wooldridge with actually running brothels, including the Bank House, the Canvas Back Lunch, and the Elssler Saloon.[165] In fact, the addresses of the taverns kept by the Wooldridge family were in the parts of town that harbored brothels. When mother and son kept a tavern at 21 Centre in 1842, they did so on a street infamous for its brothels;[166] when George kept a "Hotel" at 58 Leonard Street in 1847, he did so across from 55 Leonard, a well-known, long-term brothel address[167] and the very one that Margaret Daker, alias Ryerson, claimed when she was tried for keeping a house of prostitution in 1842 – a place that was "peculiarly annoying to the neighborhood, from the fact that the women who reside on the premises were in the habit of exposing their persons at the front windows and door."[168] Meighan, who seems to have patched up his differences with Wooldridge by 1843, puffed "The Cleopatra," a new place operated by "N. Wooldridge" (surely a relative of George) "opened for the purpose of dispensing the 'good things of this life.'" He went on to describe how the Cleopatra was different, having "charming little rooms and band boxes with locks and keys and other agreeable accompaniments." Then he asked the obvious: "How many love scrapes and scenes will be transacted there?"[169]

If Snelling and Dixon were from the same cloth, Wooldridge and Dixon were from the same bolt. Both were writers, both were interested in blackface minstrelsy (as will become especially clear in Chapter 5), and both were connected to New York's prostitution scene. I have already noted that Adeline Miller once posted bond for Dixon. Snelling liked to link Dixon with the "poor, ignorant strumpets at Julia Brown's, whose feed pensioner he is," and, more directly, with Miss Brown herself, who made "contributions to the *Polyanthos*."[170] In the fall of 1841 rumors begin to circulate that Dixon would soon marry (although there is no evidence that he ever did). A reporter for the *True Flash*, presumably Wooldridge or Dixon himself, noted that

(H)e is about to lead to the altar a daughter of a member of Congress from that State, who independent of what nature has given her has one hundred thousand GOLDEN charms. . . .

As the warm sun of summer opens the sweet flower
The Polyanthos will bloom in the fair maiden's bower.[171]

The rival *Flash* wanted to straighten the record, though:

The lady has only fifty thousand dollars in available funds and she is not a resident of Philadelphia, but of New York. She keeps a house of entertainment
for man and beast in Thomas Street and is a matron inferior in renown only
to the Roman dame Lucretia. This vestal and her *preux chevalier* will join
hearts and hands in the African Methodist Episcopal Church on Thursday,
inst., and spend the honey-moon at their winter residence, in the pleasant village of Skunk's Misery. After this, the happy pair will retire to private life and
the thought of their connubial felicity must console the public for its loss.[172]

In another satirical piece in the same issue, a "fancy ball" at Julia
Brown's is described.

George G____ led the orchestra with his face blackened with burnt cork for
the sake of symmetry; but I regret to say that he was carried out on a hand-
barrow at an early hour; much to the annoyance of his brother musicians Jem
Hazzard and black John Allen.[173] . . . The attentions of George Washington
Dixon were divided between Julia Brown and Mrs. Phoebe Doty, whom he
is shortly to lead to the hymenial altar. . . .
   A trifling controversy occurred to mar the harmony of the *reunion*. When
Mr. Dixon was about to lead Mrs. Doty to the supper room, Julia Brown disputed the pas with her, asserting that she had bought and paid for the melodist, body and soul, and had, for a year past kept his body and soul together
by her advertising patronage. On the other hand, Phoebe claimed [Dixon] as
her affianced spouse, and exhibited a written promise of marriage. The affair
became serious. Suck Jo and French Celeste had taken sides, Julia had already
lost her tiara and Phoebe had been divested of her bustle, when the entrance
of a posse of volunteer firemen, with silver badges on their backs, enforced a
neutrality.

At this point Dixon was asked for a song:

"Did you ever, ever, ever in your life ride a rail."
   "He has, more than once, and ought to know how it feels," burst from the
lips of one of his entranced auditors, and indeed, he dwelt on the miseries of
rail-rides with an unction that evinced experience and, of course, feeling. This
song was so well received that he volunteered a new version of Jem [*sic*] Crow,
written by himself, or by some half starved devil whom he has cheated out
[of] his name. It began thus,

I'm the scurviest of niggers,
   But I'd have you all to know
That I'm sorry for my errors –
   Shall I jump Jim Crow?

Dixon's alleged betrothed, Phoebe Doty, was "(d)uring the 1840s, . . . one of New York's leading prostitutes."[174]

All of this is thoroughly dizzying. I present the details of the above not as fact, but not as fable either. Truth is slippery in this case, parallel to newspapers devoted to moral reform that point the way to the most felicitous brothel. What exactly are intentions, facts, fallacies, in this kind of world, where burlesque is everything? We should not, however, lose grip of the evident truth that all the tracings here are of men with manifest seriousness of purpose (but who meanwhile liked to have a good time) and are, after the fashion of carnival and charivari, serious matters wrapped in fun.

* * * * *

DIXON TRIED OUT new careers in 1842: animal magnetist (i.e., hypnotist), spiritualist (speciality: clairvoyance), and, most significantly, professional athlete, namely as a "pedestrian" or distance walker.[175] In February he attempted to walk for forty-eight successive hours, without rest or sleep, ostensibly for the $4,000 prize to the first person to accomplish the feat;[176] but "Mr. Stevens" in fact did not agree to put up the prize, so Dixon charged admission to watch his efforts. Ever suspicious, the papers reported that "Dixon, . . . is still on his legs, although there are slanderous reports about town that he took a snooze on Monday night as to be fresh yesterday morning."[177]

Later that month he attempted to walk for fifty consecutive hours.[178] *Brother Jonathan* suggested that Dixon "walk in one direction all the time, from this part of the compass, till ocean fetches him up, and then see how far he can swim."[179] Dixon headed south that summer and walked for sixty hours consecutively in Richmond; then went to Washington, where he walked for "30 miles on the rail-road in 5 hours and 35 minutes," followed by three days and two nights on a plank.[180] When he arrived in Philadelphia he was cheered wildly "from the Pit of the Arch street Theatre" for his efforts.[181] There were reports in September that he had walked "seventy-six hours consecutively, without sleep or rest, on a platform fifteen feet long."[182] In all this (and there's much more) Dixon displayed once again his extraordinary ability to take the pulse of the times. It was at this very period that sporting matches were becoming a mania, engaged in and witnessed by the very same young, single men who made up the audience for minstrelsy; and this also at the time when musicmaking became "athleticized," with each virtuoso trying to compete with or outdo his peers. The notion of "the best" is under development here. Minstrelsy too became caught in these changes. There were "dance matches" between leading blackface (and sometimes black) dancers, such as Pelham, John Diamond, and Juba. The headlines speak loudly: "Excitement among the Sporting Community – Match between John Diamond and Juba." The *New York Sporting Whip* wrote that

The favorites are now the dancers, and he who can cut, shuffle, and attitudanize [*sic*] with the greatest facility is reckoned the best fellow and pockets the most money.

Match dances are very frequently got up, and seem to give general satisfaction, if we are allowed to judge from the crowds who throng to witness them.

We have not had a *real*, scientific, out-and-out trial of skill since that between Dick Pelham and John Diamond at the Chatham; but it appears we are soon to have another of these refined and elevating exhibitions.

A match has been made between John Diamond and a little negro called "Juba," by some of the sporting community, and is to come off in the course of a few weeks. The stake is large, and an unparalleled display will be the result.[183]

Music, sport, black and blackface, audiences and shows: Such were the inclusive components of Dixon's world too.

In early 1843 Dixon returned to the stage, for what turned out (unintentionally) to be farewell appearances. He was billed at the Bowery Amphitheatre as the "Pedestrian and Melodist" and sang "The Fireman's Call." On the same program were blackface acts by Seth B. Howes, Dan Gardner, Mr. Madigan "in a new act called 'Jim Crow, Esq., on Horseback,'" "Negro Clown" R. W. Pelham, and Billy Whitlock.[184] On 20 January Dixon appeared at the Chatham, with the billing exclaiming an all-star array: "Messrs. Whitlock! Gardner!! Rice!!! Dixon!!!!"[185] From the 23rd through the end of the month Dixon appeared at the Franklin Theatre, and on the 29th performed at the benefit for "Old Dan Emmit."[186] It is almost as if the torch were being passed in public, on the stage. At the very moment that Emmett, Whitlock, Pelham, and Frank Brower – The Virginia Minstrels – were preparing to change the nature of blackface entertainment, Dixon was to be seen and heard, and often on the same stage, but for the last time.

* * * * *

GEORGE WASHINGTON DIXON must surely be one of the most complex, eccentric, and enigmatic men ever to have crossed the American musical stage. Among his many attributes was (alas) an ability to enflame the powerful and direct their enmity against himself; yet, to his friends and fans, he was a man of estimable stature, and one not to be dismissed. His friend at the *New York Sporting Whip*, Thaddeus Meighan, shortly before his own conviction for editing an "obscene press,"[187] wrote a notice of *Dixon's Regulator* (perhaps the last venture of Dixon's editorial career) – one that could have served, with a change in tense, for Dixon's obituary.

George is a man of wonderful mould. His pedestrian feats proclaim his frame to be stronger than iron – his literary productions are an honor to himself and a credit to the Press – his knowledge of the science of animal magnetism is astonishing – his delineations of negro peculiarities are life-like and truthful – his vocal powers inexpressibly grand – and his performance of low comedy excrutiatingly [*sic*] funny, as all who witnessed his *Splash* can testify.[188] George is also a splendid orater [*sic*] – a regular Demosthenes – and with the eloquence of that somewhat notorious man he combines the wisdom of a Socrates and the satirical acumen of a Cobbett. . . . (W)hen he leaves this nasty little football of clay for a better world, millions will mourn, and the Devil will triumph.[189]

Dixon's time was passing. After his death on 2 March 1861, in New Orleans, no presses in New York, Boston, or Philadelphia found space to eulogize this remarkable life.[190]

5

Old Dan Tucker

Popular dis Courses.
Report of a Sermon
delivered by
Pompey Alexander Smash, ESQ.
At the Marlboro Chapel.

Today, in order to disoblige a 'spected white lady, I shall preach from
de following text, and as de lines at present am werry popular, I hab no
doubt but dat dey will meet wid your approbation; de words am dese,

Get out the way, old Dan Tucker,
You too late to come to supper.[1]

Tucker on de wood pile – can't count 'lebben,
Put in a fedder bed – him gwine to hebben,
His nose so flat, his face so full,
De top ob his head like a bag ob wool,
Get out de way!
Get out de way!
Get out de way! Old Dan Tucker,
Your too late to come to supper.[2]

T HE LIFE OF "ZIP COON" is illuminating. Dixon was successful so long as he spoke through blackface, but when out of it
his troubles compounded. For what he brought, unmasked, to
the printed page from the stage (where he was no longer Buffalo Dixon, but Editor Dixon) and for being quite consciously a mocking figure
too dangerous to be ignored, he was squashed and exiled.

Dixon's strategies were faulty, but his instincts were spot on; at heart, the issues were how one possesses knowledge and what one does with it. Knowledge acquired through reason and print (reason's handmaiden) was coming to establish modes of living and of value making, and many of these were at fundamental odds with traditional ways, in which moral capital was acquired by knowing the community's stories, songs, and homilies, and through spirited conversation. The old way was a performative culture of the ear; the new a mediated culture of the eye.[3] Blackface subverted "knowing" gained through image – the eye is drawn to representation, which might not be the real – just as a Western mask is not really what it appears: It conceals, and promises reordering. More significantly, however, this theoretical construct suggests that blackface was really the secondary signifier, as least from the perspective of the common people. The *noise* – the *ear* – that which always accompanies ritual representations of blackness, is a much richer indicator of the presence of inversion rituals than mere blackface. Moreover, the implied antonym of noise is not "peace and quiet," as the urban better sorts thought, but music. The English got it exactly right when they called charivari "rough music."

Once we get past sound that provides caution, alarm, or awareness, it has no intrinsic worth. Spoken language goes some ways toward encoding value in sound, but there are all sorts of problems with that enterprise, as a glance at the bulk and complexity of any unabridged dictionary makes evident. Music takes comprehension to the final degree, in that a community of listeners agree collectively on the meanings of sounds, and do so with such unanimity that music becomes a popular representation of communal values. College songs, church music, Spike Lee's movies, national anthems, the Grateful Dead, presidential inauguration ceremonies (which tend increasingly toward concerts) – all and more are about communities of shared values expressed through music. The powerful and the weak both have long expressed their respective values through sound. The music of Rev. Dr. Hawks's Episcopalian St. Thomas Church differed, I am sure, in significant ways from that heard in the small, rural, western Kentucky Southern Baptist church that nurtured me in my youth; and the music of the opera house is emphatically not hip-hop. To undo the values of the powerful, the powerless have turned to undoing their music: burlesques of Italian opera, ring shouts, the grotesque "horse fiddles" of the callithumpians, syncopation, Jimi Hendrix's version of "The Star-Spangled Banner," the *Feast of Fools:* All and many more are the patterned responses.

The powerful have a formulaic response to the ear culture of the weak: Dismiss it all as noise first, then associate it with antisocial behavior. One of the first recorded references to a musician in the English-speaking New World, in 1625, was to a "Fidlinge Rogue and Rascall" who was further accused of having "stolune the Companys Tobacco."[4] The *Quebec Gazette* spoke of charivari in 1817 and claimed that "the peace of society is disturbed night after night by the most dissonant noises suitable only to barbarians," then asked rhetorically: "Can it be reputable to our youth and others, to have it said of them, that instead of cultivating their minds, and seeking rational amusements they delight only in uncouth discordance?"[5] When the aristocratic Porter of the *Spirit of the Times* visited the Bowery Theatre he observed:

One word of the Orchestra. If not numerous, it was on this night, unique, and we fancy in phrenological parlance must have been greviously deficient in the organ of tune. It struck up what we thought an apology for the overture of "La Dame Blanche," but before we could decide whether to prefer it to the noise in the pit, lo! it seemed to have laid violent hands on the *plaintive* old melody of "*Nancy Dawson,*" which immediately gave way to something between "*Zip Coon*" and "*Yankee Doodle.*" It need hardly be added that overwhelmed with this unexpected treat, we awaited the rising of the curtain in uncontrollable "amazement and stupefaction." . . . In short, that once happy valley was now a scene of complete and utter desolation, . . . In an agony of tears we here rushed from the house.[6]

Aldabert James was hauled before the Boston Police Court in July 1838 because the watchman "inferred his intemperate habits from his acts, among which [was] his playing on the fiddle."[7] The reporter at the Dedham militia muster in 1838 versed:

The poor can but share
A crack'd fiddle in the air,
Which offends all sound morality.[8]

Is it, then, any wonder that the instruments of early stage blackface were the fiddle, the tambourine, the banjo, and the bones, in order of increasing "social noisiness?" And that Cuff in T. D. Rice's *Oh, Hush!*

or, The Virginny Cupids (1833) began his song: "Come all you Virginny gals, and listen to my noise, / Neber do you wed wid de Carolina boys"?

Of course, herein lies the reason that noise attends so successfully at moments of social slippage. Callithumpian revelers pounded kitchen utensils and shrieked and screamed, according to one report of a New Haven band.[9] On Christmas Eve 1833 "riot, noise and uproar prevailed, uncontrolled and uninterrupted in many of our central and most orderly streets."[10] In 1847 "[a] callithumpian band . . . accoutred grotesquely and with blackened faces . . . with rams horns, bells and kettles . . . shocked the very moon with their enactments."[11] The decade of the 1830s found respectable, "better sort," urban Americans attempting to curb this kind of aural violence (noise), which constantly assaulted them. After the excesses of the callithumpian bands, the *New York Evening Post* wrote, "it is high time [police] strength and . . . numbers were increased."[12] Susan Davis has shown how the establishment of the Police Department in Philadelphia and suppression of the callithumpian's caterwauling went hand in hand.[13] Moreover, in a most unambiguous assault, on 8 October 1838 the Boston City Aldermen passed an ordinance that read in part:

Sect. 3. No person shall ring or cause to be rung, unless as is provided in the first section of "An Ordinance for the regulation of horses and carriages within the City of Boston," any bell, or blow or cause to be blown any horn or other instrument, in notice of the sale of any article, or for any other purpose, in the said streets or elsewhere, unless duly licensed by the Mayor and Aldermen.[14]

This measure effectively denied those who heretofore constructed the aural environment of that most public of places, the street, access to a primary mode of expression, even livelihood. An oblique and instructive endorsement of this policy was offered by an organization of literate Bostonian wags. In an exercise that can be traced back at least to the Tuesday Club of Annapolis, Maryland, in the 1740s and 1750s,[15] middle-class white urban males in 1830s Boston grouped themselves often into societies whose reason for being was social satire. Frequently their wit manifested itself in parade and procession orders. One of these clubs, perhaps the "Mammoth Cod Association," might have been responsible for the long procession that greeted the "Striped Pig" sent

from New Orleans in 1840.[16] Among the groups and items parading
that day were the following:

> A Stuffed Alligator from the New England Museum.
> Four Trumpeters, with Conch Shells.
> Perfumer.   THE PIG.   Perfumer.
> Banner – "If in so fair a mind there reigns a fault,
> 'Tis sensibility too finely wrought."
> Committee on Swine of the Agricultural Society.
> Society of Teetotallers.
> Mayor and Aldermen.
> Harmony Band.
> Calithumpian Society.[17]
> Flouring Committee.
> Twelve Damsels, in White.
> Six Mongrel Geese – barefoot.
> Quilters of Flannel Night Gowns.
> The Anti-Swearing Society.
> Actors on Half Pay.
> Authors of Political Songs.
> The American Melodist.[18]
> Rich Newspaper Editors!
> Banner – "Gentle Shepherd, tell me where?"
> Sausage-makers, with Upturned Sleeves.
> Stray Dogs, on their last legs.
> Mason Street body-snatchers.
> Honest horse jockeys.
> Six white black birds.
> Inspectors of clam bait.
> Anti-Bell-Ringing Society.
> Two Gong Strummers.
> Constables and Turnkeys, with Hand Cuffs.
> Brigade Band.
> Presidents of Bankrupt Insurance Companies.
> Horse Marines.
> Reconnoitering Strangers from the South.
> and people generally.[19]

There is much in which to be interested here, but let me pay particular attention to the nature of the paraders. Most of them are species of

witticisms, satires, burlesques, or simply extravagantly bizarre.[20] Collectively, they establish a paradescape out of which topical, disruptive elements grin and leer. Among these are the pig itself, teetotalers, the flouring committee, the callithumpian band, Dixon, the Anti-Bell-Ringing Society (which has a kind of doubleness, as it refers to another satirical society that came about as a result of the anti-bell-ringing ordinance),[21] constables and turnkeys, the Presidents of Bankrupt Insurance Companies, and some others. However, this procession, like others of the sort, was of course a parade of the mind: No part of it was ever seen or heard! Probably the Mammoth Cod Association itself was largely a fancy, existing only as an evening's exercise in imagination and wit at a Men's Club, or on a weekend's fishing trip to Georges Bank. To have the society's name and the procession order printed in the newspaper – i.e., to have it read! – was the thing in total. Those scheduled to be seen and heard were denied their performative moments in the streets of the city. Carnival denied and order reigned![22]

The power of music might be enslaved in a similar way. A "GRAND CONCERT FOR THE BENEFIT OF THE Y.M.S.F.M.T.C.O.T.I."[23] was announced on 28 November 1838, advertised to be held the night previous! It was to feature the "Sheet Iron Band, consisting of forty-odd Instruments," obviously modeled on callithumpian ensembles. The program was printed and distributed.

PART I.

Grand Overture – "Blam! Blam! Blam!!!" – Rogers. Full Band. Symphonia – "Non Hoppo presto" – from Tuck's Opera of the "Umbrella."

Duetto in D____d flat, on two cast iron Bass-drums, obligato accompaniment on a pair of silver-bowed spectacles – by the Messrs Meryman.

Song – "Dumbar-ton Bells" – accompanied – solo-obligato – on the sheet iron octave bugle – Signora S. Katrina. Bayli.

Solo – on the sheet iron flute. This remarkable instrument is fingered only with keys, and was presented to a member of the Band, by the P.O.T.E.B. Mole Society.

Finale. Glee – Joe Smith's Requiem, or "past twelve o'clock," accompanied on a patent level humstrum.

PART II.

Introduction to the "Bright Rosy Morning," with grand flourish
of steel-traps, and obligato accompaniment on the compound
sheet iron Trombone – Towsie.

The "Crowbar Waltz," a favorite and difficult piece, as performed by the Band at the recent muster in Dedham. The
effect of this movement is so sublime, it is said, as to start
doors from their hinges! – C. W. Goings.

Grand Quartette – "Bouvons! Bouvons!!" from the celebrated
Opera, "Le petit cochon begarre," arranged for this occasion,
and to be performed on four sheet iron, stub-twist bassons –
by Todd, Larkspur, Daviski and Tuck.

The "Whistling Trio," on three pewter whistles, patent screws.

Grand Finale. "The Last Trump," a magnificent serenade,
'achieved' on the occasion of closing Charles River Bridge, for
the 'very last time' – Full Band.

Gentlemen are requested not to wear boots
with metallic heels or nails.

Doors open at 1/2 past 6,
Performances commence at 1/2 past 10, precisely.

Tickets – gratis; children half price.[24]

In brief, this was a concert that could not be but in print. Those who
cried out that it or the parade might not be as much fun as the "real"
thing were hushed with shaming and accused implicitly with having
unformed imaginations.

Mock concerts and parades glossed in a remarkably complete way
those things that the upstanding members of the Mammoth Cod Association (and other such) found potentially disruptive and transgressive.
Through the power of print they were contained, then neutered.[25]

This was happening on the cusp of 1840. My research shows a surprisingly rapid containment of the social noise of minstrelsy beginning
about the same time. The texts to blackface songs from 1828 to 1840 or
so are filled with period references to political, economic, moral, and
social issues, including the debate over slavery. Most often, the positions staked out are contrary to the interests of middle- and upper-class
Americans. Although early minstrelsy employed the palpable overlay of
the black, it did so in such a way that hope was most often the result,

even the hope of a black–white working-class alliance against slavery. There is much less chance of this kind of sentiment at the Bowery by the mid-1840s. Dialect blackface had become by then more a form of gross mockery – of blacks, of women, of the powerful too, to be sure – but a mockery that circumscribed, unlike the burlesques of the 1830s, which were limitless in hopes. As in the mock parades, mock blackface allowed for no noise, that social stuff of becoming, pregnant with possibilities. Instead, one finds songs like "Miss Lucy Long" (advertised as "new" in early 1842[26]), perhaps the most-performed blackface song of the decade, at least until songs by Stephen Foster.[27] In the James L. Hewitt edition, there are only six four-line verses, and the first is explicit: The song "isn't very long." There are only two topical items, and these are oblique (Elssler and her "Cachucha" dance and the famous physician Dr. Physick). There is no hint of anything fraught with political or social concerns. The text is "straight," requiring no insider information to unpack.

> Oh! Miss Lucy's teeth is grinning,
> Just like an ear ob corn,
> And her eyes dey look so winning
> Oh! would I'd ne'er been born.
> If she makes a scolding wife,
> As sure as she was born,
> I'll tote her down to Georgia,
> And trade her off for corn.[28]

Similarly, the music of minstrelsy came also to exclude its noise. Once a raucous, exuberant, raw, rough, vital, noisy "music" (where "proper" training, "good" tone, and "fine" ensemble were antithetical to the purpose and effect), minstrelsy became "music" of melody (the tune to "Lucy Long" is polished and formally satisfying) performed by virtuoso ("scientific") instrumentalists who advertised their formal credentials. The banjo, by way of quick example, was a handmade, preindustrial instrument played in the 1820s exclusively by blacks. Its potential for noise is clear from an 1840 playbill: "dat terror to all Pianos, Harps, and Organs, de BANJO."[29] In fact, in the early years the instrument appears to have been too wild for even the blackface stage. Mr. Leicester performed in "the Louisiana Banjou style" in October 1834, but did so on the violin![30] Leicester, about whom little more is known than that he might have been from Cincinnati and his "reputation in private life is as excellent as it is in public,"[31] continued to fake the banjo on his violin through 1836, before disappearing from the minstrel stage until 1843. He set a minor trend though, and a Mr. Hall learned to accompany his singing of "Ching a Ring," "Settin' on a Rail," and "Zip Coon" on the fiddle, in "the true banjo style."[32] Joel Sweeney was apparently the first to play a real banjo on the stage, doing so initially in New York in April 1839. Billy Whitlock claimed to have learned to play the banjo from Sweeney at about this time.[33] Sweeney by 1841 was trying to lift the banjo out of its blackness; advertisements for his playing exclaimed "scientific touches to perfection,"[34] using an adjective that stood for reason, European complication, and middle-class respectability. "Only those who have heard Sweeny [*sic*] know what music there is in a banjo."[35]

> Great Sweeny, hail! bending before thy shrine,
> I will essay thy skill to sing,
> For magic music thrills those cords of thine,
> Thou master of the Banjo-string.
> Let poets sing of Orpheus' famed lyre,
> Or Paganini's praises ring,
> More witching sweetness and melodious fire,
> Breathes softly from thy Banjo-string.[36]

In early 1843 this instrument became the heart of a *musical* ensemble – the minstrel band.[37] It soon acquired, too, the prestige of a manufactured item of commerce, replete with its own pedagogical literature. By 1893 an advertisement in *Stewart's Banjo and Guitar Journal* rejoiced that the "banjo was once monopolized by the negro minstrel performers, and hence it became associated with the black face, and was some times called the 'negro instrument' . . . [but the] banjo of today is altogether another instrument,"[38] one that was often played by white college students in their banjo clubs, with none of its original potential for noisemaking.

While Sweeney and others were converting the social work of black-face theatre into a form of musicmaking, the battle for social control of the theatre in general was nearing an end. Those working-class audiences of the 1830s who believed that theatre was participatory, as it had been to their ancestors for centuries and centuries, were replaced in the

1840s by audiences who believed theatre was better purchased than produced, as it had been by those in the first tier for a century. Management enforced a new code of behavior, one that led to the theatre becoming much quieter, more and more a private space for reflection,
in effect a temple of culture whose sacralization was complete by late
century.[39] Almost never again did white, common Americans make
musical theatre an intrinsic expression of who they were and what they
wished to be.

*****

THE BIRTH OF THE MINSTREL SHOW was truly a watershed moment, not to be understated. Those men who would make up the Virginia Minstrels – Dan Emmett, Billy Whitlock, Frank Brower, and
Dick Pelham – had appeared throughout the New York theatre season
of 1842-3, often solo, often in combination with one or two of the others, but never all together. Pelham and Whitlock (and Dixon too) all
worked at the Bowery Amphitheatre on 14 January 1843,[40] and there
were other such occasions; but there had been a more critical collabo-
ration earlier, during the Advent period. At that time Emmett and
Brower had teamed for an entertainment at the Bowery Amphitheatre
Circus titled "Negro Holiday Sports, in Carolina and Virginia," with
"new Illustrations."[41] Of the performance it was written: "Emmit's [*sic*]
banjo playing is fully equal to Jo Sweeney's, and far ahead of any other now in the United States. The dancing and Carolina negro characteristics, given by Frank Brower, are quite original and comic. . . ."[42]
Emmett and Brower could very well have known firsthand about "Negro Holiday Sports, in Carolina and Virginia," for the year before they
had jointly toured through the Carolinas and (likely) Virginia with a
"Circus and Caravan," right at the season of Misrule festivities. One
wonders, then, if the "Sports" included representation of the John Canoes, something reasonable enough to expect.

I introduce the concept of "representation" carefully and deliberate-
ly, for in it is the original and critical difference between minstrelsy before and after 1843. Most important earlier developments in the genre
concerned that which was "real" enough to the audience – noise, politics, class, gender, and so on; but representation is a simulacrum. Min-

strel representation is a phenomenon in which "Others" (blacks) are held up in deception. Moreover, despite the currency of "representation" in postmodern theoretical studies, it is not mine to use; the term belongs to Emmett and Brower. In late November 1842, at the Franklin Theatre, the bill read: "Mr. EMMET[T], the great Southern Banjo Melodist, FRANK BROWER, the perfect representation of the Southern Negro characters, and Master PIERCE the great Heelologist."[43] The genius of what the Virginia Minstrels were about needed only the melding of falsifying representation to two other bold conceptualizations – concertizing and agency – to alter forever the direction taken by blackface entertainment.

The first of these was grounded in classical economics. Blackface performers, whether in the circus ring or on the stage, seem to have earned at best about ten dollars per week.[44] Only T. D. Rice of all the early minstrels had the drawing power to command a higher salary. However, there was a new performance paradigm on the American stage at this time, one that promised significantly improved well-being to some blackface specialists, one that had been perceived earlier by George Washington Dixon. I speak of the concert. The country had been in a deep depression since the panic of 1837. Theatres had been hit hard, a fact acknowledged by the *New York Herald* on 30 November 1842 (in an issue that also carried an ad for Emmett and Brower's "Representation"): "THEATRICALS IN THE UNITED STATES. – Scarcely a theatre in the Union is now paying its expenses." The *Herald* proffered a solution: "Musical entertainments, concerts, &c., are the only affairs of the kind that are patronised" – and, thus, the only affairs of the kind that paid. When the *Herald* advertised that "Miss Browne, composer and professor of music, normally receives $30 for performances in concertos"[45] it was waving nearly a month's pay before those stuck in the theatre; and this was a paltry sum next to that commanded by such in-demand concert stars as Henry Russell.

The problem was how to reshape a medium of expression that had long been bound up with the theatre into one appropriate for the concert hall. At liminal moments in rituals of passage, in life as apparently in art, one resorts to misrule, theatrical chaos, and noise to remake the present. Emmett later told the story of how the Virginia Minstrels got their first booking.

All four [of us] were one day sitting in the North American Hotel, in the Bowery, when one of [us] proposed that . . . [we] should cross over to the Bowery Circus [the Amphitheatre] and give one of the proprietors . . . a "charivari." . . . Bringing forth [the] banjo for Whitlock to play on, [I] took the violin, Pelham the tambourine, and Brower the bones. Without any rehearsal, with hardly the ghost of an idea as to what was to follow, [we] crossed the street and proceeded to "browbeat" Uncle Nat Howes into giving [us] an engagement, the calculation being that he would succumb in preference to standing the horrible noise [we] . . . were making with [our] instruments. . . . After singing some . . . songs for him, [we] returned to the North American, where [we] resumed [our] "horrible noise" in the reading-room, which was quickly filled with spectators.[46]

By the time the group placed its ad in the *Herald* announcing their engagement, they had journied from a state of noise and charivari to one that embraced music and concert.

First Night of the novel, grotesque, original and surpassingly melodious ethiopian band, entitled the VIRGINIA MINSTRELS. Being an *exclusively musical entertainment*, combing the banjo, violin, bone castanetts, and tambourine; and entirely exempt from the vulgarities and other objectionable features, which have hitherto characterized negro extravaganzas.[47]

By 9 February, advertisements made intentions clear. In an evening at the Bowery Amphitheatre that featured the usual circus fare and was a benefit night for the Virginian Minstrels, the quartet introduced in blaring type – "A NEGRO CONCERT."[48] This is the first time that the word "concert" is allied with minstrel entertainment, but for the few telling exceptions in 1837–8 when Dixon had programmed "Zip Coon" on his concerts.

Words and names are everything in this case. What "Old Dan Tucker, & Co." chose to call themselves is important if for no other reason than their decision marked a whole genre. Nominally, "minstrels" had appeared on American stages and in concert halls before 1843. In 1833 the Tyrolese Minstrels had been in New York City;[49] the German Minstrels had come in spring 1837 and the Alpine Minstrels in the summer.[50] The Rainer Family Singers had been announced as the Tyrolean Minstrels in 1839, and hot on their heels, the Boston Minstrels in October 1840, obviously an American emulation of the European genre.[51] The Cambrian Infant Minstrels arrived later that year;[52] and through-

out 1841 and 1842 the Rainers show up everywhere, usually billed as the
Tyrolese Minstrels. Uniformly, the word "minstrels" in a performance
context was applied to (whiteface) singing groups who gave concerts in
concert halls to respectable, white middle-class audiences. That most
of these were also "families" simultaneously reassured and confirmed
the audience. It is against this backdrop that Emmett's first use of
"Ethiopian Minstrel" in late 1842[53] and "Virginia Minstrels" on 6 February 1843 assumes significance. Characteristically, Emmett's usage implied some degree of burlesque (of middle-class values and mannerisms)
but, also typically, it suggested the possibility of accommodation. From
a marketing perspective the name had the advantage of being readable
from two contrary perspectives: as satire by the common classes, and as
descriptive by the middle class. (Both groups, of course, were free to
buy tickets.) It is in the glow shed by the name that we can now read
understanding into the last two lines of the first Virginia Minstrels' ad:
"entirely exempt from the vulgarities and other objectionable features,
which have hitherto characterized negro extravaganzas." By March,
the Virginia Minstrels had further refined their approach and were unequivocally clear in the *Worcester National Aegis* that they intended to
appeal to a stalwart, family-oriented, "respectable" audience.

Chaste, Pleasing and Elegant!

The Virginia Minstrels, Who have been giving their novel and refined Concerts at the Temple in Boston, and have been so liberally patronized by the
elite of that city, beg most respectfully to announce to the Ladies and Gentlemen of Worcester, that they intend giving their last Concert at Brinley Hall,
on Wednesday Eve'g, Mar. 22, . . .[54]

An editorial notice in the same issue further polished their image.

"The Virginia Minstrels" – to-night again at Brinley Hall.

The harmony and skill with which the banjo, violin, castinets, and tamborine
are blended by these truly original minstrels, in their Ethiopian characters, is
a redeeming feature to this species of amusement, and cannot fail of making
it acceptable to the most refined and sensitive audience.

This language is much like that employed by papers like the *Aegis*
to puff appearances by the Hutchinson Family Singers at this time,
and it might well be that the Hutchinsons in a noteworthy manner

provided the germinal concept for the development of the minstrel show. When the Virginia Minstrels came to Worcester in March, they claimed to "delineate in a masterly manner, the 'holiday sports' and pastimes of the Southern Slaves, through the medium of Refrain Songs and Dittys."⁵⁵ A playbill from this period notes further that this music was like that heard "at all their Merry Meetings, such as the gathering of the Cotton and Sugar Crops, Corn Huskings, Slave Weddings and Junketings."⁵⁶ Important here is the manner of presentation. Like Henry Russell and the Hutchinson Family Singers, the Virginia Minstrels joined the functions of the lyceum and the concert and appealed to education through representation. The Minstrels were aiming directly for the middle-class Worcester audience that would have some interest in being informed on the exotic ways of southern blacks and in being entertained too, as long as it was "Chaste, Pleasing and Elegant!" The promise to the Virginia Minstrels was a big payday. It was surely not lost on them that the Hutchinson Family Singers – four performers and an agent – cleared gates of $100 for two concerts in Portsmouth, New Hampshire, in September–October 1842 and $75 in late November at Lowell. By the end of May 1843 the Hutchinsons were taking in up to $130 per concert and charging 50 cents a ticket, at a time when admission to the boxes at the Park went for that amount, and a full day's entertainment at Barnum's Museum or a night at the circus was only 25 cents.⁵⁷ All this time the Hutchinsons continued to advertise themselves as "The Granite State Minstrels."⁵⁸ Surely it is no mere coincidence that the "Ethiopian Serenaders" gave their first concert at the Chatham one week to the day after the big New York payday by the Granite State "Aeolian Vocalists" – another name used by the Hutchinsons at this time, one that resonants with that chosen by the blackface performers; or that the Congo Minstrels the next year trumpeted that "(t)heir songs are sung in Harmony in the style of the Hutchinson Family;"⁵⁹ or that the Harmoneons, a blackface minstrel troupe, were referred to by the Hutchinsons themselves in 1844 as "the Harmonian Family," the year after they had formed as the "Albino Family," "with whitened faces and flaxen wigs" – a burlesque of a burlesque.⁶⁰

The Virginia Minstrels were not interested in a program of protest against conditions suffered by working-class whites. If anything, they reinforced latent (or not so) patronizing attitudes toward slaves and blacks. With their name, concert format, and middle-class audiences came representation instead of engagement, music instead of noise, and, ultimately, issues of race instead of class.

What the Hutchinsons had that the Virginia Minstrels did not was soon remedied, for the latter hired themselves an agent. This is the necessary third stroke marking the transition from early to mature minstrelsy. To have an agent was to remove the performer a step further from the audience, to build in representation (as an agent necessarily stands for another person or thing). Agency makes possible the "show" in the modern sense, where something is portrayed, delineated, or represented in such a manner that we know it to be false, not the real thing at all! Historically, the notion forecasts groups like Christy's Minstrels (established 1844), a projection of the imagination of a man (E. P. Christy) whose calling was not as a performer but as a manager, and who set the pattern for decades to come. To arrange for agency at this pivotal moment, the Virginia Minstrels turned to a man already known to these pages: George B. Wooldridge, editor, jailbird, alleged brothel operator, and intimate of George Washington Dixon. In Wooldridge we discover a man of confused and complicated transgressive worlds of understanding (of working class and middle class, of ear culture and print culture, of irony and hermeneutics, of body and intellect, of brotherhoods and families, of brothels and homes, of noise and music), who is chosen significantly to represent blackface at a seminal moment in its history. From the perspective of the narrative, no selection could have been more ideal.

Wooldridge's agency means, in practical terms, that some details of the Virginia Minstrels' early history become available. By exploring his close (sometimes stormy) relationship with Taddeus Meighan, editor of the *New York Sporting Whip*, we unearth writings that might have been by Wooldridge himself (as was the "Dance on Long Wharf – Boston"). Each is full of abiding interest in blackface and privy to inside information. The 28 January 1843 issue of the *Sporting Whip* contains as accurate a capsule history of early blackface minstrelsy as one is likely to find during that time.

Thomas Blakely [*sic*] of the Walker-street Fountain, is the father of Negro Extravaganzists. For the benefit of some person attached to the Old Chatham Theatre, Messrs. Blakely and Sloman appeared together in the Serenade of "Coal Black Rose," and made such a favorable impression, that it was repeated nightly for some time. George Washington Dixon attended the theatre regularly, had the verses taken down, and published them as originally sung by him. Soon after[,] he adopted the *profession*. [T]hen Tom. Rice appeared with his Jim Crow, and the numerous tribe of negro singers, dancers and players, with which we are now blessed, quickly followed.

The next issue, of 4 February 1843, contains startling news, given what has been generally believed about the Virginia Minstrels (in brief, that they performed publicly for the first time at the Bowery Amphitheatre on 6 February):

The negro band, composed by Pelham, Whitlock, Emmet[t] and Brower is going to England. We hope its members will gain more money and as many wreaths there.

From this offhand comment – apparently the earliest record of the Virginia Minstrels – one gathers that they had been "a band" for some time already, a period long enough to garner some revenue and wreaths. It is further significant that the group was already planning a trip to England (as confirmed five days later in the *New York Herald*). In fact, Rice and Sweeney were doing well in London this very season, and the economy in the United States was still stagnant; the Minstrels' decision was a practical one, not at all surprising. On the 11th we learn from the *Sporting Whip* that the Minstrels had given a concert on the 4th at the Second Ward Hotel. We learn the next week that "[i]ndependent of their public qualities, each one is a 'good man and true' in his private relations." Other little bits of news appear through 4 March, after which Wooldridge went to New England with the Minstrels and the *Sporting Whip* was shut down by the authorities. Wooldridge left for England with Emmett, Brower, Whitlock, and Pelham on 21 April 1843, neatly skipping out on an indictment lately filed against him for libel.[61]

*****

FROM ALL THIS CAME not only a major genre of American popular culture, but also a song; in fact, perhaps the minstrel show arose because there was this song. "Old Dan Tucker," composed by Dan Emmett, was the most popular item on the programs of the Virginia Minstrels. It, like the Minstrels themselves, is a part of the transition, both of the old world and of the new. To examine the text on its own is to find a patchwork of themes, some reminiscent of the past, others anticipatory of the future. The first verse contains imagery of a town, a fight, the watch, and food, each a common theme in early minstrelsy. The song could apparently function as an *"Io Triumphe"* of rioters (like "Jim Crow"), on the basis of a column detailing its use by a Philadelphia mob;[62] but, excepting this single report, I know of no other such utility for "Old Dan Tucker." This is, furthermore, not a political song, like "Jim Crow" and "Zip Coon"; not once is anything remotely political mentioned in any verse of any version of the song known to me. Much more than either of the earlier two, the song is about delineation and representation – and it is not a pretty sight. Dan Tucker is stupid, horrendously ugly, with no refinement at all (in fact, he has animal characteristics), and is violent, drunk, and oversexed. In text it is of the racist genre commonly assumed to characterize minstrel songs.

However, "Old Dan Tucker" is not really about its textual matter. More like "Zip Coon" than "Jim Crow," it is about music and music-making. Here is verse 2 of "The Latest Version of Old Dan Tucker":

> We are de boys from old Virginia,
> And take de shine from Pagannini [*sic*],
> Wid our old banjo and jaw bone,
> We drive all udder music home.[63]

According to Y. S. Nathanson, it was "the best of what I have denominated the ancient negro ballads. The melody was far superior to anything that had preceded it."[64] That the music is paramount is obvious from a quick glance at the sheet music, which gives far fewer verses for reading or singing than "Jim Crow," for example, and much more music for making. Then there's the infectious tune (Musical Example 4), which Nathanson compared to Donizetti and Auber. In the refrain, especially, one hears a use of syncopation that has been entirely absent from minstrelsy, with the single qualified exception of "Zip Coon."[65] The rhythmic energy generated propels the songs along. The harmonic scheme is effective in supporting the melody. Most significantly, this is not a song for singing so much as for playing. It would, in fact, be surprising if purely instrumental "choruses" were not improvised in performance, something much more difficult to imagine with "Jim Crow." Although surely the song was danced on stage by the Virginia Minstrels, it does not really require such treatment: Four good instrumentalists picking their way through could make "Old Dan Tucker" succeed solely on the quality of its music. This is a feature that doubtless struck the Hutchinsons – musicians first, and instrumentalists as well as singers – when they chose this song in 1844 as the tune to "Get Off the Track," paradoxically and ambiguously their first song with "immediate emancipation" as a theme.

✳✳✳✳✳

BLACKFACE MINSTRELSY was delicately balanced in early 1843, at a point between riot and peace, *agon* and *ludus*, public and private, ancient and modern, community and individual, male and female, black and white, noise and music. The social energy required just to maintain this equilibrium is certainly a primary reason we are compelled to study it today. Anthropologist Victor Turner noted the attraction of "the betwixt and between" in his pathfinding study of ritual, and although his evidence was drawn from a study of African festive rituals, his observations apply equally to blackface minstrelsy.

The attributes of liminality or of liminal personae ("threshold people") are necessarily ambiguous, since this condition and these persons elude or slip through the network of classifications that normally locate states and positions in cultural space. Liminal entities are neither here nor there; they are betwixt and between the positions assigned and arrayed by law, custom, convention, and ceremonial. As such, their ambiguous and indeterminate attributes are expressed by a rich variety of symbols . . . . We are presented, in such rites, with a "moment in and out of time," and in and out of secular social structure, which reveals, however fleetingly, some recognition (in symbol if not always in language) of a generalized social bond that has ceased to be and has simultaneously yet to be fragmented into a multiplicity of structural ties.[66]

Biologists have a parallel concept, one they call the "edge effect." It characterizes the tendency of life to mass at the interstices of major ecosystems. It explains why cottonwoods congregate along a prairie creek, why wetlands are so fecund yet the deepest blue sea and the desert relatively devoid of life. It also helps us understand why human beings seek out domiciles on coasts, rivers, and at the feet of mountain ranges. Life tends toward the ambiguous edges. Few artifacts of American cultural history offered more edges than blackface minstrelsy. I have re-

Musical Example 4 (above and facing). "Old Dan Tucker" (New York: Atwill's, 1843).

flected on only some of them here, and I offer them again, in summary and in the company of their complements:

self–other   homogeneity–heterogeneity
us–them   public–private

Musical Example 4 (cont.)

equality–inequality	night–day
community–individual	dark–light
poor–rich	feast–fast
inferior–superior	fun–serious
past–present	play–work
ancient–modern	release–restraint
real–representation	free–slave
rural–urban	young–old
folk–popular	female–male
sound–text	white–black
fool–sage	disorder–order
season–time	noise–music

Like at the biological edges, life flows back and forth between the polarities, for they are dynamic couplings. Bakhtin wrote "that the most intense and productive life of culture takes place on the boundaries."[67] In blackface minstrelsy, the oppositional complements are bonded by a kind of dance at the boundary (or at the crossroads, or at "Long Wharf – Boston") that ends with an embrace, a gesture that rules out paradox and contradiction.

*****

TOO OFTEN CRITICS have seen blackface minstrelsy as only a case of inversion ritual. Were minstrelsy only about inversion, however, then Turner's classic explanation of political content in ritual would apply:

> To compensate for . . . cognitive deficiencies, juniors and inferiors, in ritual situations, may mobilize affect-loaded symbols of great power. Rituals of status reversal, according to this principle, mask the weak in strength and demand of the strong that they be passive and patiently endure the symbolic and even real aggression shown against them by structural inferiors.[68]

In an extremely important way, though, the ritual of inversion we study in blackface minstrelsy differs from that studied classically by Turner. He generally tests his theory by working from the socially low to the socially high. To fit his theory, popular working-class theatre would have developed theatricals in which the socially weak became strong, which it did in fact – in "Bowery Boy" characterizations by F. S. Chanfrau, in apocalyptic melodramas with their avenging heroes, in staged versions of the Mike Fink and Davy Crockett myths and legends. Minstrelsy's inversion, though, is from low (white common people) to even lower (blacks), which brings the (relatively) strong to a point of ritual vulnerability. Given this fundamental "inversion" of the inversion theory, we should be able to restate Turner's thesis with inverted polarities and thus describe minstrelsy, leading to a "burlesque" of the original that happens to capture truth. (Inverted terms are in italics.)

> To compensate for . . . cognitive *advantages, seniors* and *superiors,* in ritual situations, may mobilize affect-loaded symbols of *inferiority.* Rituals of status reversal, according to this principle, mask the *strong* in *weakness* and demand of the *weak* that they be *aggressive* and counter the symbolic and even real aggression shown against them by structural *superiors.*

This reading is in fact a fair description of what must have happened when white, common-class audiences viewed early blackface minstrel performances. It supports the notion that early blackface minstrelsy was a form of engaging the black "Other," and might even be supportive of action to correct the Other's social plight, as both texts and contexts suggest happened. One hates to say it, because it sounds today so naïve and openly controversial, but the inescapable conclusion is this: White working people saw an ally in the black laborer against their common superiors, not simply an inevitable enemy. Turner, however, foresaw this kind of "distortion" to his theory, and closed his study with one of his most brilliant observations, thoroughly applicable to blackface minstrelsy.

Society (*societas*) seems to be a process rather than a thing – a dialectical process with successive phases of structure and *communitas* [community without hierarchy]. There would seem to be – if one can use such a controversial term – a human "need" to participate in both modalities. Persons starved of one in their functional day-to-day activities seek it in ritual liminality. The structurally inferior aspire to symbolic structural superiority in ritual; the structurally superior aspire to symbolic communitas and undergo penance to achieve it.[69]

Caught in the middle, between class and race, white common people had to devise both upward and downward processes and rituals, as is confirmed by the bills of theatres in the Bowery and Chatham Square. The rituals that assumed structural inferiority countered the reality of social position through dynamically aggressive behavior; those of structural superiority (minstrelsy) bridged through the palliative effects of laughter.[70] Of blackface minstrelsy, we are left with the inevitable conclusion that it is engagement at the edges, not simple perversity, and that it was, in promise, one of the most powerful means developed in the century for working out the problems that follow from the magnetic attraction of marginal opposites.

In the end there is joyous ambiguity; "necessarily ambiguous," Turner called it. One suspects that a reason folk theatricals have proven so enduring is they are only vessels, not meaning itself. Their matter is fluid, special to time, place, community, and person. No two scripts are ever the same. The mummers of Northern Ireland, who might give thirty performances over the Christmas week, never gave the same show twice: Some audiences wanted the quick version, others the full treatment.[71] Not only the versions but also what they meant must have changed. Oliver Cromwell kills Saint Patrick, who is then resurrected; meanings would surely differ depending on whether the household is Protestant or Catholic. Would Miss Funny be merely funny to a family with no marriageable daughters, and thus with little interest in procreation metaphors? Blackface minstrelsy too must have been many things to many people. I can hope to trace the shape of the bottle and discern something of the chemicals therein, but I fear I shall never arrive at a single, final verity as to the quality of the wine. Instead, my conclusion has more to do with complexity and ambiguity. What I have wanted to do here is, in part, undercut the tired old story that blackface minstrelsy is about unrelenting hatred of blacks by working-class, urban white males,[72] for I believe that interpretation to be ahistorical. It ascribes meaning without understanding context, nor even human nature. It does not seek an ethnography of audience: Who were the people in the Bowery Theatre? How did they come to be there? What did they bring with them? For some in that theatre, I do not doubt that hatred and racism formed bedrock. For some, though, probably most, the basic impulse was "simply" toward entertainment. Most emphatically, we must not underestimate this fundamental human need, and dump and bury posthaste the long-standing conceit that entertainment is merely cultural detritus. For those living in Northern Ireland, or in North Carolina in 1828, or in New York's fifth ward, or in Harlem, Appalachia, or Oakland at the end of the twentieth century, with nothing more substantial than a blunt hope, entertainment is a metaphor for promise. Glassie called it "an intensification of the very best in day in day out existence."[73] If I were to believe early blackface minstrelsy to be single thing – it is, of course, many things – I would hold out for "an old ritual embracing new community through laughter and joy." This being the case, minstrelsy would assume its rightful place in American and world history as a reluctant step by new laboring-class folk into a world of their choosing, though not of their devising, from a world of their special understanding.

Epilogue

The starting-point of critical elaboration is the consciousness of what one really is, and in "knowing thyself" as a product of the historical process to date which has deposited in you an infinity of traces, without leaving an inventory.[1]

WHEN I BEGAN THE WORK leading to this book, I assumed that I would be dealing more or less objectively with a fascinating but discretely contained phenomenon of America's cultural history. However, as I have made my tracings in the graveyards of the past I have come to recognize my own image in the present; and with the emerging portrait has come a flood of questions about how this could be.

To understand, I have had to come to "know myself" in a new way, in a new light. I have had, for example, to dredge up family and community histories, memories, clues, hints, and secrets. (I would not reveal some of what I have learned under any kind of torture.) Much of my past gives support and shape to the questions that linger, so I beg indulgence.

I was born (white) into a young family in 1947, the proper nine-months-plus after my father, eighteen days discharged from the World War II U.S. Navy, married my mother. I am, thus, a bonafide baby-boomer. We lived on my grandfather's farm in Western Kentucky, emphatically southern in loyalty and attitude; my father is a native of central Mississippi, which only confirmed our sense of southernness. My mother matriculated one year at a local junior college, and my birth stymied my father's plans for college, study at which would have been a Cockrell first (a laurel that was then reserved for me). My father went to work as an apprentice in the railroad shops, and my mother "naturally" became a housewife. When the shops laid off, my father went to work driving a truck in the gravel pit down by the creek, making $1.00 per hour and providing for, by this time, three small boys. (There would be five children eventually.) His annual salary in 1952 would have been equivalent to one of about $10,688 in 1991.[2] Beyond this, though, we benefited from the advantages of a farm economy: There was a cow, some chickens, and a bounty of garden produce. In short, we were comfortable: not dirt poor by any stretch, but certainly not rich either.

I grew up doing most of the things expected of boys at that time and place (baseball, basketball, fishing, farm work), and going to school, the same rural school building for all twelve years. Politically, there was no question: We were straight-ticket Democrats, after the model exemplified by favorite son Alben W. Barkley, local boy who achieved the vice presidency during the Truman administration. As a nine-year-old I thrilled at John F. Kennedy's speech before the national convention and could not believe that the American people would really reelect Eisenhower. Religiously, a century-old rural Southern Baptist church of moderate size (150 persons or so) provided much of the social center that we enjoyed, and we were there whenever the church doors were unlocked. (I think my father, a deacon, even had a key.) Of my friends, a few were Methodists or Presbyterians, but most were Baptists. The Catholics lived in their own community up the road, went to their own schools, and interacted with us only at Halloween, when we tricked and (mostly) treated at each other's houses; I don't think I knew a Jew or an Episcopalian until my college years. My mother was the church organist and played mostly by ear, the result of family finances that afforded her only six months of piano lessons when a girl. (Exigencies in this case were the mother of her gift.) My father sang, I sang, everybody sang, loudly and with spirit, and in four parts. I was also familiar with country-western (but didn't like it much then) and, during my adolescence, was drawn deeply into rock 'n' roll; I was a little young for Elvis, who was somehow frightening to us "respectable" kids. I never once remember thinking that we were in any way different from those around us (who were probably related in some way, given the size of the family).

On the other side of the creek was "Niggertown," where many of the black people in our end of the county lived. Pete, who had a house there (a shack, we'd call it now), was my grandfather's "farmhand," but more than that, a companion. He attended my grandfather's funeral in our white church, and the ten-year-old boy in me still remembers his display of grief. Boys from "over there" would sometimes walk down the gravel road to our house, and we would have a wild, madly improvised pickup basketball game, long on extravagant moves and short on rules; but otherwise I had no truck with them. Only in my junior year was our high school integrated, and then in relatively token fashion.

However, in spite of being a product of what many might proclaim prototypical social conditioning, my attitudes about race were not what one might project. I credit my mother for this in large measure, for I vividly remember her waving a disciplining finger in my face and insisting that she "*never* wanted to see me treat a negro in *any* way different from how [I myself] wanted to be treated!" I believe that I was not alone in this aspect of my education. I remember no hateful racist talk, nor do I believe there were any student objections to the integration of our school; there was, if anything, more of a welcoming. Now, forty years later, I am left with this question: How did my mother, who today sleeps in the very room in which she was born, get such an idea – an idea, moreover, with which she upbraided us kids? Alternatively, how did my fellow students get the idea that integration was just fine? Perhaps as a result of my shaping, I never experienced any reluctance about interacting with blacks when opportunity provided. One of my very best friends in the small, state college I first attended was a black student from Arkansas, and he came home with me for the weekend on several occasions, with no thought at all on my part that this might be socially or politically unacceptable.

It was my father too: I remember his easy presence around blacks, whether in Kentucky or on Big Mama's (my great-grandmother) hardscrabble farm outside Vicksburg. I didn't know it at that time, but the whole family on that side was fraught with matters of race. To listen to my Mississippi relatives talk was to hear a conversation constantly peppered with "nigger," usually said with a sneer, condescension, or, at best, paternalism. Nonetheless, one of those relatives, a woman, apparently had a scandalously strong attraction to black men. Another, this one male, seems actually to have been married to a black woman (although the commonly euphemistic term "Indian" was applied to her background), and to have had with her a number of children, my second cousins. Clearly what my blood and kin said and what they did were very different things, a paradox that entraps those who believe that (mere) words are monolithic.

I remember vividly being hurt by the prejudice that I myself experienced when I transferred to a large, great, northern university in 1968. Students from "up North" would hear my accent, see my whiteness, and assume that they knew all they needed to know about me: "racist, a hick, and probably politically, socially, and intellectually underdeveloped." Within months, I had shucked off my telltale accent; but I was long explaining myself, particularly after accepting my first university faculty appointment in 1974 to a largely white South African university. There, after seeing up close what social destruction intense and applied racism could wreak, after sheltering "Marxist" books for friends, after seeing a colleague sentenced to seven years for his political beliefs (while we in the courtroom sang "Sikele iAfrika"), after losing a friend to the assassin's midnight shotgun, any need for "explanation" was somehow beside the point. What could possibly give representation to this kind of reality?

Is this an unusual southern personal history? Perhaps; but barring the details, I don't think so. I have spoken with a number of southern people of common background over the past several years and have heard many stories like mine. Then, too, I've spent much time observing relationships between the races in the modern-day South, where I once again happily live and work. As I leave the metropolitan areas and move among rural people of low social status, I am continually struck by how easily the races mingle.[3] Sure, there are fights, but there are also dances and romances. It still seems to me that we must not make the mistake of emphasizing the former at the expense of the latter, which to those involved are not simply psychological aberrations based upon some deep-seated guilt.

The best evidence I can forward suggesting that my personal history is not unrepresentative is to be heard throughout the music of the South, particularly what is often (and more or less incorrectly) called "white" music. Take the example of Jimmie Rodgers, the "father of country music" – for what could be more representative of what the white South once valued? The "Singing Brakeman" came along at a rough time for Americans in general and southerners in particular. His short career, from August 1927 when he made his first recording, to May 1933 when he died, spanned some of the worst years of the Great Depression. Still, at a time when the recording industry was flattened by depressed economic times (with sales slipping by 60 percent in 1931 alone),[4] from which it did not recover until after World War II, Jimmie Rodgers sold a truly extraordinary number of recordings, perhaps twelve million or more.[5] To whom? Although there is little hard evidence, one supposes they were purchased largely by white, laboring-class southerners, the ones who have made up the audience for country music since. At a time when money was extraordinarily hard to come by, the music of Jimmie Rodgers meant enough that they sacrificed in order to have his latest. And what did they buy? Basically, the blues; oftentimes unequivocally the blues – *black music*! (Just listen to "Waiting for a Train," and its beguiling amalgam of blues, Dixieland, and church-house singing.) It is hard for me to believe that these people, extraordinarily sophisticated musically, did not know what they were getting. They were, rather, getting it because of what it was![6]

One could construct similar narratives about the blackness in Hank Williams; or that in "country-western" singer Elvis Presley; or of Bill Monroe;[7] or Jerry Lee Lewis; or Carl Perkins; or the Everly Brothers – on and on, up to many of the current crop of stars. Or to me: When I sang "Were You There?" in church, in close, four-part quartet harmony, or "Just a Little Talk with Jesus" (written by a black man, Cleavant Derricks, for the white Blackwood Brothers Quartet), I had no idea that I was engaged in a form of "theft" of black culture, to use Eric Lott's phrase; it felt more like sharing, or loving. The fact is that southern American music (which is now, arguably, the music of the world) has long been dismissed as "noisy" by many in the establishment, for being, in fact, the very (rough) music of amalgamation. Happily, common people have paid no heed at all to elite views, but have continued to listen and move to this music.; for it is joy coating a heart of hope, a measure of what we have been and a promise of what we might become, all African/Americans (with slash, the mark of union, not hyphen, the mark of identity), together parts of a "world made together."[8]

*****

THE PRESENT, OF COURSE, is fraught with all sorts of currents: political, social, religious, economic, cultural, and on. It is not surprising
that we don't arrive at some kind of present understanding about the
present day, for it is always a form of debate; but the past? Especially
the distant past, more than 150 years ago! It is not for neglect, for the
topic of minstrelsy has long been of abiding interest, and the object of
much research. Nevertheless, the world I have tried to people in this
study has not been adequately described, hardly even suspected. Why?

I do not wish to suggest a conspiracy, but for a very long time there
was no tradition in minstrelsy's historiography of considering where
one stood and whence one spoke. After all, it is the descendants of the
editors, printmasters, and other powerful people who got Dixon in the
end who have continued to tell our stories, despite Zip Coon's futile
efforts to puncture their sanctimoniousness by himself pretending to be
one of them – a "larned skoler." They read (selected) words and pronounced them truth. They looked at the blackface of common people
and saw only black. They heard the musics of blackface and they proclaimed it noise. This is why, as John Higham has pointed out in the
American Quarterly, "class is among the absentees from the celebration
of diversity," for multiculturalism's "academic apostles" employ only a
"whiff of class consciousness [to] sharpen the pungent odor of subjuga-
tion and resistance."[9] As for the culture of the white working class:
There's largely been no there there! The hick, redneck, and the good
ol' boy remain just about the last cultural icons universally available for
a cheap joke.

Alternatively, the subject of my lamentation is what I myself have
become since the days of my youth. What possibly can I, now a member of the the learned elite, make of understandings shared among people who embrace paradox, who do not attempt to explain away contradiction, who are unconcerned with the slipperiness of meaning? What
am I, in other words, to make of modes and symbols that owe more to
a premodern world than to my own modern processes of comprehension?

The rhetorical formulations I use here, though, suggest answers to
the questions: Why did minstrelsy enflame such powerful social and
personal emotions? and Why have the interpretations of minstrelsy remained so rigid for a century-and-a-half? Minstrelsy might have
been *the* – or at the very least *a* – primary form of cultural mediation

between "understanding" in a premodern Old World and "understanding" in a modern, industrialized New World.[10] This cuts many ways,
and opens up many new vistas. New research makes clear the resistance
of the urban working class in Jacksonian America to industrialization,
with its clocks, bosses, subordination, grimness, and "wage slavery"
(their term, not mine). Minstrelsy attacked these institutions, and did
so using a technique that shows up in the cultural expressions of nearly all enslaved or colonized societies: seeming accommodation to the
tropes and values of the powerful, but with underlying subversion of
them and affirmation of traditional modes of understanding. In minstrelsy, captains of industry (i.e., the Lords of Rule) were surreptious-
ly ridiculed through the device of the blackface dandy, trying always to
be more than he was, and therefore absurd. Jim Crow's loose-limbed
breakdown idealized the pleasures of preindustrial days, when there was
no regard for work schedules, play was of the moment, sex was joy,
dance and music were immediately meaningful. The "seeming accommodation" I mention is, of course, with racism, an institution that benefited middle-class white America infinitely more than working-class
white America. It was to the advantage of the white middle class to
scapegoat white, common Americans by painting *them* the racists, in
the bargain cleansing their own respectably reformed consciences and
driving a wedge in the real and reasonable alliance between white and
black common Jacksonians. The means was simple: Reason would have
it that laughing with the blackface must mean laughing at the black.
Tragically, the flanking powers of reason and media convinced even
working-class folk. By the last third of the century blackface minstrelsy had become what the Virginia Minstrels forecast: a weapon by which
one group of Americans defined, marginalized, and contained another
– racism, sexism, money, power, and (capital M) Music.[11]

✳✳✳✳✳

LET ME TURN ONE last time to Jacques Attali, who wrote boldly:

Make people Forget, make them Believe, Silence them. In all three cases, music is a tool of power: of ritual power when it is a question of making people
forget the fear of violence; of representative power when it is a question of
making them believe in order and harmony; and of bureaucratic power when
it is a question of silencing those who oppose it.[12]

Attali's pessimistic tone notwithstanding, it does not necessarily have to be this way (although it often is). Common people can and sometimes do stand up for their views of the world and of life, perhaps more frequently then than now. In this spirit, Boston's Anti-Bell-Ringing ordinance was challenged head-on. On 1 December 1838, a Mr. Bacon was hauled before the police court and charged with "ringing the Exchange dinner-bell without having a license so to do from the Mayor and Aldermen." Bacon frankly acknowledged his guilt. Even the prosecutor could not divine the intent of the ordinance under which Bacon stood charged, unless it was "having recently organized and appointed a large and efficient corps of police officers, it became necessary [for the Mayor] to manufacture a batch of new crimes, in order to furnish a pretext of employment for them, ..." Nevertheless, the prosecutor prosecuted, much as, one supposes, the watchmen had watched. Bacon offered only a "common sense" defense. The judge listened and ruled that he would "confer with his colleagues, and announce his judgement on Wednesday next." The court reporter ended his column by noting that the "Court room was . . . much crowded"; he then added with simple, even naïve, surprise – "as if it had been a case of life and death."[13]

Of course, to those whose understanding was shaped by a culture that privileged sound and music, it was their very world being weighed in the balance, as the scales of justice swayed and twisted, swept by the fresh winds of great change.

Notes

-Preface

1. As so often happens – a proof of the community of ideas that governs us all in mysterious ways – I am not the first to stumble upon this means to understanding, although for a flash I thought I was. Dan Cohen, among a few others, has made both a science and an art out of reading crime reports. See especially his 1993 *Pillars of Salt, Monuments of Grace*, which publication resulted from his residence at the Commonwealth Center for Studies in American Culture at the College of William and Mary (as did – another nodal moment! – the germinal work for this study).
2. Mahar 1988 does so quite persuasively.
3. Winans 1995: 112.
4. Bakhtin 1984: 101–2.
5. Ibid.: 211–12.

Dictionariana

1. Selected from "Dictionariana" in *Boston Post*, 13 December 1836; 10, 24 January, 1 February, 2, 3, 14, 15 March, 9 August, 5 September, 3, 21 October, and 27 November 1837; 16 January, 1, 24 February, and 1 March 1838.

Prologue

1. "Jim Along Josey" (New York: Firth & Hall, 1840), verse 1.
2. From *The Dunciad*, Book Four; in Pope n.d.: 296–7.

3. New York City Municipal Archives and Record Center, New York City Court of General Sessions, Minute Books (hereafter NYCGS).
4. My account of this trial is pieced together from the report in the *New York Herald*, 15 May 1842. The trial, which lasted two full days with a decision on the third, was covered in fifty-four column inches of fine type in the *Herald*, the era's largest newspaper – an indication of general public interest.

   The relative value of money is not easy to fix; but extracting from McCusker 1992: 327, 332 an average cost factor for the period 1830–43 and dividing that into the factor for 1991, one arrives at a figure of 15.323, which can be multiplied by any dollar amount used in this study to arrive at 1991 equivalence. Hence, Magnus was fined about $1532 in 1991 dollars.
5. From NYCGS, 23 May 1842.
6. One could read the verse as if "jim" were also a verb. I note that *Webster's Second International Dictionary* includes "jim-around," a term used in the mining industry to refer to a handy man; but I know of no other evidence that suggests an alternative reading.
7. The *Libertine*, 15 June 1842. All the women listed here were also well-known Boston prostitutes.
8. Fanny Elssler, the French ballet danseuse, was one of the most popular performers then appearing on the American stage.
9. Winans 1984: 81. It was published in 1842 by James L. Hewitt of New York.
10. Published in 1840 by Firth & Hall (New York).
11. Published in 1840 by Firth & Hall.
12. The term "legitimate theatre" is problematic, for it implies an "illegitimate theatre." I can find no easy way out of the dilemma, however, and will therefore stick with the term, and employ "legitimate" throughout this book to mean "conventional theatrical entertainment," as opposed to popular blackface minstrel theatre, and with no implied aspersions on other forms of theatre and their audiences.
13. Torbert 1986: ix.

1. Blackface on the Early American Stage

1. From F. Reynolds 1809: n.p.
2. One might compound such from many sources, but among the canonic works are Wittke 1930; Nathan 1962; Green 1970; and Toll 1974.
3. Respectively, Odell 1927–48; Smither 1944; and Wilson 1935.
4. That is, Willis 1924.
5. Among the more useful of these histories are Shockley 1977 and W. T. Hill 1971. I should point out that many of these histories are not complete in their details for the periods they purportedly cover. Even the venerable Odell volumes are shot through with omissions, and sometimes even errors. A rough estimate is that one can reconstruct only somewhat less than half the stage

history of New York from Odell, and the more lowbrow he deemed the production, the more likely it was not recorded.

6. Counting minstrel-type pieces, the total jumps to 233 blackface productions.

7. For the record, the second ten are *Jack Robinson and His Monkey* (57), *The Moorish Page* (47), *Norman Leslie* (41), *Robinson Crusoe* (39), *Nick of the Woods* (38), *Inkle and Yarico* (37), *A Day after the Fair* (32), *The Aethiop* (31), *High, Low, Jack, and the Game* (25), and *The Foulah Slave* (14).

8. The most-performed minstrel plays through 1843 were those by Thomas D. Rice. They were *Oh Hush!* or, *The Virginny Cupids* (premiered 1833, 138 performances), *The Virginny Mummy* (1835, 96), *Bone Squash Diavolo* (1835, 69), *Jumbo Jum* (1838, 39), *The Foreign Prince* (1839, 22), and *Othello Travestie* (1836, 18). One should note, however, that minstrel-type songs were probably the most performed of all blackface entertainments, partly for obvious production-related reasons. By far the most popular minstrel song during the period was "Jim Crow," for which I have been able to document 433 performances.

9. In particular, see Grimsted 1968; Buckley 1984; Meserve 1986; Levine 1988; Allen 1991; McConachie 1992.

10. See C. D. Johnson 1975; Bank 1993.

11. I have not been able to find Hackett's version of *Jonathan in England*. It appears, though, that the blackfaced characters in his version were extremely minor. I doubt that many (any?) of the points I make below would need modification were I to locate Hackett's version. Still, it would have been nice to read *Jonathan in England*, especially if, as Hodge claims (1964: 136): "[w]ith the possible exception of Samuel Woodworth's *The Forest Rose*, it was probably the most widely played theatre piece in America before 1850."

12. From Peake n.d.: 28.

13. Ibid.: 18.

14. *Spirit of the Times*, 4 May 1833.

15. F. Reynolds 1809: 11.

16. This is the father (d. 1829) of famed nineteenth-century tragedian William Charles Macready. See Downer 1966: 5–7.

17. McCready 1821: 28. A "bochro" is pidgen for "buckra," or a white man.

18. Ibid. For more on the blackface tradition and mumming, see Chapter 2.

19. Ibid.: 29.

20. Bickerstaffe 1825: 15.

21. Information on Hackett's life is widely available; for a summary see Wilmeth and Miller 1993: 216; for more detailed information see Hodge 1964: 85–151.

22. Wilmeth and Miller 1993: 232; see also Hodge 1964: 155–218, and Hill 1853 (his autobiography).

23. Wilmeth and Miller 1993: 302; see also Hodge 1964: 221–39.

24. Odell 1928: 3:655ff. *The Kentuckian* was a revision made in 1833 by William Bayle Bernard, a substantial rewrite of John Augustus Stone's *The Lion of the West*, which was in turn based on James K. Paulding's two-act farce on (likely) the life of Davy Crockett – a relationship that was denied by Paulding.

Hackett played Nimrod Wildfire (Crockett's persona) in the first production. In addition to Paulding, Stone, and Bernard 1954 see Shackford 1956: 253–64 for a discussion of Crockett's legend and its relation to *The Lion of the West*.

25. *Boston Post*, 7 June 1834. Hodge 1964: 282 is obviously in error when he dates the premier on 8 May 1835 in Philadelphia.
26. Barnett n.d.: 5.
27. Ibid.: 6.
28. Hodge 1964: 172.
29. Jones n.d.: 9.
30. Quoted in Hill 1853: 169–70. This scene was apparently omitted in later (mid-century and after?) productions.
31. Moody 1966: 147.
32. Woodworth 1825: 1.
33. Quoted in Saxton 1990: 122.
34. Ibid.: 123.
35. Woodworth 1825: 13–14.
36. Ibid.: 39.
37. Saxton 1990: 123.
38. *New York Sporting Whip*, 18 February 1843. See also Grimsted 1968: 56.
39. This is a term favored by the paper when referring to the productions of the Bowery Theatre, with its highly wrought melodramas and minstrel performances; the Bowery was Rice's favored venue when in New York at this time.
40. *Spirit of the Times*, 20 February 1841.
41. See McConachie 1988.
42. This and the next quotation are from Adams 1836: 209; those that ensue are from ibid.: 209–10, 211, and 215, respectively.
43. *Spirit of the Times*, 23 September 1837. It is instructive to note too that Porter chose to reprint the full text of Adams's article, shortly after its initial publication, in his 5 March 1836 edition.
44. Quoted in McConachie 1992: 15.
45. *Courier and Enquirer*, 20 September 1833.

2. Blackface in the Streets

Portions of this chapter were first published in my "Callithumpians, Mummers, Maskers, and Minstrels: Blackface in the Streets of Jacksonian America," in *Theatre Annual* (Cockrell 1996a).

1. Description of a feast in Antibes; quoted in Chambers 1903: 1:317.
2. From "The Age We Live In," quoted in the *Flash*, 10 December 1842.
3. *New York Herald*, 16 May 1842.
4. *Spirit of the Times*, 1 December 1832.
5. Ibid., 26 September 1840; emphasis in the original.
6. On theatre riots, see especially Grimsted 1972; McConachie 1985, 1992; Gilje 1987: 246–53; and Butsch 1995.

7. See Levine 1988: esp. 11–81 for a study of the importance of Shakespeare to the "lowbrows."
8. See McConachie 1992 for a full and superb study of melodrama among the working classes; I have learned much from this book.
9. See Gilje 1987: 257–60 for more descriptions of callithumpian bands; also S. G. Davis 1988: 103–9. The origin of the term *callithumpian* is problematic. Gilje 1987: 254 traces it to a compound of the Greek word for "beautiful," *kalli*, with the English *thump*. S. G. Davis 1988: 98 cites lexicographic sources that claim it was derived from a dialect word in eighteenth-century western England referring to "Jacobins, radical reformers, and 'disturbers of order at Parliamentary elections.'" I would like to suggest yet another derivation, one that follows from a notion developed later in this book: that a primary opposition to the chaotic, noisy world of public street rituals (like callithumpian bands) is the interior, private world of harmony, expressed by music. In New York in the early nineteenth century, before the term callithumpian appears in common usage, a quasi-secret, obviously upper-crust chamber music society existed, which surely sponsored its own "band" (orchestra) of music. It called itself the Calliopean Society, after the Greek muse of music (Odell 1927–48: 1:416, 2:68, 2:185, 3:74), and was an apt and timely target for burlesque, punctuated with a loud and noisy "thump."

There are competing etymologies, some even contemporaneous and often offered in the essential spirit of the callithumpian moment. For instance, the *Boston Post* (23 March 1840) defined the term as "a compound of two words in the Symmeseholian language – viz., 'cali,' which signifies brethren, and 'thump,' which signifies affection or friendship; and thus 'Calithumpian' stands for the 'affectionate brotherhood.'" A breakthrough? Alas, no. "Symmeseholian" is a burlesque on the quack theories of John Cleve Symmes, who believed that there was at 82° N. lat. an enormous opening in the earth; if one were to follow the path there into the center of the earth one would discover an idyllic world of plenty (Brewer 1900: 1068–9). Clearly the *Post* is trying to make the callithumpians appear absurd by association. The same paper offered on 16 April 1840 an article on "The Calathumpian Society" by "Zeno." This piece claimed for the society "venerable antiquity," traced references to it in the writings of Thucydides, Plato, Demosthenes, and Herodotus, among other ancient Greeks, and noted that "in Pliny's letters we read, 'that the order of the Calathumpians was the most renowned in the state, not excepting that of the Albigenses.'" The article promised that "a learned and elaborate volume is in preparation . . . which will do ample justice" to the history of the society. Of course, the *Post* confirmed only the burlesquing of history, not history itself.

10. There is no generally agreed-upon name to embrace the whole family of rituals, although S. G. Davis (1988: 203n) suggests "folk dramas," and Laroque (1991) "la fête" (translated as "seasonal entertainments"). I prefer "folk theatricals," which emphasizes the essential theatrical quality of the ritual without implying written text.

The best detailed overview of the whole family of rituals is probably to be found in Laroque, specifically in his pt. 1; he limits himself, of course, to the state of "la fête" during the time of Shakespeare.

11. See Gilje 1987: 21–3.
12. See ibid.: 260.
13. Interestingly, Bartlett 1848: 74, s.v. "charivari," notes it was "(c)ommonly pronounced shevaree." He also parallels the functions of charivari and callithumpian bands by cross-referencing them (pp. 61, 75).
14. This "policing" function complemented that of the married, family-oriented segment of the community, which was, of course, primarily responsible for perpetuating the existence of the community via procreation.
15. See Alford 1959; Thompson 1972, 1992; N. Z. Davis 1975.
16. See N. Z. Davis 1975: 97.
17. Kinser 1990: 21.
18. Flint 1826: 140.
19. See Bakhtin 1984: 214 for more on the tradition of bells in festive theatricals; also Nissenbaum 1996.
20. Shoemaker 1959: 73. Of course, Santa Claus is implicit in this model, and the cultural icon was developed, not surprisingly, in the 1820s and 1830s. On any aspect of Christmas see the wonderful book by Stephen Nissenbaum, *The Battle for Christmas* (1996).
21. Kinser 1990: 107.
22. S. White 1994; see also Piersen 1988, especially the chapter on "Black Kings and Governors."
23. Quoted in Kinser 1990: 335.
24. Eights 1867; quoted in Abrahams and Szwed 1983: 325. See also S. White 1988.
25. Quoted in Piersen 1988: 122. Election Day was closely related to Pinkster; see Reidy 1978.
26. On this, see MacMillan 1926; Reid 1942; Walser 1971; Ping 1980; Fenn 1988; Sands 1989, 1991.
27. Throop 1851: 384–5.
28. Jacobs 1861: 179.
29. See, for example, MacMillan 1926: 54. On kunering in general, see Walser 1971; Ping 1980; Stuckey 1987: 64–73; Fenn 1988.
30. Reid 1942: 353.
31. Lewis 1829; quoted in Abrahams and Szwed 1983: 241.
32. Bettelheim 1988: 56.
33. "Characteristic Traits . . ." 1797, quoted in Abrahams and Szwed 1983: 234–5.
34. Scott 1833: 2:63.
35. C. R. Williams 1826; quoted in Abrahams and Szwed 1983: 249.
36. Dirks 1987: 167–8.
37. Scott 1833: 2:71.
38. Cassidy 1966: 50.
39. See also Belisario 1838.
40. De La Beche 1825; quoted in Abrahams and Szwed 1983: 249.

41. Nugent 1839; quoted in Abrahams and Szwed 1983: 235.
42. Abrahams 1967: 462.
43. See Bettelheim 1988: 69.
44. Chambers 1903: 1:394. For a pungent overview of mumming and its impact on American folk culture, see Rammel 1990: chaps. 4–6.
45. For example, see Lake 1931.
46. For information on the structure of mumming see Tiddy 1923: 71–3; Chambers 1933: 13; Gailey 1969, 1974; Brody 1970; Dirks 1979a: 94–6; and Glassie 1983, among many other sources.
47. By laying out this logic I do not wish to vitiate the underside of the ritual understanding, for the equation of darkness and evil is a cornerstone of modern-day racism. On this see Jordan 1968: 7–11.
48. Glassie 1983: 117.
49. Simms 1978.
50. See Richardson 1976. For an interesting and recent example of the tenacity of this ritual see Pentzell 1977.
51. Quoted in Welch 1966: 525.
52. Breck 1877: 35.
53. See Shoemaker 1959: 21ff.
54. *Philadelphia North American,* 21 December 1913; quoted in ibid.: 23.
55. Shoemaker 1959: 23.
56. *York (Pa.) Sunday Gazette,* 24 December 1905; quoted in ibid.: 84. In corroboration, S. G. Davis (1982: 191) believes that it was "likely that Afro-Americans contributed much to the shape of Christmas revelry [in Philadelphia], in part as a result of "the steady influx of blacks from the coastal South where slaves [had] developed distinct mumming traditions."
57. An example to serve me here, one easily at hand: Abolitionist Asa Hutchinson of the Hutchinson Family Singers noted in his 1844 journal that he was reading James Phillippo's *Jamaica: Its Past and Present* (1843), in which a John Canoe festival is detailed. This episode can be found in Cockrell 1989: 189.
58. Throop 1851: 384–5.
59. *Philadelphia Sunday Dispatch,* 26 December 1858; quoted in Shoemaker 1959: 87.
60. Ibid., 24 December 1876; quoted in Shoemaker 1959: 23.
61. S. G. Davis 1982: 198.
62. Elizabeth J. Galt to J. H. Strobia, fall 1847, Galt Family papers, Swem Library, College of William and Mary; my thanks to Thad Tate for pointing out this reference to me.
63. See Thompson 1992: 3–4; also Alford 1959, 1968.
64. See Palmer 1978. Moore 1991 posits some benefits to some Indiana communities in the 1920s.
65. My problem is remarkably similar to that treated by François Laroque in his *Shakespeare's Festive World* (1991), although in a very different time and place. His treatment of relationships between the folk/popular and social/theatrical contexts has guided me in many ways.

66. S. G. Davis 1982: 188–9.
67. *Boston Post*, 26 May 1840.
68. One might want to compare this cover with the definition of *charivari* provided by Cotgrave in his 1611 dictionary: "A publicke defamation, or traducing of; a foule noise made, blacke *Santus* rung, to the shame, and disgrace of another; hence, an infamous (or infaming) ballade sung, . . ." (n.p.).
69. For instances, see *Spirit of the Times*, 26 August 1837; *Boston Post*, 7 March 1837.
70. This relationship is claimed in Nathan 1962: 166. Since Nathan relied upon a collection that was made long after the initial popularity of the minstrel song, the evidence is not conclusive. Even if morris dancers borrowed the tune from minstrelsy instead of the other way round, this is some oblique evidence of their mutuality.
71. Cf. Puck in *Midsummer Night's Dream:* "I am sent with broom before / To sweep the dust behind the door" (Act 5, scene 1).
72. *Spirit of the Times*, 30 January 1841.
73. The evidence associating minstrelsy with folk theatricals is also rich in the period after my study. The 1861 New Orleans Mardi Gras featured "a band of nigger minstrels, playing nigger music, [who] marched around, having at their head a comical effigy of Old Abe Lincoln, riding a rail of his own splitting" (quoted in Kinser 1990: 97). Immediately after the Civil War, the Mobile Mardi Gras was suspended by demoralized citizenry in favor of performances by the "Lost Cause Minstrels," replete with blackface, costumes, banjos, and all (Kinser 1990: 99). The Christmas Day 1874 edition of the *Easton (Pa.) Morning Dispatch* reported that the belsnickels "were out in full force last night, with banjos and bones" (quoted in Shoemaker 1959: 79).

   A most intriguing shard linking mumming with blackface minstrelsy comes from the *Philadelphia North American* in its 21 December 1913 edition: "The mummers, direct from anciently merrie England, have been shouldered off by Philadelphia's Christmas on to its New Year. In the early part of the nineteenth century the mummers appeared on Christmas eve, instead of New Year's eve, and they went from house to house, after the homely English fashion, singing their waits' songs and seeking dole of pence and cakes – and got it. That practice lasted right on up to twenty years ago. . . . Probably the man who did most to keep alive the old spirit of sheer comic humor was Eph Horn, in after years famed as the most popular nigger minstrel. Eph organized a band of mummers that belonged around Sixth and South streets, and it was he who supplemented the character of George Washington – the patriotic substitute for the British Saint George – and our own peculiar Cooney Cracker, . . ." (quoted in Shoemaker 1959: 23). Eph Horn was, in fact, born in Philadelphia, in 1818, and from about 1847 until his death in 1877 was one of the stage's leading blackface impersonators (E. L. Rice 1911: 27). It is unlikely that anyone can document that the young Eph Horn was a mummer, but note the supposition that follows from reporting the association so confidently: To readers in 1913 it was obviously not surprising that a blackface minstrel would once have been a mummer.

74. The devil throughout much of the nineteenth century was represented to be black, not red as today. Faris 1969: 138, notes that the devil carried several cognomens in rural Newfoundland: "Black Man," "Blackie," "Old Mummer," and "Old Nick" (cf. "St. Nick") among them.

75. Helm 1969 discusses this play and includes a copy of its text. The most sophisticated treatment comparing blackface in European folk theatricals with possible influences on American minstrelsy is Rehin 1975b; see also Pickering 1986: 78. On all-blackface plays see Chambers 1933: 85.

76. On morris dancing, see Chambers 1903: 1:199; Sharp 1911; Needham 1936; or Barrand 1991.

77. Needham 1936: 26; Chamber 1903: 1:199.

78. *Courier and Enquirer*, 28 February 1834; 3 April 1834; 14 April 1834.

79. Ibid., 23 January 1835; emphasis in the original.

80. Playbill for 23 January 1836, HTC.

81. *New York Herald*, 23–6 December 1839.

82. Quoted in Shoemaker 1959: 74.

83. See ibid.: 73–85.

84. Carmichael 1833: 2:289, reported that at Christmas allowance time the slaves "flour each other's black faces and curly hair, and call out, 'look at he white face! and he white wig!'"

85. Scott 1833: 2:73.

86. Bakhtin 1984: 39. Bakhtin's dictum and its application to blackface minstrelsy was demonstrated to me when Professor Charles Hamm of Dartmouth College shared a video he had made of the 1991 "Annual Minstrel Show" held in Tunbridge, Vermont. The show was replete with blackfaced line of comics and singers, featuring endmen and an Interlocutor (in whiteface). Sponsored by the Civic Club, the blackface performers (all male) were, according to Hamm, "farmers, loggers, school teachers, the road commissioner, and the justice of the peace" (Hamm 1995: 355). But for the association many of us carry of minstrel blackface with racism (and it is not clear that the bulk of the audience made this association), there was nothing explicitly racist about the show; by this I mean that none of the jokes, repartee, or songs dealt with sensitive racial matter. The jokes, which were exclusively the domain of the blackface characters, were what we might generously call Rabelaisian, and were generally concerned, in Bakhtin's formulation, with "lower bodily strata." A mild (for this particular occasion) but characteristic example, one that occurred right at the beginning of the show, set the tone:

ENDMAN: Mr. Interlocutor. What can a swan do, that a goose can almost do, that a duck can't do, that a lawyer oughta do?

INTERLOCUTOR: I give up.

MR. TAMBO: Stick his bill up his ass.

Likely, out of blackface, these citizens honor a social code that circum-
scribes this kind of folk humor in mixed company and prohibits its public
display. Nevertheless, the mixed audience (by age and gender; all were, however, white) accepted blackface as appropriate removal from the ordinary and
laughed joyously at each risqué punch line or slam at political authority.

87. Gluckman 1954: 125.
88. Dirks 1987: 167–8.
89. Eights 1867: 325.
90. Marsden 1788: 229–30.
91. "Characteristic Traits . . ." 1797, quoted in Abrahams and Szwed 1983: 233.
92. C. R. Williams 1826: 250. Of course, "My Long-Tail Blue" was one of the
    most popular early minstrel songs, first performed in 1833 according to my
    records.
93. Throop 1851: 384.
94. Shoemaker 1959: 74.
95. Widdowson and Halpert 1969: 157.
96. Shoemaker 1959: 23.
97. Exceptions to the switching of gender from male to female can be found in
    the earliest years of minstrelsy. Occasionally, white women performed black-
    face female roles, such as Rose in "Coal Black Rose." More frequently, how-
    ever, females cross-dressed and blacked up. For example, Miss Wray, "sev-
    en years old," was a minor hit in 1835 with her version of "Jim Crow."
98. The thorny issue of audience sociology is broached in the upcoming section.
99. Historians have only recently begun to explore the early and worldwide pop-
    ularity of minstrelsy. See Rehin 1975b, 1981; Pickering 1986; Cockrell 1987;
    Blair 1990.
100. See in particular, Lott 1993a; also Saxton 1975; Roediger 1991.
101. See Winans 1984: 95–6 on the way burlesque works in minstrelsy.
102. See S. G. Davis 1988: 98–100.
103. Glassie 1983: 48, 89.
104. Ibid.: 138.
105. See, for instances, *Spirit of the Times,* 25 February 1837, 2 February 1839.
106. Glassie 1983: 90, 92. Glassie glosses the term "goodmanning" as "locally syn-
     onymous with the verb to encourage."
107. Ibid.3: 31.
108. See the brilliant study by John F. Szwed (1975).
109. Bakhtin 1984: 45.
110. Kinser 1990: 318.
111. I base this percentage on a twenty-five-cent ticket, common for pit admission,
     and a laborer's daily wage of seventy-five cents. To support the appropriate-
     ness of this wage I note a corroborating account in the *New York Herald,* 5
     May 1842, and the work of Sean Wilentz, which shows that the average male
     annual wage of workers in 1850 New York City was $297.12. (Wilentz 1984:
     405). At the extreme, the *Boston Post* (16 September 1834) was shocked to re-
     port that one John Follett "was obliged to work for $1.80 cents a week, and

maintain his mother out of it, ..." Compare these figures to the $500–600 computed in Blumin 1989: 110 to be necessary annually for the maintenance of a family in modest living conditions.

112. Halpert 1969: 53.
113. Levine 1988 traces this progression brilliantly.
114. Dirks 1979a: 97.
115. Glassie 1983: 31, 83–6.
116. Halpert 1969: 44.
117. *Christian World*, 24 December 1891; quoted in Shoemaker 1959: 82. This citation leads one to wonder if Santa too isn't supposed both to frighten and beguile little children. If the intention is not there, the reality certainly is, as home photo albums across the United States, filled with obligatory Christmas snapshots of screaming or suspicious children on the laps of department-store Santas, would surely verify.
118. See in particular R. Williams 1973: 10–2.

3. *Jim Crow*

Portions of this chapter were first published in my "Jim Crow, Demon of Disorder," in *American Music* (Cockrell 1996b).

1. From the "London correspondent" of the *New York Express*, dated 29 December 1836; quoted in *Spirit of the Times*, 25 February 1837.
2. Ludlow 1880: 327–8.
3. *New York Herald*, 27 April 1837.
4. Cowell 1844: 86; confirmed by *Cincinnati Commercial Advertiser*, 28 January 1830.
5. Cf. *Louisville Public Advertiser*, 30 November 1830.
6. Cowell 1844: 87. There is suggestive evidence that young Cowell sang in blackface. His father wrote that his son was asked to sing at a concert of "the *fashionables*" and that he was "to give his 'Negro Melodies' *with a white face*," as if this were an exception to normal performance practice (Cowell 1844: 88; emphasis added); whereas at a Louisville performance in late 1830 Master Cowell was advertised to sing "'Coal Black Rose' – in character" (*Louisville Public Advertiser*, 30 November).
7. Cowell 1844: 87. According to Cowell (p. 66), "[Tom Blakeley] was the first to introduce *negro singing* on the American stage, and his 'Coal Black Rose' set the fashion for African melodies. . . ." A verse to the "Jim Crow" published by Willig in Baltimore acknowledged the debt: "Oh de Coal Black rose, / Once was all de go / But now she find a ribal / In Mister Jim Crow."
8. Smith 1868: 65; emphases in the original. Smith's arrangement with Drake is corroborated in the *Louisville Public Advertiser*, 20 September 1830.
9. Ludlow 1880: 392.
10. *Louisville Public Advertiser*, 18 September 1830.
11. Ibid., 22 September 1830.

12. Ibid., 29 September 1830.
13. *Spirit of the Times*, 28 April 1832, copied two lines of an "Old Song," obviously "Jim Crow": "Come all ye bold Kentuckians, / I'd have you for to know, &c."
14. *Courier and Enquirer*, 8 November 1832.
15. Ibid., 31 August 1833.
16. The financial dimensions of Rice's success were significant. Some newspapers even credited him with keeping the Bowery Theatre afloat. The *New York Herald* (23 February 1841) claimed that he earned the "trifle of $5000 for his several engagements during the season" at the Chatham Square Theatre. He accumulated enough to build a mansion on Long Island Sound, where he often retired during the off-season.
17. *Spirit of the Times*, 11 June 1836, 22 October 1836.
18. *New York Herald*, 27 August 1837. Almack's was a popular and exclusive dance palace.
19. *Spirit of the Times*, 26 August 1837; quoted from *The Star*.
20. *Boston Post*, 26 July 1838.
21. *New York Herald*, 8 August 1837; the wedding took place on 29 June 1837 in London, at St. John's Church, Westminster.
22. *Boston Semi-Weekly Courier*, 10 August 1837.
23. *London Sunday Times*, 9 July 1837, quoted in *Spirit of the Times*, 2 September 1837.
24. *Spirit of the Times*, 2 September 1837; *New York Herald*, 29 July 1837.
25. *Spirit of the Times*, 30 March 1839. Rice returned to the United States in June 1840, according to the *Boston Post*, 15 June 1840.
26. *Bell's Life*, quoted in *Spirit of the Times*, 21 January 1843.
27. Rice's biography is pieced together here from my own reading of primary sources and a multitude of secondary sources, most prominently: E. L. Rice 1911: 7–11; *DAB:* 15:545–6; Ramshaw 1960; Dormon 1969; Hitchcock and Sadie: 1986.
28. *New York Herald*, 13 October 1840.
29. Quoted in *Spirit of the Times*, 2 December 1837. In the original a "not" was inserted between "would" and "patronize" in the first line. This, of course, changes completely the meaning of the sentence; but the rest of the article suggests that the "not" was unedited in the typesetting, perhaps a residue of a previously more convoluted rhetorical flourish. I have removed it.
30. *New York Herald*, 8 April 1842. The character of "Bowery Boys" has been discussed in many places. See, for example, McConachie 1992: 122; Butsch 1994. The Chatham was at this time New York's "lowest" theatre.
31. Ibid., 30 August 1837.
32. Ibid., 29 July 1837.
33. *Figaro in London*, 17 September 1836; quoted in *Spirit of the Times*, 12 November 1836.
34. Quoted in *Spirit of the Times*, 7 January 1837, 4 February 1837.
35. Ibid., 29 September 1838.

36. Ibid., 2 February.
37. *Boston Post*, 25 May 1840.
38. Ibid., 23 November 1840.
39. Of more than tangential significance on this point is Leonard L. Richards's 1970 classic study, *"Gentlemen of Property and Standing,"* where the same group is defined. I suspect that the great scholarly confusion over class during this period, especially in work that has looked at theatre audiences and society, derives in part from privileging traditional Marxist economic definitions of class over one that includes social status. To be unmarried (in action, if not also in fact) and male put one in a "social class" irrespective of income, one that attended minstrelsy and that supported mob action, among other such sports. To be married, male, and (especially) with family established for one an entirely different social space. I have seen nothing to counter my belief that the male cohort for minstrelsy was based to a considerable extent on marital and family status.

   In an oblique but telling narrative, I like how a "prominent leader" functioned in the sociology of a charivari that occurred in Eufaula, Alabama, in February 1843, and its aftermath: "A Mr. William Edwards, who had been committing various misdemeanors about town (such as fighting, drinking, rowdying, and so on), was taken by the citizens, and placed upon that most pleasant of all things, a fine three-cornered rail, and escorted by a band of tin pails, cowbells, &c., carried across the river into Georgia. An ex-Marshall of our town, who was the prominent leader of this movement, as soon as Edwards was in Georgia, slipped back across the bridge to console Edwards' wife, for the loss, disgrace, &c., of her husband. Edwards, however, concluding he was the proper one to comfort the lady in affliction, also slipped back, and finding the ex-Marshall in bed with his better half, drew a knife, and cut him all to pieces, splitting his nose, lips, and cutting him seriously, and perhaps mortally, in the body" (*New York Herald*, 28 February 1843).
40. *New York Transcript*, 15 April 1836.
41. NYCGS: 10 July 1835. There is some confusion about Rice's conviction, for the *New York Transcript*, 11 July 1835, noted that he and others of his fellow defendants were found not guilty. NYCGS: 13 July 1835 shows that "George Rice judged not guilty on assault," perhaps a correction to the entry of the 10th.
42. *New York Transcript*, 5 April 1835.
43. *Courier and Enquirer*, 23 December 1833; *Mazeppa* was the theatrical hit of that season for the Bowery Theatre.

   It is not manifestly clear from the record the relation this woman had to Rice – she could have, conceivably, been his mother – yet context seems to suggest an amorous relationship. (Interestingly, no evidence survives suggesting that Rice was married, or divorced, before his union to Charlotte Gladstone in 1837.) Whatever the kinship reading, my general point still stands.
44. Ca. 1837–40; Broadsides Collection, AAS.
45. Broadsides Collection, John Hay Library, Brown University.

46. I date the publication of this song on the basis of a note in the *Spirit of the Times*, 2 February 1833: "New Music: E. Riley, 29 Chatham St., has published since our last . . . the comic extravaganza, 'Jim Crow,' with a full length lithography [*sic*] of Mr. T. Rice, . . ."

47. Sometimes Jim Crow claims to have arrived from "Tuckyhoe," geographically a section in tidewater Northern Virginia, but this word was (and is) popularly assumed to refer to Kentucky. I should note for the sake of balance that Jim Crow was on some occasions identified as a fiddler from Virginia, but another verse in the same song would always place him farther west.

48. There is significant literature on this topic by Smith-Rosenberg 1985: 90–108; Saxton 1990: 78–84; and others. The general literature on Crockett is vast, but see especially (in addition to Smith-Rosenberg and Saxton) Shackford 1956; Wolfe 1989.

49. "Jim Crow" (Boston: Leonard Deming, ca. 1837–40); Broadside Collection, AAS.

50. "Jim Crow" (sheet music) (New York: Atwill's, ca. 1833). The "lion of the west" is a reference to Nimrod Wildfire, main character in the novel and the derived play of the same title (later renamed *The Kentuckian*), both popularly believed to be based on the life and legend of Davy Crockett.

51. "Jim Crow" (sheet music) (Baltimore: George Willig, ca. 1833).

52. E. Riley edition (see n. 46).

53. George Willig edition.

54. E. Riley edition.

55. Saxton 1975: 17, passim.

56. "Jim Crow" (sheet music) (Baltimore: John Cole, ca. 1833). The pun, of course, is on the name of Henry Clay, the defeated Whig presidential candidate in the election of 1832 and leader of anti-Jacksonian forces in the Senate. (It was Clay who proposed the compromise Tariff of 1833, easing tensions between the federal government and South Carolina over the latter's controversial nullification of earlier federal tariffs.)

57. *Lowell Courier*, 14 October 1843; no issues of this journal appear to be extant. Also note that in *Deacon Snowball's Negro Melodies* 1843: [17–18] there can be found "Latest Jim Crow; or, The Infancy of John Tyler," a thorough satire on the President of the United States.

One might even make the case that excessive drinking during the Jacksonian period was something of a political gesture, for as Rorabaugh 1979: 248 has documented, merchants and manufacturers were among the lowest consumers of alcohol, whereas laborers, canal builders, and riverboatmen were among the highest. This might help explain why so frequently drunks picked up by the watch were attended to because they were supposedly singing or dancing to "Jim Crow." For a representative sample see *Boston Post*, 28 September 1833, 15 February 1834, 27 January 1838; *New York Evening Tattler*, 9 October 1839.

58. *Courier and Enquirer*, 19 August 1834. The *Alexandria Gazette*, 18 August 1834, noted too that the rioters, "so far as we can learn, had their faces painted."

59. *Boston Post,* 16 August 1834.
60. Ibid. Cf. Blumin 1989: 139 where he examines pianos as middle-class icons denoting social standing.
61. *Trial of John R. Buzzell* 1834: 64. The month before the burning of the convent, "Jim Crow" had been used in another riotous context. The New York riots in July 1834 featured working-class, white male attacks on theatres (about which more in Chapter 4), churches, middle-class abolitionists, and blacks (who might have been the scapegoats for the abolitionists). One reporter noted that the rioters, while in a black church, "struck up a Jim Crow chorus" (*New York Times,* quoted in *Boston Morning Post,* 18 July 1834).
62. *Trial of John R. Buzzell* 1834: 78, 84.
63. My thanks to Dan Cohen for freely given insights into the convent burning.
64. *British Whig,* 27 April 1837, quoted in Palmer 1978: 30. "Mawworm" was the main character in *The Hypocrite,* a favorite farce of the day adapted by Isaac Bickerstaffe from Molière's *Tartuffe.*
65. Ramshaw 1960: 40–1. The citation is, alas, undocumented.
66. *Cork Herald,* quoted in *Spirit of the Times,* 13 May 1837.
67. Nathanson 1855: 72.
68. I would suggest, moreover, that the material culture that is part of the sheet music to "Jim Crow," "Coal Black Rose," "Clare de Kitchen," "Long Time Ago," and other early minstrel songs has been fundamentally misinterpreted. Scholars had usually assumed that these are either predominantly texts or, at the other extreme, songs (music) first. However, if they are at base theatrical pieces (which does not negate their value as either text or sound), then there is a rationale for the form in which they appear: relatively expensive pieces of sheet music that typically include a lithograph on the cover. Someone in, for example, Bangor, Maine, who wished to perform "Jim Crow" in the local theatre could order a copy of the sheet music from Boston or New York, find there a selection of appropriate verses, the tune, the harmony (optional, of course), and an illustration of appropriate costuming with attendant gestures and dispositions – virtually all that was needed to mount a performance. In fact, when the Bangor Theater's possessions were sold at auction in 1837, among the items offered were "Jim Crow's Song" and "raggy pants," suggesting that someone might have done "jis so" (*Spirit of the Times,* 16 September 1837).
69. *Louisville Public Advertiser,* 4 October 1830.
70. Ibid., 7 October 1830; emphases in the original. The reference to "localities" [or "local sayings"] may be found in a passage quoted earlier from the *Louisville Public Advertiser* (see n. 12).
71. Ludlow 1880: 392; emphases in the original. This assertion remains undocumented.
72. See Abrahams 1992 for a fine study of this tradition, although I must respectfully disagree with his conclusion that blackface minstrelsy is a direct result of southern corn-husking traditions, "Jim Crow" notwithstanding.
73. Tucker 1970: 116–17; emphases added.

74. Ibid.
75. Quoted in *Spirit of the Times*, 13 May 1837.
76. Hamm 1979: 121–2.
77. Quoted in *Spirit of the Times*, 4 February 1837.
78. Hone 1889: 1:266.
79. *New Haven Standard*, quoted in *Pennsylvania Gazette*, 6 June 1833.
80. *Philadelphia Daily Chronicle*, 26 December 1833, quoted in Shoemaker 1959: 86.
81. *Philadelphia Daily Evening Bulletin*, 27 December 1859, quoted in Shoemaker 1959: 87.
82. *Philadelphia Public Ledger*, 2 January 1847, quoted in S. G. Davis 1988: 105; *New York Herald*, 2 January 1843.
83. *Harrisburg Telegraph*, 26 December 1879, quoted in Shoemaker 1959: 80.
84. *Philadelphia North American*, 25 December 1861, quoted in Shoemaker 1959: 87.
85. Latrobe 1980: 204.
86. Eights 1867, quoted in Abrahams and Szwed 1983: 382.
87. "Characteristic Traits . . ." 1797, quoted in Abrahams and Szwed 1983: 233.
88. Williams 1826, quoted in Abrahams and Szwed 1983: 249.
89. This watershed moment has been much documented and discussed, but see especially Moody 1958; Levine 1988: 63–8; McConachie 1992: 145–50. Not everyone seems to agree on the number of dead; I rely on the count of my friend and colleague Bruce McConachie.
90. Attali 1985: 6.
91. Throughout this account, I have modernized punctuation.
92. On blacks who performed minstrel songs, see, for instances, *Evening Tattler*, 25 January 1840; *New York Herald*, 4 September 1841; *Spirit of the Times*, 5 January 1842. On black audiences for minstrelsy, I note that ticket prices for "colored persons" are advertised at Baltimore's New Theatre during the very time that Dixon was singing "Clare de Kitchen" and likely other blackface songs (*Baltimore Patriot*, 2 November 1832). In New York, Police Court records frequently show African-American attendance at the theatres – for example, that of "Sam Jonsing," who "was most decidedly noisy on Monday night at the Chatham Theatre" (*New York Herald*, 11 August 1841). My research largely supports David Grimsted (1968: 53) in his assertion that "Negroes in northern theaters shared the gallery with Caucasians."
93. Perhaps, even probably, other towns and cities as well, but my research did not extend systematically to many of them.
94. *Boston Post*, 26 October 1842.
95. Ibid., 25 August 1835 and 17 November 1840.
96. *New York Herald*, 26 December 1841.
97. Ibid., 21 October 1839.
98. This account is reconstructed from a report in the *Evening Tattler*, 25 January 1840. Another account of racial mixing in gambling houses can be read in the *New York Herald*, 28 February 1842.

99. On the often quite good race relations between the "lower sorts" in the periods before see Roediger 1991: 24, and A. Vaughan 1989, who admits (somewhat reluctantly, to be sure) the possibility that lower-class whites showed "signs of eroding prejudice [on becoming] more familiar with black men and women," and that "the upper class may then have reinvigorated a waning racist ideology among the poor whites to prevent a united working class" (348). On this topic also see G. S. Rowe's 1989 study "Black Offenders, Criminal Courts, and Philadelphia Society in the Late Eighteenth Century," which chronicles criminal activities where blacks and whites worked in teams and "numerous parties where 'whites, blacks and mulattoes [were] all dancing together.'" Rowe concluded that "the lower classes of both races often accepted each other on terms of equality much more readily than did their social betters" (695).

100. *New York Herald*, 4 September 1841.

101. Dickens 1842: 36. Although Dickens never mentioned the name of the establishment, a note in the *New York Herald*, 11 November 1842, makes it clear. The best treatment of Juba, though it is shot through with errors, is still Winter 1948.

102. Toll 1974: 43. Nathan 1962: 83–5 has a good general discussion of the double shuffle.

103. *Boston Post*, 11 August 1835. One assumes, from the report, that all the dancers were also white.

104. *New York Herald*, 9 August 1841.

105. *Evening Tattler*, 29 January 1840. The "pigeon wing" is another black dance, in which the dancer jumps into the air and clicks his legs, heels, or ankles together (Nathan 1962: 85).

106. *Baltimore Patriot*, 19 October 1833.

107. *New York Herald*, 1 September 1841.

108. Nathan 1962: 92. Abrahams 1992: 102 claims that "the term breakdown [refers] to the customary slave dance [and] was common in the South from the early nineteenth century."

109. *New York Daily Express*, 14 September 1840. Juba's proper name is usually recorded as William Henry Lane; there were competing claims to the name "Juba," though, by at least two black dancers, and perhaps this is the "other" one. I wish to thank George A. Thompson, Jr., for pointing out this reference to me.

110. *New York Herald*, 28 December 1842. The easy possibility exists, since the descriptions of black dances are almost always by whites, that the names for once-white dances have thus been applied descriptively to black dance practice.

111. Toll 1974: 66 has estimated that roughly the same number of early blackface minstrel songs opposed slavery as supported it.

112. *The American Comic Songster* 1834: 80.

113. Published January 1833 (see n. 46).

114. *New York Express*, 13 April 1839.

115. Flour, the color of which is the inverse of blackness as well as a symbol of fecundity, was often used during this time to ridicule sterility. (See, for example, the *New York Evening Post*, 2 January 1828, and its account of callithumpians bombarding a tavern.) Of course, flouring is still a tradition at the New Orleans Mardi Gras, with vestiges remaining of its original meaning.

116. *Boston Post*, 18 June 1840. In a mocking article on the "floured tragedian," the *Post* of 15 June 1840 had claimed: "The Secretary of the Calithumpian Society requests us to state, that no vote was ever passed authorizing the flouring of Mr Shales, and that he could prove that Shales had purchased an exemption from flouring, by giving the requisite number of 'throws,' but unfortunately the Treasurer has gone to Texas, carrying with him the records, and all the moveable property of the Society."

117. Ibid., 5 May 1834, and 8 September 1835. The *Post*, a Democratic paper, is not a good source for accurate information about Davy Crockett, who by 1835 had fallen out with the party of Jackson. Nonetheless, it is clear that Crockett and Jim Crow often appeared at the theatre the same evening, that advertisements touted both appearances, and that together they were an undeniable draw. Even if apocryphal, the mythical qualities of such a union are undeniable.

4. Zip Coon

1. From "Some Passages in the Life of G. W. Dixon, the American Coco la Cour," in *The Flash*, 11 December 1841. The comparative "Coco la Cour" remains a mystery to me, in spite of a tantalizing (and brief) reference to him in Hugo's *Les Misérables;* my thanks to Carol Rifelj for the citation.

2. From "Zip Coon on the Go-Ahead Principle" (Boston: Leonard Deming, ca. 1834); Broadside Collection, AAS.

3. I base this dating on the fact that the song was new to the *Boston Post* on 31 October 1833 when it noted: "Jim Crow has a rival at the south, in the person of one Zip Coon."

4. "Zip Coon" (sheet music) (New York: Atwill's, 1834).

5. An excellent study of honor is that of Gorn 1985, which has redirected my thinking about many things. Although this piece is about the "Southern Backcountry," there are consequential parallels with northern, urban working-class life, a point I shall develop further toward the end of this chapter.

6. "Zip Coon" is, in this regard, like many songs of the early minstrel period, which generally treat issues of honor, status, and social positioning. In response to Roediger 1991: 124, who believes that the exclusion of blacks from the early minstrel stage is proof of its essential racist nature, I would claim that the social and political dimensions of early minstrelsy's inherent protest manifestly could not proceed from the mouths of African Americans; hence early minstrelsy's whiteness and the lack of convincing proof that it is unequivocally about race.

7. On this publication see Goertzen and Jabbour 1987, especially p. 125, which treats "Zip Coon" and its tune family. I am generally indebted to Paul Wells, Director of the Center for Popular Music, Middle Tennesse State University, for his guidance and expertise on all matters relating to fiddle tunes. Wells and McLucas 1997 provide the fullest discussion of the development and evolution of the tune called popularly today "Turkey in the Straw."

8. *New York Herald*, 25 May 1837; see also Flint 1826: 295.

9. I base this date on the admission information gathered by the New Orleans Charity Hospital, 27 February 1861, which stated that the patient was then sixty years old. The *Flash* for 11 December 1841 noted that he "was born some forty years ago, . . ." The 1808 date given generally in most biographical sources is surely wrong.

10. This information is compiled from the *Sunday Mercury*, 19 September 1841, and the *Flash*, 11 December 1841. Neither source is in agreement on all points: The *Mercury* claims Dixon was born in Baltimore; the *Flash* insists on Alexandria, Virginia (whereas he seems, in fact, to have been born in Richmond). The *Flash*, especially, was not the most objective of sources, but there is precious little else on which to base Dixon's early biography.

11. Thayer 1976/1986: 1:126.

12. Sankus 1981: 227.

13. Odell 1927–48: 3:354.

14. Thayer 1976/1986: 1:188–9.

15. Ibid.: 207.

16. *Virginia Herald*, issues throughout February 1829; Thayer 1976/1986: 221.

17. Odell 1927–48: 3:400, 413, 421; *Flash*, 11 December 1841. Dixon is sometimes given credit for performing "Coal Black Rose" as early as 1827 (see, e.g., Greenwood 1909: 124)

18. Odell 1927–48: 3:472.

19. Phelps 1880: 145.

20. He might have resided in Philadelphia during some of this time, although city directories cannot verify it. My basis for this suggestion is a notice in the *Boston Post*, 13 February 1837, which asserted that "Dixon was living in Philadelphia" at the time "Ritner was ran against Gov. Wolf." Wolf and Ritner faced each other in 1829 and 1832, but only in 1832 was Wolf the governor.

21. Dixon 1830, 1834: [3]. The crowd estimate might, of course, be by Dixon himself; it is surely an exaggeration.

22. On fire departments see Laurie 1973.

23. Ireland 1867b: n.p.

24. *Baltimore Patriot*, 4 December 1832.

25. I have no chronicle of his whereabouts at all from 5 February 1833 to 27 January 1834.

26. Dixon had answered "editor" to the question of occupation at time of admittance into the New Orleans Charity Hospital where he died.

27. *Flash*, 11 December 1841.

28. 18 January 1834.

29. Notice copied in the *Harrisburg Telegraph*, 18 January 1834.
30. Quoted in *Boston Post*, 21 February 1834.
31. Quoted in New York's *Courier and Enquirer*, 27 January 1834.
32. Thayer 1976/1986: 2:160.
33. I have no hard evidence to support this. The *Boston Post* (31 October 1833) dates the song to 1833 and places it in the South. Farrell was singing the song by 1834 in the North, and billing himself "from the southern theaters" (Odell 1927–48: 4:25). I note too that E. L. Rice 1911: 6 claims for Farrell that he was "the original 'Zip Coon.'"
34. See the *Courier and Enquirer* for that date.
35. Ibid., 25 March 1834.
36. 19 June 1834, Arch Street Theatre (Ireland 1867b: anonymous account).
37. See Kerber 1967.
38. See McConachie 1985; on theatre riots in general see Butsch 1995.
39. *Commercial Advertiser*, 10 July 1834.
40. *New York Sun*, 11 July 1834.
41. My interpretation here follows the lead of an editorial in the *Boston Post* (15 July 1834): "In one sense, the abstract questions of abolition, intermarriage, &c., had nothing to do with these outbreakings of popular fury. . . . Scarcely one in a thousand of the citizens of New York look upon the doctrine of familiar intercourse and intermarriage between blacks and whites, with any other feelings than those of loathing and destestation – yet the few, whose tastes and inclinations prompt them to befriend it, would have been suffered to go on their way rejoicing, without any other opposition than public opinion calmly and discreetly expressed, had they not carried their efforts far beyond the bounds of decency and propriety. . . . When they [the abolitionist leaders] took it upon themselves to regulate public opinion upon this point, and to brand as thieves and accomplices, all who refused to acquiesce in their smutty tastes, is it not wonderful that their temerity bought down upon them not only the denunciations of an insulted community, but the violence of an infuriated populace."
42. *New York Transcript*, 14 July 1834; quoted in *Boston Post*, 15 July 1834.
43. Advertisement for 9 January 1835 concert in Worcester, Massachusetts (Hill 1853: 9).
44. *Boston Post*, 20 May 1835; *Dixon's Daily Review*, 25 May 1835, which refers to the first issue "four weeks ago."
45. *Dixon's Daily Review*, 25 May 1835; emphases in the original.
46. Dixon 1834: 4.
47. *Dixon's Daily Review*, 25 May 1835.
48. Ibid.
49. Dixon's later manifest fixation on women and sexuality might well give support to Carroll Smith-Rosenberg's point that "sexuality and the family, because of their primitive psychic and social functions, serve as reservoirs of physical imagery through which individuals seek to express and rationalize

their experience of social change" (1985: 90). It was, indeed, a world in the throes of immense change.

50. *Boston Post,* 11 June 1835.
51. Ibid., 30 June 1835.
52. Ibid., 1 July 1835.
53. Ibid., 6 August 1835.
54. *Boston Semi-Weekly Courier,* 22 February 1836; *Boston Post,* 24, 25, 26 February 1836.
55. *Boston Post,* 23 February 1836.
56. Quoted in ibid., 11 March 1836.
57. Ibid., 12 April 1836; 29 April 1836.
58. "The Fireman's Call" (Boston: C. H. Keith, n.d.)
59. Odell 1927–48: 4:61.
60. I thus tend to agree with Blumin 1989, who argues against the neo-Marxist perspective and claims that there was both the concept and the fact of an urban American middle-class during this period, although it was ill-defined and sometimes amorphous to be sure. However, Dixon (and the others in his cohort that we shall meet later in this chapter) were quite obviously and consciously trying to move "up" to something, and it surely was not the elite class, which was way out of reach. (One needed too much money for that.) With the proper education, "taste," and refinement one aspired to improving living conditions and social status.
61. Suggesting a paying audience of about 140 persons, at the advertised fifty cents per ticket.
62. *New York Transcript,* 2 June 1836.
63. The narrative of the trial is reconstructed from the *New York Transcript,* 16 June 1836, and from the *Boston Post* account quoted in the *Spirit of the Times,* 18 June 1836.
64. *Flash,* 11 December 1841.
65. *Spirit of the Times,* 2 July 1836.
66. *Lowell Journal,* 27 July 1836.
67. *Boston Post,* 24 December 1836.
68. On labor abolitionism see Jentz 1977; Magdol 1986; Aptheker 1989; Shapiro 1989.
69. *Boston Post,* 30 January 1837.
70. Quoted in *Boston Times,* 4 February 1837. The quote from Alexander Pope is from *The Dunciad* (n.d.), a section of which I included at the head of my "Prologue" to this study.
71. All quotations are from the *Boston Post,* 2 February 1837, which my account of the hearing follows.
72. Ibid., 4 February 1837.
73. Quoted in ibid., 13 February 1837.
74. Ibid., 15 February 1837.
75. Quoted in ibid., 18 February 1837.

76. *Lowell Patriot,* 22 February 1837.
77. *Boston Post,* 18 March 1837.
78. Ibid., 18 April 1837.
79. *Lowell Courier,* 27 April 1837.
80. *Boston Post,* 21 April 1837.
81. Ibid., 25 August 1837.
82. Letter to Charles S. Brewster, 28 July 1837, Misc. Manuscripts, Massachusetts Historical Society. This letter and another of 14 July 1837 both mention an "article" that is owed Brewster; the *Portsmouth Journal* (29 July) reported that Dixon was in debt to Brewster for "fourteen dollars, with interest," likely the "article" in question (one that was finally paid).
83. *Spirit of the Times,* 26 August 1837; emphasis in the original.
84. *Boston Post,* 29 January 1838.
85. Ibid., 6 December 1837.
86. Dixon typically began his concerts at 7 o'clock until, by my record, 27 April 1837, when he pushed commencement back to the more "respectable" 8:00 P.M. At this time, circuses, theatres, and the like – venues for the common sort – usually started their programs at 7:00 or 7:30 P.M., more appropriate for audiences who might have early working hours.
87. *Bedford Enquirer,* quoted in the *Harrisburg Pennsylvania Telegraph* for 18 January 1834.
88. *Portland Eastern Argus,* 5 August 1837; emphasis in the original.
89. *Lowell Courier,* 18 April 1837.
90. *Boston Post,* 11 December 1837.
91. Ibid.
92. *Daily Gazette and Comet,* 23 March 1861.
93. HTC folder: "Minstrels – History of, Manuscript"; undated; the anonymous, handwritten note is obviously late century, and might have been penned by T. Allston Brown.
94. Dixon's "campaign" is pieced together from the *Boston Post,* 11 December 1837, and the *Boston Evening Transcript,* 11 and 14 December 1837.
      For the record, Dixon might during his time in Boston have also tried to start up a paper called the *Sun* and another one named the *Star,* but no proof of these appears to be extant (*Flash,* 11 December 1841).
95. *Boston Post,* 25 January 1838.
96. Ibid., 7 February 1838.
97. *Flash,* 11 December 1838.
98. *Boston Post,* 28 February 1838.
99. The first issue was published in early June, according to the *Boston Post,* 8 June 1838.
100. Ibid., 20 June 1838.
101. For more details of this story see Dudden 1994: 69–70.
102. On at least two other earlier occasions Hamblin had responded to perceived insult with force. A relatively minor barroom brawl is documented in the *New York Transcript,* 6 October 1834. A far more serious assault was that on

New York Herald editor James Gordon Bennett, which resulted in a two-day trial and Hamblin's conviction. (See *New York Herald*, 17 February 1837 and subsequent issues.)

103. *New York Transcript*, quoted in *Boston Post*, 31 July 1838. Arbaces was a character in *The Last Days of Pompeii*, a role for which Hamblin was renowned.
104. Quoted in *Spirit of the Times*, 1 September 1838.
105. *Polyanthos*, 17 January 1841.
106. This issue appears not to be extant; I date the article from its listing as "People's Evidence," NYCGS: 15 April 1839.
107. *New York Herald*, 21 December 1838.
108. In this kind of charge Dixon was one of a string of editors from this time who fixated on exposing the illicit sexual doings of the clergy. See P. C. Cohen 1995.
109. New York City Municipal Archives, Watch Returns.
110. *New York Herald*, 1 January 1839.
111. Ibid., 19 May 1840.
112. He very nearly succeeded too, and many were the claims and rumors in coming years that Dixon was a creole. The fact of the matter is that there is no hard evidence whatsoever that Dixon, a man of oft-noted swarthy complexion, was in any significant proportion of mixed blood, and a great deal of evidence to the contrary. Even William Snelling, an editor of the *Flash* who, we shall see, was not kindly disposed toward Dixon, acknowledged that he was not born in "the arid sands of the Gold coast; neither is it true that he is the grandson of the king of Congo. . . . Therefore notwithstanding his inimitable performance of 'Zip Coon' and other sable worthies, which some assert is too natural for mere imitation, we affirm that he is as white as so dusky a man can be" (*Flash*, 11 December 1841).
113. *New York Herald*, 8 January 1839.
114. Ibid.; emphasis in the original. By my count only two persons had died.
115. On prostitution in New York and on Miller see Gilfoyle 1992; M. W. Hill 1993. By several tabulations reported in *McDowall's Journal* (May 1833), there were 220–500 brothels in New York at that time; the lower figure is generally corroborated by Gilfoyle's research. Prostitution thrived in other cities as well, with even staid and ostensibly puritanical Boston having as many as 105 (*Boston Mercantile Journal*, quoted in *McDowall's Journal*, February 1834).
116. NYCGS: 6 February 1839.
117. *New York Herald*, 16 April 1839.
118. NYCGS: 20 April 1839.
119. *New York Dispatch;* quoted in the *Boston Post*, 23 April 1839.
120. *Polyanthos*, 26 April 1839.
121. *New York Herald*, 19 April 1839.
122. *McDowall's Journal*, January 1833; emphasis in the original.
123. *Courier and Enquirer*, 15 March 1834.
124. I do not intend to suggest that McDowall acted alone. New York penny-press papers such as the *Sun* were also involved in the moral reform movement.

125. 31 October 1841. The editors of the *Flash* had – familiar story! – just been indicted for publishing an obscene newspaper.
126. *New York Sporting Whip*, 25 February 1843.
127. I do not intend to suggest that those who mediated charivari possessed wisdom any less finite than did those who performed it. Both enjoyed some successes in shaping public mores, and both on occasion weakened the social fabric by attacking the innocent. E. P. Thompson wrote powerfully to this point in an article on rough music (1992: 20): "Where it is enacted upon an evident malefactor – some officious public figure or a brutal wife-beater – one is tempted to lament the passing of the rites. But the victims were not all of this order. They might equally be some lonely sexual non-conformist, some Sue Bridehead and Jude Fawley living together out of holy wedlock. And the psychic terrorism which could be brought to bear upon them was truly terrifying: the flaring and lifelike effigies, with their ancient associations with heretic-burning and the maiming of images – the magical or daemonic suggestiveness of masking and of animal-guising – the flaunting of obscenities – the driving out of evil spirits with noise." Like so much in the worlds under study here – most of which exist on the margins between the performance and the word, between joy and terror – meanings, rights, and responsibilities were not often sharply defined.
128. *New York Herald*, 19 April 1839.
129. Ibid., 11 November 1843.
130. Saxton 1990: chap. 9 is devoted to a study of George Wilkes, who also later bought and edited the *Spirit of the Times;* Schiller 1981 contains an excellent analysis of the *Police Gazette*, its history, and its audience.
131. *New York Weekly Herald*, 27 April 1839.
132. NYCGS: 10, 11 May 1839.
133. *New York Express*, 14 May 1839.
134. *Boston Post*, 20 May 1839.
135. *New York Weekly Herald*, 27 April 1839.
136. *Flash*, 18 December 1841.
137. *New York Express*, 13 May 1839.
138. *DAB:* 8:416–17.
139. *New York Herald*, 17 May 1839.
140. *Polyanthos*, 6 March 1841; see also *Flash*, 18 December 1841. See Delarue 1976: 5, 9 for reproductions of two woodcuts of Elssler that appeared originally in the *Polyanthos*.
141. *Polyanthos*, 17 January 1841.
142. Ibid., 16 February 1841.
143. Ibid., 27 March 1841; reproduced in Browder 1988: 36.
144. Browder 1988: 44 claims authorship of this pamphlet for Dixon; for it see [Dixon] 1841. During the years he remained in New York, Dixon never let Restell work quietly and unobtrusively. In 1846 he planned a public protest meeting, posted handbills, addressed the crowd (some called it a mob), and

encouraged "the people" to take matters into their own hands if the authorities would not act for them to rid the social blight (Browder 1988: 65–6).

145. *Sunday Mercury,* 12 September 1841. Curiously, a few days later, while still convalescent, Dixon was himself charged with assault and battery, against one Peter D. Formal "while the latter was tearing down certain notices that George had placed upon his bulletin in Broadway" (*New York Herald,* 11 November 1841; NYCGS: 31 August 1841, 16 September 1841).

146. *Sunday Mercury,* 19 September 1841.

147. *Uncle Sam,* 18 September 1841. The iceberg allusion is beyond my ken.

148. NYCGS.

149. *New York Herald,* 11 November 1841.

150. NYCGS. The *New York Herald* of 14 November 1842 suggests further that Adeline Miller, the madame who had bailed Dixon in 1839, was also connected in some mysterious way to the *Flash.* We learn moreover that the *Herald* thought the *Flash* "was patronised by the bad society of New York, and especially written for their benefit and amusement."

151. NYCGS.

152. NYCGS; *Flash,* 11 December 1841.

153. NYCGS. A hung jury was the result. An account of the trial can be found in the *New York Herald,* 15 January 1842; a somewhat more colorful, if biased, version is found in Snelling's *Flash,* 22 January 1842.

154. NYCGS: 21 January 1842.

155. Ibid.: 14, 15, 28 September 1842.

156. I note also the existence of a French satirical paper founded in 1832, entitled *Charivari,* which featured the cartoons of Daumier and was prosecuted twenty times by Louis Philippe's government (N. Z. Davis 1975: 123).

157. *New York Herald,* 11 December 1841.

158. *Flash,* 18 December 1841.

159. These quotations and all other information found in this discussion were abstracted from the *Flash,* 11 and 18 December 1841.

160. *DAB:* 17:382.

161. *Flash,* 18 December 1841.

162. *Courier and Enquirer,* 21 August 1835; New York City directories, 1833 and after.

163. *Flash,* 22 January 1842.

164. *Weekly Rake,* 30 July 1842.

165. *Flash,* 22 January 1842; *Weekly Rake,* 30 July 1842.

166. Gilfoyle 1992: 45.

167. M. W. Hill 1993: 185 details the prostitutes at this address during 1835–56.

168. *New York Herald,* 21 June 1842. A somewhat different account of Mrs. Ryerson's establishment was published in the *Flash* two days later, a newspaper for which at that time Wooldridge was coeditor: "We next dropped into Mrs. Ryerson's, No. 58 Leonard street. A party of fashionable bucks sat round a table in the front room, enjoying themselves with wine, and uttering stale

jests, as for instance, 'I'll put you in the Whip,' &c. They were attended by the lovely hostess. This establishment is decorated and furnished in the most costly and magnificent style. We had an agreeable chat with a lively French ballet dancer, and also with the sweet Miss Louisa ____, the most beautiful frail one Leonard street can boast of."

169. *Weekly Rake*, 28 January 1843.
170. *Flash*, 18 December 1841. It is not patently clear to me what Snelling inferred by "contributions."
171. *True Flash*, 4 December 1841.
172. *Flash*, 18 December 1841; unattributed quotations in the remainder of this section are from the same source.
173. I have not been able to unmask "George G." It appears that the orchestra, though, comprised a white, a black, and a blackface!
174. Gilfoyle 1992: 72.
175. *New York Herald*, 12 September 1842.
176. Ibid., 7 February 1842.
177. Ibid., 9 February 1842.
178. Ibid., 21 February 1842.
179. Quoted in the *Lowell Courier*, 19 July 1842.
180. Ibid., 13 August 1842; *New York Herald*, 30 August 1842.
181. *New York Herald*, 21 August 1842.
182. *Lowell Courier*, 13 September 1842.
183. *New York Sporting Whip*, 28 January 1843.
184. *New York Herald*, 14 January 1843.
185. Ireland 1867b: n.p. This must have been George Rice, for T. D. Rice was in England at this time.
186. *New York Herald*, 29 January 1843. He also appeared at the Bowery Amphitheatre during this time on at least one occasion.
187. Ibid., 16 March 1843.
188. A character in Rodwell's farce *The Young Widow; or, a Lesson for Lovers*. The first record I have of Dixon playing this part is 21 August 1829, at the Chatham, and the last at the Front Street Theatre in Baltimore on 9 November 1832 (see the playbill in the second section of this chapter).
189. *New York Sporting Whip*, 4 March 1843.
190. This leaves the last eighteen of Dixon's years still unwritten. He continued to be involved in local political and moral issues in New York until about 1846. It appears from some witnesses that he was in a party of filibusters that encamped on Mexico's Yucatan in 1847. In keeping with the tradition of radical republicanism, the filibusters hoped to effect America's "Manifest Destiny" through annexation of ever more territory. By about 1848 Dixon had relocated to New Orleans. There, the Poydras Market, "by night and day, was the home of this waif upon society. . . . The 'General' was not without friends who contributed an odd 'five' to him when too frail to move about. His errors were those of the head, rather than of the heart. We knew him well, and fully believe that he would not knowingly have injured the most helpless. –

He was, perhaps, his own worst enemy; but however mistaken in the purpose of his life, he has now gone to his long account, and we freely cover him with the mantle of charity" (*Mirror*, quoted in *Baton Rouge Daily Gazette and Comet*, 23 March 1861).

At the time of his death, according to the Charity Hospital admission books for 1861–2 (p. 94), he was sixty years old, a native of Richmond, an editor by occupation, a resident of New Orleans for twelve years, and had been sick with "phthisis" (pulmonary tuberculosis) for nine months.

5. Old Dan Tucker

1. *Boston Satirist*, 1 September 1843.
2. Dan Emmett, "Old Dan Tucker" (sheet music) (New York: Atwill's, 1843), verse 3.
3. I think this kind of formulation helps us appreciate the Jacksonian fixation with puns and conundrums. Black Billy asked: "Why are the ladies' dresses like money in a will? Because it's a leg-i-see." (*Spirit of the Times*, 4 May 1833). "Why is a cold like a division in Congress? Because sometimes the eyes have it, and sometimes the noes" (Ibid., 30 March 1833). "When a child's leg is growing, why does it resemble Africans? – Give it up? Because its knee-grows, too!" (Ibid., 9 May 1840). In all these, and countless others like them, one must see the words and hear them simultaneously. The tension and the joke are generated by a contest of the worlds of the ear and the eye. In the late twentieth century, print and sight are triumphant, and conundrums are dead, perhaps a result of cause and effect.
4. Quoted in Maurer 1950: 511; the musician, John Utie, was also a member of the House of Burgesses.
5. *Quebec Gazette*, 9 October 1817; quoted in Palmer 1978: 58.
6. *Spirit of the Times*, 3 January 1835. Tellingly, the next column began with this announcement: "The Opera. We are happy to be able to announce that the Italian Opera will be revived next week. . . ."
7. *Boston Post*, 28 July 1838.
8. Ibid., 13 September 1838.
9. *New Haven Standard*, quoted in *Pennsylvania Gazette*, 6 June 1833.
10. *Philadelphia Daily Chronicle*, 26 December 1833; quoted in Shoemaker 1959: 87.
11. *Philadelphia Public Ledger*, 2 January 1847; quoted in S. G. Davis 1988: 105.
12. *New York Evening Post*, 2 January 1828; on this question see generally Gilje 1987: 259–60.
13. S. G. Davis 1986: 109. Of course the callithumpians knew the issue was one of power. Charivari had ritually assumed the policing role for centuries; now that important form of social control was manifestly being usurped by the authorities and their lieges, the police. In this light it is interesting to note the great number of blackface minstrel songs that refer derisively to the watch.

14. Quoted in *Constitution of the Anti-Bell-Ringing Society* 1839: 4.
15. See Breslaw 1988.
16. The Striped Pig phenomenon was in reply to a Massachusetts law passed in 1838, which proclaimed that liquor could be bought only in quantities of fifteen gallons. One intention was to encourage temperance, but it effectively banned liquor by the drink and bore hardest upon the lower classes, because as the *Boston Post*, 8 March 1839, wrote: "[P]ure water is such a luxury, poor men, of course, can't expect it, and unless they can buy fifteen gallons at a time, what right have they to either spirits, wine or water?" An enterprising exhibitor at a muster in Dedham offered a free drink with every ticket to see his "striped pig," and effectively circumvented the law.
17. One can hardly help but take pleasure at the clamor and clash produced by grouping the Harmony Band with callithumpians, an almost Ivesian moment.
18. Dixon!! – and not even his first appearance in a mock parade. For the mock "Fourth of July, 1839" parade in Boston, a slot was reserved for the "American Melodist from Sing Sing"; Dixon was, of course, in the penitentiary during this holiday (*Boston Post*, 4 July 1839).
19. Ibid., 28 March 1840; quoted in *Spirit of the Times*, 4 April 1840. I have reluctantly edited the "order of procession," for the original is twice this length.
20. On the general phenomenon of satire and burlesque, with application for this earlier period, see the insightful book by Robert C. Allen (1991).
21. See the sixteen-page burlesque *Constitution of the Anti-Bell-Ringing Society* (1839) in the collections of the AAS.
22. My reading here is buttressed by S. White 1994, where he concludes, among other important points, that the parade supplanted festival in the nineteenth century.
23. The initials stand for the "Young Men's Society for Meliorating the Conditions of the Indians." See their entertaining mock Fourth of July parade that same year (*Boston Post*).
24. *Boston Post*, 28 November 1838.
25. Perhaps the best example of this is the "Calathumpian Quick Step," by John Friedhiem [*sic*] (Boston: Henry Prentiss, 1840). One might expect the noise of the callithumpians in a piece so named, but in fact discord is virtually nonexistent. The reason is in the dedication – "to the Calathumpian Society," a group, as the lithographed cover portrait reassures, that comprises respectable men who enjoy satirizing the callithumpian movement, thereby containing it. The kind of music "that made night hideous" would have undone their whole purpose. The composer of the piece is the very same who sued Dixon in 1837 for obtaining concert receipts by false pretenses, the very charge against which Dixon defended himself by scandalously (and disingenuously) pleading *non compos mentis*.
26. *New York Herald*, 13 January 1842.
27. Winans 1984: 83.

28. "Lucy Long" (sheet music) (New York: James L. Hewitt, 1842).
29. "Diamond" file, HTC.
30. *Boston Post,* 15 October 1834.
31. Ibid., 20 February 1837; *New York Transcript,* 8 February 1836.
32. Ibid., 17 January 1837.
33. Undated clipping from the *New York Clipper,* HTC.
34. Playbill, Bowery Theatre, 18 March 1841, AAS.
35. *Boston Post,* 9 December 1841.
36. Ibid., 21 December 1841.
37. Winans 1984: 71.
38. Quoted in Linn 1991: 21.
39. Levine 1988 and Butsch 1994 trace this progression most persuasively.
40. *New York Herald,* 14 January 1843.
41. Ibid., 1 January 1843; it appears that the duo had given the show two days earlier as well.
42. Ibid., 31 January 1842.
43. Ibid., 28 November 1842. It is significant, too, that more and more on the minstrel stage "Others" represented "Others," that representation itself becomes politicized. The second generation of minstrels performers and composers – Emmett, Sweeney, George Christy, Dan Bryant, Stephen Foster, and many others – were Irish Americans. They were part of the development whereby minstrel shows became, to a certain extent, a product by and for Irish Americans. The Irish, who occupied a "low Other" social niche with black Americans, claimed a triumph over blacks in issues of power and control – representation! – on the stage and in the streets, with the draft riots of 1863 being only the bloodiest instance (see Lott 1993a: 94–6). Irishness was not a significant part of minstrelsy during the first generation, so the point was then moot. Rice had an Irish name, but he and his family had been in the United States long before the immigration waves of the 1820s and 1840s, and he never drew attention to his roots. There is even evidence that Dixon was virulently anti-Irish; a report from the end of 1843 had it that Dixon shot someone in the thigh over an argument about the Native American Party (the Know-Nothings), "of which George is a leading member" – this in the first year of the movement's existence (*Lowell Courier,* 21 December 1843).
44. Compare the reminiscence on the Virginia Minstrels in *New York Clipper,* 19 May 1877.
45. *New York Herald,* 5 May 1842.
46. *New York Clipper,* 19 May 1877.
47. *New York Herald,* 6 February 1843; emphasis added.
48. Ibid., 9 February 1843.
49. *Courier and Enquirer,* 16 July 1833; this group was the first incarnation of the Rainer Family Singers.
50. *New York Herald,* 27 March 1837, 29 August 1837.
51. Ibid., 25 November 1839, 23 December 1839.

52. Ibid., 21 October 1840; they were also called the Hughes Family Singers.
53. Ibid., 19 December 1842.
54. *Worcester National Aegis,* 22 March 1843.
55. Hill 1853: 29. Likely an "s" and a comma were omitted between "Refrain" and "Songs," much as I might wish for the telling elision.
56. Quoted in Finson 1994: 178. I suspect that a "Junketing" is linguistic slippage from "Jonkonnuing."
57. Moreover, this is at a time when money had deflated 18 percent since 1841 and 29 percent since 1837 (McCusker 1992: 327).
58. Hill 1853: 32; Cockrell 1989: 86, 88, 140. On ticket prices see, for example, theatre and concert ads in the *New York Herald,* 11 May 1843.
59. Baltimore, 31 May 1844 playbill; quoted in Nathan 1962: 158.
60. Cockrell 1989: 297; E. L. Rice 1911: 28.
61. NYCGS: 22 March 1843. Wooldridge returned later that summer and shows up subsequently in the city directories as an "agent" and the proprietor of a constabulary. An undated article from the *New York Clipper* in the HTC claims that Wooldridge was later known pseudonymously as "Tom Quick" and wrote a popular column for the *Leader.*
62. *New York Sporting Whip,* 28 January 1843. Here the military was arrayed against the "Hallow Guards," a street gang headed by "the celebrated Stovepipe Bill," who led the assemblage in:

    I went down town de udder night,
    I heard a noise, I seen a fight,
    Dar was the watchman running round,
    When he heard old Tucker's come to Town.

    (Full chorus by 100 persons)

    Oh, get out de way,
    Oh, get out de way,
    Oh, get out de way, old Dan Tucker,
    Your too late to come to supper.

63. *Deacon Snowball's Negro Melodies* 1843: [11].
64. Nathanson 1855: 74.
65. "Zip Coon" in places suggests a syncopated treatment, although the notation does not actually indicate it.
66. Turner 1969: 95–6.
67. Bakhtin 1986: 2.
68. Turner 1969: 175–6.
69. Ibid.: 203.
70. Lott 1991: 237–8 is supportive at this point.
71. Glassie 1983: 85.
72. Lott 1993a and I share similar conclusions, but employ different methods to arrive at them.
73. Glassie 1983: 121.

Epilogue

1. Gramsci 1971: 324.
2. This figure is derived from cost factors found in McCusker 1992: 331–2.
3. This phenomenon is little studied. One of the few pieces to deal with race relations among common southerners is Fink 1980, who examines a powerful political and labor coalition between black and white in turn-of-the-century Richmond.
4. Sanjek 1988: 3:117; in addition, radio was affecting sales of recordings, which had fallen from annual revenues of $106 million in 1921 to $16.9 million in 1931.
5. Porterfield 1979: 381.
6. There is even some evidence that the impulse that led to the development of the blues came from black–white interaction. In the 1840s whites frequently employed the term "blue" or "blues" to describe a depressed mental state. (For example, see my edition of the Hutchinson Family journals [Cockrell 1989], where the singers use the expression on several occasions.) The *Boston Post* on 1 January 1840 copied a black-dialect article from the *New Orleans* [!!] *Picayune*, entitled "A Negro with the Blues." In this "Sam Jonsing" admits:

   > "I feels bad – I'se got what de white folks calls de bloos, and de wos sort at dat, dat's what I has, Pete Gumbo."
   > "De what you call 'em, Sam?"
   > "De bloos – de raal indigo bloos."
   > "Dars whar you corner dis child, Sam; you's ahead ob me dis time. Now if it don't make any 'terial difference to you, I'd just like to hear you explanity wat dis bloos is."
   > "Wy, wy, Pete, you don't know notin. I tort you'd more 'quaintance wid de fiosify ob de human mind. Woll, you see, when a man's got de bloos he looks forard into de commin footoority jest as though he was gwine to draw a blank in de big lottery – he feels like as if all de delightsum prizes in dis low down scene hadn't a single number on 'em. Wen he gets in de mornin he feels bad, and wen goes to bed at night he feels wusser. He tinks dat his body is made ob ice cream, all 'cept his heart, and dat – dat's a piece ob lead in de middle. All sorts ob sights are hubbering around, and red monkeys is buzzing about his ears. Dar, dem's what I got now, and dem's what I calls de bloos."

   One would love to hear what Bessie Smith (or Jimmie Rodgers, for that matter) would have done with the "red monkeys . . . buzzing about his ears."
7. As Robert Cantwell has done so brilliantly, even to pondering the relationship of minstrelsy with bluegrass. See Cantwell 1984: chap. 11.
8. I invoke Mechal Sobel's (1987) title here intentionally, to suggest that this made world extends from, at least, the "black and white values in eighteenth-century Virginia" (Sobel's subtitle) to the present. My point here is supported by Cantwell 1984: 264.
9. Higham 1993: 202.

10. Toulmin 1990 is particularly insightful on this problem.
11. In support of this conclusion I note that all the evidence used in Baker 1983: 213–43 to prove the essentially racist nature of minstrelsy comes from the years after the period of my study. Virtually the same thing can be said about Saxton 1990: chap. 7, and other such studies.
12. Attali 1985: 19; Attali has been a guide to much of this work, in often mysterious and inexplicable ways.
13. *Boston Post*, 3 December 1838.

Bibliography

Abbreviations

AAS   American Antiquarian Society, Worcester, Massachusetts.

DAB   Johnson, Allen, and Dumas Malone, eds. *Dictionary of American Biography.* 1928–36. New York: Charles Scribner's Sons.

HTC   Harvard Theatre Collection, Harvard University, Cambridge, Massachusetts.

NYCGS New York City Municipal Archives and Record Center, New York City Court of General Sessions, Minute Books.

Works

Abrahams, Roger D. 1967. "The Shaping of Folklore Traditions in the British West Indies." *Journal of Inter-American Studies* 9: 456–80.

    1968. "'Pull Out Your Purse and Pay': A St. George Mumming from the British West Indies." *Folklore* 79: 176–201.

    1970. "Patterns of Performance in the British West Indies." In Whitten and Szwed 1970: 163–80.

    1992. *Singing the Master: The Emergence of African American Culture in the Plantation South.* New York: Pantheon Books.

Abrahams, Roger D., and John F. Szwed, eds. 1983. *After Africa: Extracts from British Travel Accounts and Journals of the Seventeenth, Eighteenth, and Nineteenth Centuries concerning the Slaves, Their Manners, and Customs in the British West Indies.* New Haven, Conn.: Yale University Press.

Adams, Henry W. 1955. *The Montgomery Theatre, 1822–1835.* Tuscaloosa: University of Alabama Studies.

Adams, John Quincy. 1836. "The Character of Desdemona." *American Monthly Magazine* (March): 209–17.

Aimes, Hubert H. S. 1905. "African Institutions in America." *Journal of American Folklore* 18: 15–25.

Alford, Violet. 1959. "Rough Music or Charivari." *Folklore* 70: 505–18.

———. 1968. "The Hobby Horse and Other Animal Masks." *Folklore* 79: 122–34.

Allen, Robert C. 1991. *Horrible Prettiness: Burlesque and American Culture.* Chapel Hill: University of North Carolina Press.

The American Comic Songster: A Collection of All the Wit, Humour, Eccentricity, and Originality in Song, Which the Present Day Has Produced. 1834. New York: G. J. Shaw.

Aptheker, Herbert. 1989. *Abolitionism: A Revolutionary Movement.* Boston: Twayne Publishers.

Arac, Jonathan. 1987. *Critical Genealogies: Historical Situations for Postmodern Literary Studies.* New York: Columbia University Press.

Artaud, Antonin. 1958. *The Theater and Its Double.* Trans. Mary Caroline. New York: Grove Weidenfeld.

Attali, Jacques. 1985. *Noise: The Political Economy of Music.* Trans. Brian Massumi. Theory and History of Literature Series, vol. 16. Minneapolis: University of Minnesota Press; originally published Paris: Presses Universitaires de France, 1977.

Austin, William W. 1987. *"Susanna," "Jeanie," and "The Old Folks at Home": The Songs of Stephen C. Foster from His Time to Ours.* 2d ed. Urbana: University of Illinois Press.

Babcock, Barbara A., ed. 1978. *The Reversible World: Symbolic Inversion in Art and Society.* Austin: University of Texas Press.

Baker, Jean H. 1983. *Affairs of Party: The Political Culture of Northern Democrats in the Mid-Nineteenth Century.* Ithaca, N.Y.: Cornell University Press.

Bakhtin, Mikhail M. 1984. *Rabelais and His World.* Trans. Hélène Iswolsky. Cambridge, Mass.: MIT Press; originally published Moscow: Khudozhestvennaya Literatura, 1965.

———. 1986. *Speech Genres and Other Late Essays.* Ed. Caryl Emerson and Michael Holquist. Trans. Vern W. McGee. Austin: University of Texas.

Bank, Rosemarie K. 1993. "Hustlers in the House: The Bowery Theatre as a Mode of Historical Information." In *The American Stage: Social and Economic Issues from the Colonial Period to the Present,* ed. Ron Engle and Tice L. Miller, pp. 47–64. Cambridge: Cambridge University Press.

Barclay, Alexander. 1826. *A Practical View of the Present State of Slavery in the West Indies. . . .* London: Smith, Elder.

Barnett, Morris. n.d. *Yankee Peddler; or, Old Times in Virginia: A Farce in One Act.* New York: Samuel French.

Barrand, Anthony G. 1991. *Six Fools and a Dancer: The Timeless Way of the Morris.* Plainfield, Vt.: Northern Harmony Publishing.

Barthelemy, Gerard. 1987. *Black Face, Maligned Race: The Representation of Blacks in English Drama from Shakespeare to Southerne.* Baton Rouge: Louisiana State University Press.

Bartlett, John Russell. 1848. *Dictionary of Americanisms: A Glossary of Words and Phrases, Usually Regarded as Peculiar to the United States.* New York: Bartlett & Welford.

Baskervill, Charles Read. 1920. "Dramatic Aspects of Medieval Folk Festivals in England." *Studies in Philology* 17: 19–87.

——— 1929. *The Elizabethan Jig and Related Song Drama.* Chicago: University of Chicago Press.

Bastin, B. 1979. "Black Music in North Carolina." *North Carolina Folklore* 27: 2–19.

Bates, Arlo. 1888. "Shivaree." *American Notes and Queries* 1 (20 October): 297.

Bauman, Richard. 1972. "Belsnickling in a Nova Scotia Island Community." *Western Folklore* 31, no. 4: 229–43.

Beckwith, Martha Warren. 1923. *Christmas Mummings in Jamaica: Music Recorded in the Field by Helen H. Roberts.* Poughkeepsie, N.Y.: Vassar College.

Belisario, I. M. 1838. *Sketches of Character in Illustration of the Habits of the Negro Population of Jamaica.* Kingston, Jamaica: n.p. Excerpted in Bettelheim 1988.

Belk, Russell W. "A Child's Christmas in America: Santa Claus as Deity, Consumption as Religion." *Journal of American Culture* 10, no. 1 (Spring): 87–100.

Berger, Peter, and Hansfried Kellner. 1973. *The Homeless Mind: Modernization and Consciousness.* New York: Random House.

Bethel, Edward Clement. 1978. "Music in the Bahamas: Its Roots, Development and Personality." M.A. thesis, University of California–Los Angeles.

Bettelheim, Judith. 1979. "The Afro-Jamaican Jonkonnu Festival: Playing the Forces and Operating the Cloth." Ph.D. diss., Yale University.

——— 1988. "Jonkonnu and Other Christmas Masquerades." In Nunley and Bettelheim 1988: 39–83.

Bettelheim, Judith, John Nunley, and Barbara Bridges. 1988. "Caribbean Festival Arts: An Introduction." In Nunley and Bettleheim 1988: 31–7.

Bickerstaffe, Isaac. 1825. *The Padlock: A Comic Opera in Two Acts.* New York: Charles Willey.

Blair, John G. 1990. "Blackface Minstrels in Cross-Cultural Perspective." *American Studies International* 28, no. 2: 52–65.

Blair, Walter. 1976. "Charles Mathews and His 'A Trip to America.'" *Prospects* 2: 1–23.

Bluestein, Gene. 1972. *The Voice of the Folk: Folklore and American Literary Theory.* Amherst: University of Massachusetts Press.

Blumin, Stuart. 1973. "Residential Mobility within the Nineteenth-Century City." In *The Peoples of Philadelphia: A History of Ethnic Groups and Lower-Class Life, 1790–1940,* ed. Allen F. Davis and Mark H. Haller, pp. 37–52. Philadelphia: Temple University Press.

1989. *The Emergence of the Middle Class: Social Experience in the American City,*
1760–1900. Cambridge: Cambridge University Press.

Bolton, H. Carrington. 1890. "Gombay, A Festal Rite of Bermudian Negroes."
Journal of American Folklore 3: 222–6.

Bordman, Gerald. 1984. *The Oxford Companion to American Theatre.* New York:
Oxford University Press.

Boskin, Joseph. 1986. *Sambo: The Rise and Demise of an American Jester.* New
York: Oxford University Press.

Bourdieu, Pierre. 1984. *Distinction: A Social Critique of the Judgment of Taste.*
Trans. Richard Nice. Cambridge, Mass.: Harvard University Press.

"Bowery Theatre." 1840. *The Knickerbocker; or, New-York Monthly Magazine* 16
(July): 84.

Bowra, Sir Maurice. 1966. "Ritualization of Human Cultural Activities: Dance,
Drama, and the Spoken Word." *Philosophical Transactions of the Royal Soci-*
ety Series B 251: 387–92.

Bowron, P. 1973. "The Minstrels and the Geordies; or, The American Influence
on Tyneside Song." *English Dance and Song* 35, no. 4: 132–5.

Brantlinger, Patrick. 1990. *Crusoe's Footprints: Cultural Studies in Britain and Amer-*
ica. New York: Routledge.

Bratton, J. S. 1981. "English Ethiopians: British Audiences and Black-Face Acts,
1835–1865." *Yearbook of English Studies* 11: 127–42.

Breck, Samuel. 1877. *Recollections of Samuel Breck with Passages from His Note-*
Books (1771–1862). H. E. Scudder, ed. London: S. Low, Marston, Searle,
& Rivington.

Breslaw, Elaine G., ed. 1988. *Records of the Tuesday Club of Annapolis, 1745–56.*
Urbana: University of Illinois Press.

Brewer, E. Cobham. 1900. *The Reader's Handbook of Famous Names in Fiction, Al-*
lusions, References, Proverbs, Plots, Stories, and Poems. Rev. ed. Philadelphia:
J. B. Lippincott Co.

Bristol, Michael D. 1985. *Carnival and Theater: Plebeian Culture and the Structure*
of Authority in Renaissance England. London: Methuen.

Brody, Alan. 1970. *The English Mummers and Their Plays: Traces of Ancient Mys-*
tery. Publications in Folklore and Folklife Series. Philadelphia: University of
Pennsylvania Press.

Brookes, Chris. 1988. *A Public Nuisance: A History of the Mummers Troupe.* Social
and Economic Studies Series. St. John's: Memorial University of Newfoundland Press.

Browder, Clifford. 1988. *The Wickedest Woman in New York: Madame Restell, the*
Abortionist. Hamden, Conn.: Archon Books.

Brown, T. Allston. 1874. "The Origin of Negro Minstrelsy." In Day 1874: 5–
10.

1903. *History of the New York Stage.* Reprint, New York: Benjamin Blom, 1969.

Browne, Ray B. 1960. "Shakespeare in America: Vaudeville and Negro Minstrelsy." *American Quarterly* 12: 374–91.

Buckley, Peter G. 1984. "To the Opera House: Culture and Society in New York City, 1820–1860." Ph.D. diss., State University of New York–Stony Brook.

Burdine, Warren Buster, Jr. 1991. "The Evolution of the Images of African-American Characters in the American Commercial Musical." Ph.D. diss., City University of New York.

Burke, Peter. 1978. *Popular Culture in Early Modern Europe*. New York: New York University Press.

Burns, Rex. 1976. *Success in America: The Yeoman Dream and the Industrial Revolution, 1825–1860*. Amherst: University of Massachusetts Press.

Butsch, Richard. 1994. "Bowery B'hoys and Matinee Ladies: The Re-Gendering of Nineteenth-Century American Theater Audiences." *American Quarterly* 46: 374–405.

1995. "American Theater Riots and Class Relations, 1754–1849." *Theatre Annual: A Journal of Performance Studies* 48: 41–59.

Campbell, Charles. 1828. *Memoirs*. Glasgow: J. Duncan & Co. Excerpted in Abrahams and Szwed 1983.

Campbell, Marie. 1938. "Survival of the Old Folk Drama." *Journal of American Folklore* 51: 10–24.

Cantwell, Robert. 1984. *Bluegrass Breakdown*. Music in American Life Series. Urbana: University of Illinois Press.

Capp, Bernard. 1977. "English Youth Groups and *The Pinder of Wakefield*." *Past and Present* 76 (August): 127–33.

Carmichael, Mrs. A. C. 1833. *Domestic Manners and Social Conditions of the White, Coloured and Negro Population of the West Indies*. London: Whittaker, Treacher, & Co.

Case, Sue-Ellen, and Janelle Reinelt, eds. 1991. *The Performance of Power: Theatrical Discourse and Politics*. Iowa City: University of Iowa Press.

Cassidy, Frederic G. 1966. "'Hipsaw' and 'John Canoe.'" *American Speech* 41: 45–51.

Cawte, E. C. 1972a. "Even More about the Mummers' Play." *Journal of American Folklore* 85: 250–2.

1972b. "The Revesby Sword Play." *Journal of American Folklore* 85: 250.

Cawte, E. C., Alex Helm, and N. Peacock. 1967. *English Ritual Drama: A Geographical Index*. London: Folk-Lore Society.

"The Celebrated Opera of – Oh, Hush." 1833. *New-York Mirror: Devoted to Literature and the Fine Arts*, 5 October, 110.

Chamberlain, A. F. 1888. "Charivari." *American Notes and Queries* 1 (27 October): 311–12.

Chambers, E. K. 1903. *The Medieval Stage*. 2 vols. Oxford: Clarendon Press.

1933. *The English Folk-Play*. Oxford: Clarendon Press.

Champe, Flavia Waters. 1983. *The Matachines Dance of the Upper Rio Grande: History, Music, and Choreography*. Lincoln: University of Nebraska Press.

"Characteristic Traits of the Creolian and African Negroes in Jamaica, &c. &c." 1797. *Colombian Magazine*. Excerpted in Abrahams and Szwed 1983.

Chase, Alice C. 1888. "The 'Shivaree.'" *American Notes and Queries* 1 (29 September): 263–4.

Christian, W. Asbury. 1912. *Richmond: Her Past and Present*. Richmond, Va.: L. H. Jenkins.

Clapin, Sylva. 1897. *New Dictionary of Americanisms*. New York: Century Dictionary.

Clapp, William W., Jr. 1853. *A Record of the Boston Stage*. Boston: James Munroe.

Clarke, Mathew St. Clair (attrib.). 1833. *Sketches and Eccentricities of Colonel David Crockett of West Tennessee*. New York: J. & J. Harper.

Cline, Ruth H. 1958. "Belsnickles and Shanghais." *Journal of American Folklore* 71: 164–5.

Cockrell, Dale. 1987. "Of Gospel Hymns, Minstrel Shows, and Jubilee Singers: Toward Some Black South African Musics." *American Music* 5: 417–32.

———. 1989. *Excelsior: Journals of the Hutchinson Family Singers, 1842–1846*. Sociology of Music Series, no. 6. Stuyvesant, N.Y.: Pendragon Press.

———. 1996a. "Callithumpians, Mummers, Maskers, and Minstrels: Blackface in the Streets of Jacksonian America." *Theatre Annual* 49: 15–34.

———. 1996b. "Jim Crow, Demon of Disorder." *American Music* 14, no. 2 (Summer): 161–84.

Cohen, Daniel A. 1993. *Pillars of Salt, Monuments of Grace: New England Crime Literature and the Origins of American Popular Culture, 1674–1860*. Commonwealth Center for the Study of American Culture Series. New York: Oxford University Press.

Cohen, Patricia Cline. 1992. "Unregulated Youth: Masculinity and Murder in the 1830s City." *Radical History Review* 52: 33–52.

———. 1995. "Ministerial Misdeeds: The Onderdonk Trial and Sexual Harassment in the 1840s." *Journal of Women's History* 7, no. 3: 34–57.

Colman, George. n.d. *Jonathan in England: A Comedy in Three Acts (Altered from . . . "Who Wants a Guinea?")*. Boston: William V. Spencer.

Constitution of the Anti-Bell-Ringing Society. 1839. Boston: Henry P. Lewis.

Conway, Cecelia. 1995. *African Banjo Echoes in Appalachia: A Study of Folk Traditions*. Knoxville: University of Tennessee Press.

Cotgrave, Randle, comp. 1611. *A Dictionarie of the French and English Tongues*. With an Introduction by William S. Woods. London: Printed by Adam Islip. Reprint, Columbia, S.C.: University of South Carolina Press, 1950.

Couvares, Francis G. 1984. *The Remaking of Pittsburgh: Class and Culture in an Industrializing City, 1877–1919*. Albany: State University of New York Press.

Cowell, Joseph. 1844. *Thirty Years Passed among the Players in England and America: Interspersed with Anecdotes and Reminiscences of a variety of persons, directly or indirectly connected with the drama . . .* New York: Harper & Bros.

Craigie, William A., and James R. Hulbert, eds. 1938. *A Dictionary of American English*. Chicago: University of Chicago Press.

Crockett's Yaller Flower Almanac, for '36, Snagsville, Salt-River: Published by Boon Crockett, and Squire Downing, Skunk's Misery, Down East. 1835. New York: Elton.

Crow Quadrilles. 1840. Philadelphia: John F. Nunns.

Crowley, Daniel J. 1956. "The Traditional Masques of Carnival." *Caribbean Quarterly* 4: 194–223.

Damon, S. Foster. 1934. "The Negro in Early American Songsters." *Bibliographical Society of America Papers* 28, no. 2: 132–63.

1936. *Series of Old American Songs*. Providence, R.I.: Brown University Library.

Davidson, Frank C. 1952. "The Rise, Development, Decline, and Influence of the American Minstrel Show." Ph.D. diss., New York University.

Davis, Alva L., and Raven I. McDavid, Jr. 1949. "'Shivaree': An Example of Cultural Diffusion." *American Speech* 24: 251.

Davis, Natalie Zemon. 1971. "The Reasons of Misrule: Youth-groups and Charivaris in Sixteenth-Century France." *Past and Present* 50: 41–75.

1975. *Society and Culture in Early Modern France: Eight Essays*. London: Duckworth.

Davis, Susan G. 1982. "'Making Night Hideous': Christmas Revelry and Public Order in Nineteenth-Century Philadelphia." *American Quarterly* 34: 185–99.

1988. *Parades and Power: Street Theater in Nineteenth-Century Philadelphia*. Berkeley: University of California Press; originally published Philadelphia: Temple University Press, 1986.

Day, Charles H. 1874. *Fun in Black; or, Sketches of Minstrel Life*. New York: DeWitt.

De Caro, Francis A., and Tom Ireland. 1988. "Every Man a King: Worldview, Social Tension and Carnival in New Orleans." *International Folklore Review* 6: 58–66.

De La Beche, H. T. 1825. *Notes on the Present Conditions of the Negroes in Jamaica*. London: T. Cadell.

Deacon Snowball's Negro Melodies. 1843. New York: Turner & Fisher.

Dean, Bennett Wayne. 1971. *Mardi Gras, Mobile's Illogical Whoopededo*. Chicago: Adams Press.

Dean-Smith, Margaret. 1958. "The Life-Cycle Play or Folk Play,' *Folklore* 49: 237–53.

1963. "Disguise in English Folk-Drama." *Folk Life* 1: 97–101.

Delarue, Allison, ed. 1976. *Fanny Elssler in America*. New York: Dance Horizons.

Denning, Michael. 1987. *Mechanic Accents: Dime Novels and Working-Class Culture in America*. London: Verso.

Dennison, Sam. 1982. *Scandalize My Name: Black Imagery in American Popular Music*. New York: Garland Publishing.

Devine, George John. 1940. "American Songster 1806–1815." M.A. thesis, Brown University.

Dibdin, [Charles]. 1799. *A Collection of Songs, selected from the Works of Mr. Dibdin, to which are added, the newest and most favourite American Patriotic Songs*. Philadelphia: H. & P. Rice.

Dickens, Charles. 1842. *American Notes for General Circulation*. New York: Harper & Bros.

Dirks, Robert. 1979a. "The Evolution of a Playful Ritual: The Garifuna's John

Canoe in Comparative Perspective." In *Forms of Play of Native North Americans*, ed. Edward Norbeck and Claire R. Farrer, pp. 89–109. St. Paul: West Publishing.

1979b. "John Canoe: Ethnohistorical and Comparative Analysis of a Carib Dance." *Actes du XLIIe Congrès International des Americanistes* 6: 487–501.

1987. *The Black Saturnalia: Conflict and Its Ritual Expression on British West Indian Slave Plantations.* Gainesville: University of Florida Press.

Dixon, George Washington. 1830. *Oddities and Drolleries of Mr. G. Dixon, The celebrated American Buffo Singer. . . .* New York: George G. Sickels.

1834. *Dixon's (The Celebrated Buffo Singer) Oddities. Glorious Collection of Nerve Working, Side Cracking, Care Destroying, Mouth Tormenting Songs; as Sung by Mr. G. Dixon, . . .* New York: D. Felt & Co.

[ ]. 1841. *Trial of Madame Restell, alias Ann Lohman for abortion and causing the death of Mrs. Purdy.* New York: n.p.

Dobbin, Jay D. 1986. *The Jombee Dance of Montserrat: A Study of Trance Ritual.* Columbus: Ohio St. University Press.

Dominguez, Virginia B. 1986. *White by Definition: Social Classification in Creole Louisiana.* New Brunswick, N.J.: Rutgers University Press.

Dormon, James H. 1969. "The Strange Career of Jim Crow Rice." *Journal of Social History* 3 (Winter): 109–22.

Douce, Francis. 1839. *Illustrations of Shakespeare and of Ancient Manners: With Dissertations on the Clowns and Fools of Shakespeare; on the Collection of Popular Tales entitled Gesta Romanorum, and on the English Morris Dance.* London: T. Tegg.

Douglas, Mary. 1986. *Purity and Danger: An Analysis of the Concepts of Pollution and Taboo.* London: Ark; originally published London: Routledge & Kegan Paul, 1966.

Downer, Alan S. 1966. *The Eminent Tragedian William Charles Macready.* Cambridge, Mass.: Harvard University Press.

Dudden, Faye E. 1994. *Women in the American Theatre: Actresses and Audiences 1790–1870.* New Haven, Conn.: Yale University Press.

The Early Minstrel Show. 1985. New York: New World Records NW 338.

Edelstein, Tilden G. 1982. "Othello in America: The Drama of Racial Intermarriage." In *Region, Race, and Reconstruction: Essays in Honor of C. Vann Woodward*, ed. J. Morgan Kousser and James M. McPherson, pp. 179–97. New York: Oxford.

Eights, James. 1867. "Pinkster Festivities in Albany Sixty Years Ago." In *Collections on the History of Albany*, ed. Joel Munsell, vol. 2, pp. 323–7. Albany: by the author.

Ely, Melvin. 1992. *The Adventures of Amos 'n' Andy: A Social History of an American Phenomenon.* New York: Free Press.

Emery, Lynne Fauley. 1972. *Black Dance in the United States from 1619 to 1970.* Palo Alto, Ca.: National Press Books.

Engle, Gary D., ed. 1978. *This Grotesque Essence: Plays from the American Minstrel Stage.* Baton Rouge: Louisiana University Press.

Epstein, Dena J. 1977. *Sinful Tunes and Spirituals: Black Folk Music to the Civil War.* Urbana: University of Illinois Press.

Espiñosa, Aurelio M. 1985. *The Folklore of Spain in the American Southwest.* Norman: University of Oklahoma Press.

Faris, James C. 1969. "Mumming in an Outport Fishing Settlement: A Description and Suggestions on the Cognitive Complex." In Halpert and Story 1969a: 128–44.

Fenn, Elizabeth A. 1988. "'A Perfect Equality Seemed to Reign': Slave Society and Jonkonnu." *North Carolina Historical Review* 65, no. 2: 127–53.

Fenton, William N. 1987. *The False Faces of the Iroquois.* Norman: University of Oklahoma Press.

Fink, Leon. 1980. "'Irrespective of Party, Color or Social Standing': The Knights of Labor and Opposition Politics in Richmond, Virginia." In *The Southern Common People: Studies in Nineteenth-Century Social History,* ed. Edward Magdol and Jon L. Wakelyn, pp. 289–311. Contributions in American History Series, no. 86. Westport, Conn.: Greenwood Press.

Finson, Jon W. 1994. *The Voices That Are Gone: Themes in Nineteenth-Century American Popular Song.* New York: Oxford University Press.

Flint, Timothy. 1826. *Recollections of the Last Ten Years, Passed in Occasional Residences and Journeyings in the Valley of the Mississippi . . .* Boston: Cummings, Hilliard, & Co.

Foner, Eric. 1976. *Tom Paine and Revolutionary America.* New York: Oxford University Press.

———. 1980. *Politics and Ideology in the Age of the Civil War.* New York: Oxford University Press.

Foner, Philip S. 1941. *Business and Slavery: The New York Merchants and the Irrepressible Conflict.* Chapel Hill: University of North Carolina Press.

Forrest, John. 1984. *Morris and Matachin: A Study of Comparative Choreography.* Sheffield, England: University of Sheffield Press.

Frederickson, George. 1971. *The Black Image in the White Mind: The Debate on Afro-American Character and Destiny, 1817–1914.* New York: Harper & Row.

Gailey, Alan. 1969. *Irish Folk Drama.* Cork: Mercier Press.

———. 1974. "Chapbook Influences on Irish Mummers' Plays." *Folklore* 85: 1–22.

Gaines, Francis Pendleton. 1925. *The Southern Plantation: A Study in the Development and the Accuracy of a Tradition.* New York: Columbia University Press.

Galbreath, C. B. 1904. *Daniel Decatur Emmett.* Columbus: F. J. Heer.

Gardner, W. J. 1873. *A History of Jamaica from its Discovery by Christopher Columbus to the Year 1872 . . .* London: E. Stock.

Geertz, Clifford. 1973. *The Interpretation of Cultures.* New York: Basic Books.

Gilfoyle, Thomas. 1992. *City of Eros: New York City, Prostitution, and the Commercialization of Sex, 1790–1920.* New York: W. W. Norton.

Gilje, Paul A. 1987. *The Road to Mobocracy: Popular Disorder in New York City, 1763–1834.* Institute of Early American History and Culture Series. Chapel Hill: University of North Carolina Press.

Glassie, Henry. 1983. *All Silver and No Brass: An Irish Christmas Mumming.* Phila-

Bibliography

delphia: University of Pennsylvania Press; originally published Bloomington: Indiana University Press, 1975.

Gluckman, Max. 1954. *Rituals of Rebellion in South-East Africa.* Manchester, England: Manchester University Press.

1955. *Custom and Conflict in Africa.* Oxford: Blackwell.

ed. 1962. *Essays on the Ritual of Social Relations.* Manchester, England: Manchester University Press.

Goertzen, Chris, and Alan Jabbour. 1987. "George P. Knauff's *Virginia Reels* and Fiddling in the Antebellum South." *American Music* 5: 121–44.

Gombrich, E. H. 1966. "Ritualized Gesture and Expression in Art." *Philosophical Transactions of the Royal Society Series B* 251: 393–401.

Goody, Jack, Joan Thirsk, and E. P. Thompson, eds. 1976. *Family and Inheritance: Rural Society in Western Europe, 1200–1800.* Cambridge: Cambridge University Press.

Gorn, Elliott J. 1985. "'Gouge and Bite, Pull Hair and Scratch': The Social Significance of Fighting in the Southern Backcountry." *American Historical Review* 90: 18–43.

1986. *The Manly Art: Bare-Knuckle Prize Fighting in America.* Ithaca, N.Y.: Cornell University Press.

Gramsci, Antonio. 1971. *Selections from the Prison Notebooks of Antonio Gramsci.* Ed. and trans. Quinton Hoare and Geoffrey Nowell-Smith. New York: International Publishers.

Green, Alan W. C. 1970. "'Jim Crow,' 'Zip Coon': The Northern Origins of Negro Minstrelsy." *Massachusetts Review* 11, no. 2: 385–97.

Greenberg, Kenneth S. 1985. *Masters and Statesmen: The Political Culture of American Slavery.* Baltimore: Johns Hopkins University Press.

Greenblatt, Stephen. 1991. *Marvelous Possessions: The Wonder of the New World.* Chicago: University of Chicago Press.

Greene, Laurence. 1937. *The Filibuster: The Career of William Walker.* Indianapolis: Bobbs–Merrill Co.

Greenwood, Isaac J. 1909. *The Circus: Its Origin and Growth prior to 1835: With a Sketch of Negro Minstrelsy.* New York: William Abbatt.

Grimsted, David. 1968. *Melodrama Unveiled: American Theater and Culture, 1800–1850.* Chicago: University of Chicago Press.

1972. "Rioting in Its Jacksonian Setting." *American Historical Review* 77: 361–97.

Gruber, William E. 1986. *Comic Theatres: Studies in Performance and Audience Response.* Athens: University of Georgia Press.

Gutman, Herbert G. 1976. *Work, Culture and Society in Industrializing America: Essays in American Working-Class and Social History.* New York: Vintage Books.

Hall, Kim F. 1991. "Sexual Politics and Cultural Identity in *The Masque of Blackness.*" In Case and Reinelt 1991: 3–18.

Hall, Lillian A. 1920. "Some Early Black-Face Performers and the First Minstrel Troupe." *Harvard Library Notes* (October): 39–45.

Hall, Stuart. 1975. *Resistance through Rituals: Youth Subcultures in Post-war Britain.* London: Hutchinson.

Halpert, Herbert. 1969. "A Typology of Mumming." In Halpert and Story 1969a: 34–61.

Halpert, Herbert, and G. M. Story, eds. 1969a. *Christmas Mumming in Newfoundland: Essays in Anthropology, Folklore, and History.* Toronto: University of Toronto Press, for Memorial University of Newfoundland.

Halpert, Herbert, and G. M. Story. 1969b. "Newfoundland Mummers' Plays: Three Printed Texts." In Halpert and Story 1969a: 186–207.

Halttunen, Karen. 1982. *Confidence Men and Painted Women: A Study of Middle-Class Culture in America, 1830–1870.* New Haven, Conn.: Yale University Press.

Hamm, Charles. 1979. *Yesterdays: Popular Song in America.* New York: W. W. Norton.

    1995. "The Last Minstrel Show?" In *Putting Popular Music in Its Place,* pp. 354–66. Cambridge: Cambridge University Press.

Hanley, Miles L. 1933. "Charivaria II: 'Serenade' in New England." *American Speech* VIII (April): 24–6.

Hatch, James V. 1970. *Black Image on the American Stage: A Bibliography of Plays and Musicals, 1770–1970.* New York: DBS Publications.

    1989. "Here Comes Everybody: Scholarship and Black Theatre History." In Postlewait and McConachie 1989: 148–65.

Havig, A. R. 1977. "American Historians and the Study of Popular Culture." *Journal of Popular Culture* 11, no. 1: 180–92.

Haywood, Charles, 1966. "Negro Minstrelsy and Shakespearean Burlesque." In *Folklore and Society: Essays in Honor of Benj. A. Botkin,* ed. Bruce Jackson, pp. 77–92. Hatboro, Pa.: Folklore Associates.

Hazen, Margaret Hindle, and Robert M. Hazen. 1992. *Keepers of the Flame: The Role of Fire in American Culture, 1775–1925.* Princeton, N.J.: Princeton University Press.

Heath-Coleman, Philip. 1985. "Forrest and Matachin: An Assessment of John Forrest's 'Morris and Matachin.'" *Folk Music Journal* 5, no. 1: 83–96.

Helm, Alex. 1965. "In Comes I, St. George." *Folklore* 76: 118–36.

    1969. *The Chapbook Mummers' Plays: A Study of the Printed Versions of the North-West of England.* Ibstock, Leicester: Guizer Press.

Hewes, George R. T. 1834. *A Retrospect of the Boston Tea-Party, with a Memoir of George R. T. Hewes, a Survivor of the Little Band of Patriots who Drowned the Tea in Boston Harbour in 1773.* New York: James Hawkes.

Hewitt, Roger. 1983. "Black through White: Hoagy Carmichael and the Cultural Reproduction of Racism." *Popular Music* 3: 33–50.

Higham, John. 1993. "Multiculturalism and Universalism: A History and Critique." *American Quarterly* 45: 195–219.

Hill, Benjamin Thomas. 1853. "Worcester Amusements, 1798–1854." Scrapbook, AAS.

Hill, Errol. 1972. *The Trinidad Carnival, Mandate for a National Theatre.* Austin: University of Texas Press.

———. 1984. *Shakespeare in Sable: A History of Black Shakespearean Actors.* Amherst: University of Massachusetts Press.

Hill, George Handel. 1853. *Scenes from the Life of an Actor.* New York: Garrett & Co.

Hill, Marilynn Wood. 1993. *Their Sisters' Keepers: Prostitution in New York City, 1830–1870.* Berkeley: University of California Press.

Hill, West T., Jr. 1971. *The Theatre in Early Kentucky, 1790–1820.* Lexington: University Press of Kentucky.

Hirsch, Susan E. 1978. *Roots of the American Working Class: The Industrialization of Crafts in Newark, 1800–1860.* Philadelphia: University of Pennsylvania Press.

Hitchcock, H. Wiley, and Stanley Sadie, eds. 1986. *The New Grove Dictionary of American Music.* London: Macmillan.

Hobsbawm, Eric J. 1959. *Social Bandits and Primitive Rebels: Studies in Archaic Forms of Social Movement in the Nineteenth and Twentieth Centuries.* Glencoe, Ill.: Free Press.

Hodge, Francis. 1964. *Yankee Theatre: The Image of America on the Stage, 1825–1860.* Austin: University of Texas Press.

Holmberg, Carl Bryan, and Gilbert D. Schneider. 1986. "Daniel Decatur Emmett's Stump Sermons: Genuine Afro-American Culture, Language, and Rhetoric in the Negro Minstrel Show." *Journal of Popular Culture* 19, no. 4: 27–38.

———. 1994. "Things That Go Snap-Rattle-Clang-Toot-Crank in the Night: Halloween Noisemakers." In Santino 1994: 221–46.

Holmes, William F. 1969. "Whitecapping: Agrarian Violence in Mississippi, 1902–1906." *Journal of Southern History* 35: 165–85.

Homberger, Eric. 1994. *Scenes from the Life of a City: Corruption and Conscience in Old New York.* New Haven, Conn.: Yale University Press.

Hone, Philip. 1889. *The Diary of Philip Hone, 1828–1851.* Ed. Bayard Tuckerman. New York: Dodd, Mead & Co.

Honour, Hugh. 1989. *The Image of the Black in Western Art: From the American Revolution to World War I,* vol. 2, *Black Models and White Myths.* Cambridge, Mass.: Harvard University Press.

Hoole, W. Stanley. 1946. "Shakespeare on the Ante-bellum Charleston Stage." *Shakespeare Association Bulletin* 21: 37–45.

Horlick, Allan Stanley. 1975. *Country Boys and Merchant Princes: The Social Control of Young Men in New York.* Lewisburg, Pa.: Bucknell University Press.

Hunter, G. K. 1967. "Othello and Colour Prejudice": Annual Shakespeare Lecture of the British Academy. *Proceedings of the British Academy* 53: 139–63.

Hutton, Lawrence. 1891. *Curiosities of the American Stage.* New York: Harper & Bros.

Ireland, Joseph N. 1867a. *Records of the New York Stage.* New York: T. H. Morrell.

1867b. *Records of the New York Stage, from 1750 to 1860: Extended and Extra-Illustrated for Augustin Daly by Augustus Roedteberg.* New York, T. H. Morrell.

Jackson, Bruce, ed. 1967. *The Negro and His Folklore in Nineteenth Century Periodicals.* Publications of the American Folklore Society, Bibliographical and Special Series 18. Austin: University of Texas Press.

[Jacobs, Mrs. Harriet]. 1861. *Incidents in the Life of a Slave Girl, Written by Herself.* . . . Ed. L. Maria Child. Boston: for the author.

Jameson, Frederic. 1982. *The Political Unconscious: Narrative as a Socially Symbolic Act.* Ithaca, N.Y.: Cornell University Press.

Jefferson, Joseph. 1897. *The Autobiography of Joseph Jefferson.* New York: Century Co.

Jentz, John B. 1977. "Artisans, Evangelical and the City: A Social History of Abolition and Labor Reform in Jacksonian New York." Ph.D. diss., City University of New York.

Jim Crow's Vagaries, or Black Flights of Fancy: Containing a Choice Collection of Nigger Melodies: To Which Is Added the Erratic Life of Jim Crow. n.d. London: Orlando Hodgson.

Johnson, Claudia D. 1975. "That Guilty Third Tier: Prostitution in Nineteenth-Century American Theaters." *American Quarterly* 27: 575–84.

Johnson, Paul E., and Sean Wilentz. 1994. *The Kingdom of Matthias: A Story of Sex and Salvation in 19th-Century America.* New York: Oxford University Press.

Jones, David. 1973. *Before Rebecca.* London: Allen Lane.

Jones, Eugene H. 1988. *Native Americans as Shown on the Stage, 1753–1916.* Metuchen, N.J.: Scarecrow Press.

Jones, J. S. n.d. *The Green Mountain Boy: A Comedy in Two Acts.* Boston: William V. Spencer.

Jordan, Winthrop D. 1968. *White over Black: American Attitudes Toward the Negro, 1550–1812.* Institute of Early American History and Culture Series. Chapel Hill: University of North Carolina.

Joyner, Charles W. 1971. *Folk Song in South Carolina.* Columbia: University of South Carolina Press.

1984. *Down by the Riverside: A South Carolina Slave Community.* Urbana: University of Illinois Press.

Kelley, Brooks Mather. 1974. *Yale: A History.* New Haven, Conn.: Yale University Press.

Kendall, John Smith. 1947. "New Orleans' Negro Minstrels." *Louisiana Historical Quarterly* 30 (January): 128–48.

Kerber, Linda K. 1967. "Abolitionists and Amalgamators: The New York City Race Riots of 1834." *New York History* 48, no. 1: 28–39.

Kerns, Virginia, and Robert Dirks. "John Canoe." *National Studies* 3, no. 6: 1–15.

K[innard], J. K., Jr. 1845. "Who Are Our National Poets?" *Knickerbocker Magazine* 26 (October): 331–41.

Kinser, Samuel. 1990. *Carnival, American Style: Mardi Gras at New Orleans and Mobile.* Chicago: University of Chicago Press.

Kirby, E. T. 1971. "The Origin of the Mummers' Play." *Journal of American Folklore* 84: 275–88.

Kmen, Henry A. 1962. "Old Corn Meal: A Forgotten Urban Negro Folksinger." *Journal of American Folklore* 75: 29–34.

Kolin, Philip C. 1983. *Shakespeare in the South: Essays on Performance.* Jackson: University Press of Mississippi.

Kreyling, Michael. 1987. *Figures of the Hero in Southern Narrative.* Baton Rouge: Louisiana State University Press.

Kurath, Gertrude Prokosch. 1949. "Mexican Moriscas: A Problem in Dance Acculturation." *Journal of American Folklore* 62: 87–106.

———. 1957. "The Origin of the Pueblo Indian Matachines." *El Palacio* 64, no. 9: 10.

Lake, H. Coote. 1931. "Mummers' Plays and the Sacer Ludus. *Folk Lore* 42: 141–9.

Laroque, François. 1991. *Shakespeare's Festive World: Elizabethan Seasonal Entertainment and the Professional Stage.* Trans. Janet Lloyd. Cambridge: Cambridge University Press; originally published Paris: Presses Universitaires de France, 1988.

Latrobe, Benjamin. 1980. *Journals.* Ed. Edward C. Carter II, John C. Van Horne, and Lee W. Formwalt. New Haven: Yale University Press.

Laurie, Bruce. 1973. "Fire Companies and Gangs in Southwark: The 1840s." In *The Peoples of Philadelphia: A History of Ethnic Groups and Lower-Class Life, 1790–1940,* ed. Allen F. Davis and Mark H. Haller, pp. 71–88. Philadelphia: Temple University Press.

———. 1980. *Working People of Philadelphia, 1800–1850.* Philadelphia: Temple University Press.

———. 1989. *Artisans into Workers: Labor in Nineteenth-Century America.* New York: Noonday.

Lawrence, Vera Brodsky. 1988. *Strong on Music: The New York Music Scene in the Days of George Templeton Strong, 1836–1875,* vol. 1, *Resonances: 1836–1850.* New York: Oxford University Press.

Leonard, William Torbert. 1986. *Masquerade in Black.* Metuchen, N.J.: Scarecrow Press.

Levine, Lawrence W. 1977. *Black Culture and Black Consciousness: Afro-American Folk Thought from Slavery to Freedom.* New York: Oxford University Press.

———. 1988. *Highbrow/Lowbrow: The Emergence of Cultural Hierarchy in America.* Cambridge, Mass.: Harvard University Press.

Lewis, Arthur Ansel. 1937. "American Songsters 1800–1805." M.A. thesis, Brown University.

Lewis, Matthew Gregory. 1829. *Journal of a West-India Proprietor, Kept during a Residence in the Island of Jamaica.* London: J. Murray.

Lhamon, W. T., Jr. In press. *Raising Cain: Blackface Performance in Its Lore Cycle.* Cambridge, Mass.: Harvard University Press.

Lichman, Simon. 1981. "The Gardener's Story and What Came Next: A Contextual Analysis of the Marshfield Paper Boys' Mumming Play." Ph.D. diss., University of Pennsylvania.

Linn, Karen. 1991. *That Half-Barbaric Twang: The Banjo in American Popular Culture.* Urbana: University of Illinois.

Lippard, George. 1853. *New York: Its Upper Ten and Lower Million.* Upper Saddle River, N.J.: Pregg Press.

Lipsitz, George. 1990. *Time Passages: Collective Memory and American Popular Culture.* Minneapolis: University of Minnesota Press.

Litwack, Leon F. 1961. *North of Slavery: The Negro in the Free States, 1790–1860.* Chicago: University of Chicago Press.

Logan, Olive. 1879. "The Ancestry of Brother Bones." *Harper's Monthly* 58: 687–98.

Long, Edward. 1774. *The History of Jamaica.* London: T. Lowndes. Reprint, London: F. Cass, 1970.

Lorenz, K. Z. 1966. "The Psychobiological Approach: Methods and Results: Evolution of Ritualization in the Biological and Cultural Spheres." *Philosophical Transactions of the Royal Society Series B* 251: 273–84.

Lott, Eric. 1991. "'The Seeming Counterfeit': Racial Politics and Early Blackface Minstrelsy." *American Quarterly* 43: 223–54.

——— 1992. "Love and Theft: The Racial Unconscious of Blackface Minstrelsy." *Representations* 39 (Summer): 23–50.

——— 1993a. *Love and Theft: Blackface Minstrelsy and the American Working Class.* New York: Oxford University Press.

——— 1993b. "White Like Me: Imperial Whiteness and Racial Cross-Dressing." In *Cultures of U. S. Imperialism,* ed. Amy Kaplan and Donald E. Pease, pp. 474–95. Durham, N.C.: Duke University Press.

Lower, Charles B. 1983. "Othello as Black on Southern Stages, Then and Now." In Kolin 1983: 199–228.

Ludlow, Noah Miller. 1880. *Dramatic Life as I Found It.* St. Louis: G. I. Jones.

McConachie, Bruce A. 1985. "'The Theatre of the Mob': Apocalyptic Melodrama and Preindustrial Riots in Antebellum New York." In *Theatre for Working-Class Audiences in the United States, 1830–1980,* ed. Bruce A. McConachie and Daniel Friedman, pp. 17–46. Contributions in Drama and Theatre Studies Series, no. 14. Westport, Conn.: Greenwood Press.

——— 1988. "New York Operagoing, 1825–50: Creating an Elite Social Ritual." *American Music* 6: 181–92.

——— 1991. "New Historicism and American Theater History: Toward an Interdisciplinary Paradigm for Scholarship." In Case and Reinelt 1991: 265–71.

——— 1992. *Melodramatic Formations: American Theatre and Society, 1820–1870.* Iowa City: University of Iowa Press.

McCready, William. 1821. *The Irishman in London; or, The Happy African.* Philadelphia: Thomas H. Palmer.

McCusker, John J. 1992. *How Much Is That in Real Money? A Historical Price Index for Use as a Deflator of Money Values in the Economy of the United States.* AAS.

MacMillan, Dougald. 1926. "John Kuners." *Journal of American Folklore* 39: 53–7.

Magdol, Edward. 1986. *The Antislavery Rank and File: A Social Profile of the Abolitionist Constituency.* Westport, Conn.: Greenwood Press.

Mahar, William J. 1985. "Black English in Early Blackface Minstrelsy: A New Interpretation of the Sources of Minstrel Show Dialect." *American Quarterly* 37: 260–85.

  1988. "'Backside Albany' and Early Blackface Minstrelsy: A Contextual Study of America's First Blackface Song." *American Music* 6: 1–27.

  1991. "Ethiopian Skits and Sketches: Contents and Contexts of Blackface Minstrelsy, 1840–1890." *Prospects* 16: 241–79.

Manning, Frank E. 1973. *Black Clubs in Bermuda: Ethnography of a Play World.* Ithaca, N.Y.: Cornell University Press.

Marks, Morton Allen. 1972. *Performance Rules and Ritual Structures in Afro-American Music.* Ph.D. diss., University of California–Berkeley.

Marsden, Peter: 1788. *An Account of the Island of Jamaica.* Newcastle: Printed for the author by S. Hodgson.

Mason, Jeffrey D. 1991. "The Politics of *Metamora*." In Case and Reinelt 1991: 92–110.

  1993. *Melodrama and the Myth of America.* Bloomington: Indiana University Press.

Mathews, Mrs. Anne. 1839. *A Continuation of the Memoirs of Charles Mathews, Comedian.* Philadelphia: Lea & Blanchard.

Mathews, Charles. 1824. *The London Mathews; Containing an Account of This Celebrated Comedian's Trip to America. . . .* Philadelphia: Simon Probasco.

Matthews, Brander. 1915. "Rise and Fall of Negro Minstrelsy." *Scribner's Magazine* 57 (June): 754–9.

Maurer, Maurer. 1950. "The 'Professor of Musick' in Colonial America." *Musical Quarterly* 36: 511–24.

Mayer, David. 1969. *Harlequin in His Element: The English Pantomime, 1806–1836.* Cambridge, Mass.: Harvard University Press.

Meine, Franklin J., ed. 1955. *The Crockett Almanacks, Nashville Series, 1835–1838.* Chicago: Caxton Club.

Meserve, Walter J. 1977. *An Emerging Entertainment: The Drama of the American People to 1828.* Bloomington: Indiana University Press.

  1986. *Heralds of Promise: The Drama of the American People during the Age of Jackson, 1829–1849.* Westport, Conn.: Greenwood Press.

Moody, Richard. 1944. "Negro Minstrelsy." *Quarterly Journal of Speech* 30 (October): 321–8.

  1955. *America Takes the Stage: Romanticism in American Drama and Theatre, 1750–1900.* Bloomington: Indiana University Press.

  1958. *The Astor Place Riot.* Bloomington: Indiana University Press.

1966. *Dramas from the American Theatre: 1769–1909.* Bloomington: Indiana University Press.

Moore, Leonard J. 1991. *Citizen Klansmen: The Ku Klux Klan in Indiana, 1921–1928.* Chapel Hill: University of North Carolina Press.

Moreau, Charles C., comp. 1891. "Negro Minstrelsy in New York." Unpublished manuscript in HTC.

Napier, A. David. 1986. *Masks: Transformation and Paradox.* Berkeley: University of California Press.

Nathan, Hans. 1945. "Negro Impersonation in Eighteenth Century England." *Notes* 2: 245–54.

——— 1946. "Charles Mathews, Comedian, and the American Negro." *Southern Folklore Quarterly* 10, no. 3: 191–7.

——— 1962. *Dan Emmett and the Rise of Early Negro Minstrelsy.* Norman: University of Oklahoma Press.

[Nathanson, Y. S.] 1855. "Negro Minstrelsy – Ancient and Modern." *Putnam's Monthly; a Magazine of American Literature, Science, and Art* 5, no. 25 (January): 72–9.

Needham, Joseph. 1936. "The Geographical Distribution of English Ceremonial Dance Traditions." *Journal of the English Folk Dance and Song Society* 3, no. 1: 1–45.

Nevin, Robert P. 1867. "Stephen C. Foster and Negro Minstrelsy." *Atlantic Monthly* 22 (November): 608–10.

Newcomb, Bobby. 1882. *Tambo: His Jokes and Funny Sayings with which is incorporated Hints to the Amateur Minstrel.* New York: Wehman.

Newell, W. W. 1896. "Christmas Maskings in Boston." *Journal of American Folklore* 9: 178.

Nichols, Thomas L. 1840. *Journal in Jail, Kept during a Four Months' Imprisonment for Libel.* Buffalo: A. Dinsmore.

Nicoll, Allardyce. 1963. *The World of Harlequin.* Cambridge: Cambridge University Press.

Nissenbaum, Stephen. 1993. "Revisiting 'A Visit from St. Nicholas': The Battle for Christmas in Early Nineteenth-Century America." In *The Mythmaking Frame of Mind: Social Imagination and American Culture,* ed. James Gilbert, Amy Gilman, Donald M. Scott, Joan W. Scott, pp. 25–70. Belmont, Ca.: Wadsworth Publishing Co.

——— 1996. *The Battle for Christmas.* New York: Alfred A. Knopf.

Noble, Madeleine M. 1973. "The White Caps of Harrison and Crawford Counties, Indiana: A Study in the Violent Enforcement of Morality." Ph.D. diss., University of Michigan.

Norbeck, Edward. 1963. "African Rituals of Conflict." *American Anthropologist* 65: 1254–79.

Nugent, Maria. 1839. *A Journal of a Voyage to, and Residence in, the Island of Jamaica, from 1801 to 1805, . . .* London: T. & W. Boone.

Nunley, John. 1988. "Masquerade Mix-up in Trinidad Carnival: Live Once, Die Forever." In Nunley and Bettelheim 1988: 85–117.

Nunley, John, and Judith Bettelheim, eds. 1988. *Caribbean Festival Arts: Each and Every Bit of Difference.* Seattle: University of Washington Press.

Oakes, R. A. 1888. "Charivari." *American Notes and Queries* 1 (27 October): 312.

Odell, George C. D. 1927–48. *Annals of the New York Stage.* 15 vols. New York: Columbia University Press.

Oinas, Felix J. 1963. "Spirits, Devils, and Fugitive Soldiers." *Journal of American Folklore* 76: 225–30.

Oliver, James, and Lois E. Horton. 1979. *Black Bostonians: Family Life and Community Struggle in the Antebellum North.* New York: Holmes & Meier.

O'Neill, Francis. 1913. *Irish Minstrels and Musicians.* Chicago: Regan Publishing House.

"Origins of Jim Crow." 1841. *Boston Transcript,* 27 May.

Ostendorf, Berndt. 1982. *Black Literature in White America.* Totowa, N.J.: Harvester.

Owsley, Frank L. 1949. *Plain Folk of the Old South.* Baton Rouge: Louisiana State University Press.

Palmer, Bryan D. 1978. "Discordant Music: Charivaris and Whitecapping in Nineteenth-Century North America." *Labour/ Le travailleur* 1: 4–62.

———. 1990. *Descent into Discourse: The Reification of Language and the Writing of Social History.* Philadelphia: Temple University Press.

Paskman, Dailey. 1928. *"Gentlemen, Be Seated!": A Parade of the American Minstrels.* Rev. ed. New York: Clarkson N. Potter Press.

Patterson, Cecil Lloyd. 1961. "A Different Drum: The Image of the Negro in the Nineteenth-Century Popular Song Books." Ph.D. diss., University of Pennsylvania.

Paulding, James Kirke, John Augustus Stone, and William Bayle Bernard. 1954. *The Lion of the West, Retitled The Kentuckian; or, A Trip to New York: A Farce in Two Acts.* Ed. James N. Tidwell. Stanford, Ca.: Stanford University Press.

Peake, Richard Brinsley. n.d. *The Hundred Pound Note: A Farce, in Two Acts.* London: John Cumberland.

Pearse, Andrew. 1956. "Carnival in Nineteenth Century Trinidad." *Caribbean Quarterly* 4: 175–93.

Pentzell, Raymond J. 1977. "A Hungarian Christmas Mummers' Play in Toledo, Ohio." *Educational Theatre Journal* 29: 178–98.

Phelps, H. P. 1880. *Players of a Century: A Record of the Albany Stage.* Albany, N.Y.: Joseph McDonough.

Phillippo, James M. 1843. *Jamaica: Its Past and Present.* New York: Saxton & Miles.

Pickering, Michael. 1986. "White Skin Black Masks: 'Nigger' Minstrelsy in Victorian Britain." In *Music Halls: Performance and Style: Popular Music in Britain,* ed. J. S. Bratton, pp. 78–90. Milton Keynes: Open University Press.

Piersen, William D. 1988. *Black Yankees: The Development of an Afro-American Subculture in Eighteenth-Century New England.* Amherst: University of Massachusetts Press.

Pieterse, Jan Nederveen. 1992. *White on Black: Images of Africa and Blacks in Western Popular Culture.* New Haven, Conn.: Yale University Press.

Ping, Nancy. 1980. "Black Musical Activities in Antebellum Wilmington, North Carolina." *Black Perspective in Music* 8: 139–60.

Pope, Alexander. n.d. *The Dunciad,* ed. James Sutherland. Reprint, New York: Oxford University Press, 1943.

Porterfield, Nolan. 1979. *The Life and Times of America's Blue Yodeler: Jimmie Rodgers.* Urbana: University of Illinois Press.

Postlewait, Thomas, and Bruce A. McConachie, ed. 1989. *Interpreting the Theatrical Past: Essays in the Historiography of Performance.* Iowa City: University of Iowa Press.

Preston, Michael J. 1972. "The Revesby Sword Play." *Journal of American Folklore* 85: 51–7.

Rammel, Hal. 1990. *Nowhere in America: The Big Rock Candy Mountain and Other Comic Utopias.* Folklore and Society Series. Urbana: University of Illinois Press.

Ramshaw, Molly Niederlander. 1960. "Jump, Jim Crow! A Biographical Sketch of Thomas D. Rice (1808–1860)." *Theatre Annual* 17: 36–47.

Rawick, George P., ed. 1972–9. *The American Slave: A Composite Autobiography.* Westport, Conn.: Greenwood Press.

Rede, Leman Thomas, and Francis C. Wemyss. 1859. *The Guide to the Stage.* New York: Samuel French.

Rehin, George F. 1975a. "The Darker Image: American Negro Minstrelsy through the Historian's Lens." *American Studies* 9: 365–73.

1975b. "Harlequin Jim Crow: Continuity and Convergence in Blackface Clowning." *Journal of Popular Culture* 9, no. 3: 682–701.

1981. "Blackface Street Minstrels in Victorian London and Its Resorts: Popular Culture and Its Racial Connotations as Revealed in Polite Opinion." *Journal of Popular Culture* 15, no. 1: 19–38.

Reid, Ira De A. 1942. "The John Canoe Festival." *Phylon* 3: 349–70.

Reidy, Joseph P. 1978. "'Negro Election Day' and Black Community Life in New England, 1750–1860." *Marxist Perspectives* 1: 102–17.

Reynolds, David S. 1988. *Beneath the American Renaissance: The Subversive Imagination in the Age of Emerson and Melville.* New York: Alfred A. Knopf.

Reynolds, Frederick. 1809. *Laugh When You Can.* Boston: Oliver Greenleaf.

Reynolds, Harry. 1928. *Minstrel Memories: The Story of Burnt Cork Minstrelsy in Great Britain from 1836 to 1927.* London: A. Rivers, Ltd.

Rice, Edward LeRoy. 1911. *Monarchs of Minstrelsy from Daddy Rice to Date.* New York: Kenny.

Rice, Thomas Dartmouth. c. 1833. *Oh, Hush! or, The Virginny Cupids.* In Engle 1978: 1–12.

1835. *The Virginia Mummy: A Negro Farce.* Arr. Charles White. New York: French.

Richards, Leonard L. 1970. *"Gentlemen of Property and Standing": Anti-Abolition Mobs in Jacksonian America.* New York: Oxford University Press.

Richardson, Alice I. 1976. "Mummers' Plays in the Americas." Ph.D. diss., New York University.

Ritchey, David. 1982. *A Guide to the Baltimore Stage in the Eighteenth Century: A History and Day Book Calendar*. Westport, Conn.: Greenwood Press.

Roach, Joseph. 1996. *Cities of the Dead: Circum-Atlantic Performance*. New York: Columbia University Press.

Robb, John Donald. 1980. *Hispanic Folk Music of New Mexico and the Southwest: A Self-Portrait of a People*. Norman: University of Oklahoma Press.

Robinson, Philip. 1994. "Harvest, Halloween, and Hogmanay: Acculturation in Some Calendar Customs of the Ulster Scots." In Santino 1994: 3–23.

Roediger, David R. 1991. *The Wages of Whiteness: Race and the Making of the American Working Class*. London: Verso Press.

Rogin, Michael. 1992a. "Blackface, White Noise: The Jewish Jazz Singer Finds His Voice." *Critical Inquiry* 18: 417–53.

——— 1992b. "Making America Home: Racial Masquerade and Ethnic Assimilation in the Transition to Talking Picture." *Journal of American History* 79: 1050–77.

Romero, Brenda Mae. 1993. "The Matachines Music and Dance in San Juan Pueblo and Alcalde, New Mexico: Contexts and Meanings." Ph.D. diss., University of California–Los Angeles.

Rorabaugh, W. J. 1979. *The Alcoholic Republic: An American Tradition*. New York: Oxford University Press.

Rourke, Constance. 1931. *American Humor: A Study of the National Character*. New York: Harcourt, Brace & Co. Reprint, Tallahassee: Florida State University Press, 1986.

Rowe, G. S. 1989. "Black Offenders, Criminal Courts, and Philadelphia Society in the Late Eighteenth Century." *Journal of Social History* 22 (Spring): 685–95.

Rudé, George. 1964. *The Crowd in History: A Study of Popular Disturbances in France and England, 1730–1848*. New York: John Wiley & Sons.

Runcie, John. 1972. "'Hunting the Nigs' in Philadelphia: The Race Riot of August 1834." *Pennsylvania History* 32: 187–218.

Ryman, Cheryl. 1984. "Jonkonnu, a Neo-African Form." *Jamaica Journal* 17, no. 1: 13–23.

Sacks, Howard L., and Judith R. Sacks. 1988. "Way Up North in Dixie: Black–White Musical Entertainment in Knox County, Ohio." *American Music* 6: 409–27.

——— 1993. *Way Up North in Dixie: A Black Family's Claim to the Confederate Anthem*. Washington, D.C.: Smithsonian Institution Press.

Saldaña, Nancy H. 1966. "La Malinche: Her Representation in Dances of Mexico and the United States." *Ethnomusicology* 10: 298–309.

Salvaggio, John. 1992. *New Orleans' Charity Hospital: A Story of Physicians, Politics, and Poverty*. Baton Rouge: Louisiana State University Press.

Sampson, Henry T. 1980. *Blacks in Blackface: A Source Book on Early Black Musical Shows*. Metuchen, N.J.: Scarecrow Press.

Sands, Rosita M. 1989. "Conversation with Maureen ('Bahama Mama') DuValier and Ronald Sims: Junkanoo Past, Present, and Future." *Black Perspective in Music* 17: 93–108.
  1991. "Carnival Celebrations in Africa and the New World: Junkanoo and the Black Indians of Mardi Gras." *Black Music Research Journal* 11: 75–92.
Sanjek, Russell. 1988. *American Popular Music and Its Business.* New York: Oxford University Press.
Sankus, Patricia Helen. 1981. "Theatrical Entertainments and Other Amusements in Salem, Massachusetts, from the Colonial Period through the year 1830." Ph.D. diss., Tufts University.
Santino, Jack, ed. 1994. *Halloween and Other Festivals of Death and Life.* Knoxville: University of Tennessee Press.
Saxton, Alexander. 1975. "Blackface Minstrelsy and Jacksonian Ideology." *American Quarterly* 27: 3–28.
  1990. *The Rise and Fall of the White Republic: Class Politics and Mass Culture in Nineteenth-Century America.* London: Verso.
Shank, Theodore. 1956. "The Bowery Theatre, 1826–1836." Ph.D. diss., Stanford University.
Schiller, Dan. 1981. *Objectivity and the News: The Public and the Rise of Commercial Journalism.* Philadelphia: University of Pennsylvania Press.
[Scott, Michael]. 1833. *Tom Cringle's Log.* Philadelphia: E. L. Carey & A. Hart.
Shackford, James Atkins. 1956. *David Crockett: The Man and the Legend.* Chapel Hill: University of North Carolina Press.
Shapiro, Herbert. 1989. "Labor and Antislavery: Reflections on the Literature." *Nature, Society and Thought* 2: 471–90.
Sharp, Cecil J. 1911. *The Sword Dances of Northern England, . . .* London: Novello.
Shattuck, Charles H. 1976/1987. *Shakespeare on the American Stage,* 2 vols. Washington, D.C.: Folger Shakespeare Library.
Sherman, Alfonso. 1964. "The Diversity of Treatment of the Negro Character in American Drama Prior to 1860." Ph.D. diss., Indiana University.
Shockley, Martin Staples. 1977. *The Richmond Stage: 1784–1812.* Charlottesville: University Press of Virginia.
Shoemaker, Alfred L. 1959. *Christmas in Pennsylvania: A Folk-Cultural Study.* Kutztown, Pa.: Pennsylvania Folklife Society.
Sider, Gerald M. 1977. *Mumming in Outport Newfoundland.* Toronto: New Hogtown Press.
Simms, Norman. 1978. "Ned Ludd's Mummers Play." *Folklore* 89: 166–78.
Singleton, Esther. 1968. *Dutch New York.* New York: B. Blom.
Smith, Horatio. 1833. *Festivals, Games, Amusements: Ancient and Modern.* With additions by Samuel Woodworth. New York: J. & J. Harper.
Smith, Sol. 1868. *Theatrical Management in the West and South for Thirty Years.* New York: Harper & Bros.
Smith-Rosenberg, Carroll. 1985. *Disorderly Conduct: Visions of Gender in Victorian America.* New York: Alfred A. Knopf.

Smither, Nelle. 1944. *A History of the English Theatre in New Orleans.* New York: Benjamin Blom.

Snyder, Robert William. 1986. "The Voice of the City: Vaudeville and the Formation of Mass Culture in New York Neighborhoods, 1880–1930." Ph.D. diss., New York University.

Sobel, Mechal. 1987. *The World They Made Together: Black and White Values in Eighteenth-Century Virginia.* Princeton: Princeton University Press.

Southern, Eileen. 1975. "Black Musicians and Early Ethiopian Minstrelsy." *Black Perspective in Music* 3: 77–99.

Southern, Eileen, and Josephine Wright, comp. 1990. *African-American Traditions in Song, Sermon, Tale, and Dance, 1600s–1920: An Annotated Bibliography of Literature, Collections, and Artworks.* Greenwood Encyclopedia of Black Music Series. Westport, Conn.: Greenwood Press.

Stansell, Christine. 1986. *City of Women: Sex and Class in New York, 1789–1860.* New York: Alfred A. Knopf.

Stearns, Marshal, and Jean Stearns. 1968. *Jazz Dance: The Story of American Vernacular Dance.* New York: Macmillan.

Story, G. M. 1969. "Mummers in Newfoundland History: A Survey of the Printed Record." In Halpert and Story 1969a: 165–85.

Stott, Richard B. 1990. *Workers in the Metropolis: Class, Ethnicity, and Youth in Antebellum New York City.* Ithaca, N.Y.: Cornell University Press.

Stuckey, Sterling. 1987. *Slave Culture: Nationalist Theory and the Foundations of Black America.* New York: Oxford University Press.

Suthern, Orrin Clayton, II. 1971. "Minstrelsy and Popular Culture." *Journal of Popular Culture* 4, no. 3: 658–73.

Szwed, John F. 1966. *Private Culture and Public Imagery: Interpersonal Relations in a Newfoundland Peasant Society.* St. John's: Institute of Social and Economic Research, Memorial University of Newfoundland.

———. 1970. "Afro-American Musical Adaptation." In Whitten and Szwed 1970: 219–27.

———. 1975. "Race and the Embodiment of Culture." *Ethnicity* 2: 19–33.

Taussig, Michael T. 1986. *Shamanism, Colonialism, and the Wild Man: A Study in Terror and Healing.* Chicago: University of Chicago Press.

Thayer, Stuart. 1976/1986. *Annals of the American Circus . . .* 2 vols. Vol. 1, Manchester, Mich.: by the author; vol. 2, Seattle: by the author.

Thompson, E. P. 1968. *The Making of the English Working Class.* Harmondsworth: Penguin.

———. 1971. "The Moral Economy of the English Crowd in the Eighteenth Century." *Past and Present* 50: 76–136.

———. 1972. "'Rough Music': Le charivari anglais." *Annales: Économies, sociétés, civilisations* 27, no. 2: 285–312.

———. 1992. "Rough Music Reconsidered." *Folklore* 103: 3–26.

Thorpe, Alice Louis. 1935. "American Songsters of the Eighteenth Century." M.A. thesis, Brown University.

[Throop, George Higby]. 1851. *Bertie; or, Life in the Old Field,* . . . Philadelphia: A. Hart.

Tiddy, R. J. E. 1923. *The Mummers' Play.* Oxford: Oxford University Press.

Toll, Robert C. 1974. *Blacking Up: The Minstrel Show in Nineteenth-Century America.* New York: Oxford University Press.

Toulmin, Stephen. 1990. *Cosmopolis: The Hidden Agenda of Modernity.* Chicago: University of Chicago Press.

Trial of John R. Buzzell, before the Supreme Judicial Court of Massachusetts, for arson and burglary in the Ursuline convent at Charlestown. 1834. Boston: Russell, Odiorne & Metcalf.

Tucher, Andie. 1994. *Froth & Scum: Truth, Beauty, Goodness, and the Ax Murder in America's First Mass Medium.* Chapel Hill: University of North Carolina.

Tucker, George. 1970. *The Valley of Shenandoah; or, Memoirs of the Graysons.* With an Introduction by Donald R. Noble, Jr. Chapel Hill. University of North Carolina Press. Originally published 1824.

Turner, Victor. 1969. *The Ritual Process: Structure and Anti-Structure.* Chicago: Aldine.

1977. "Frame, Flow, and Reflection: Ritual and Drama as Public Liminality." In *Performance in Postmodern Culture,* ed. Michel Benamou, pp. 33–55. Madison, Wisc.: Coda.

ed. 1982. *Celebrations: Studies in Festivity and Ritual.* Washington, D.C.: Smithsonian Institution Press.

1986. *The Anthropology of Performance.* New York: PAJ Publications.

Vaughan, Alden. 1989. "The Origins Debate: Slavery and Racism in Seventeenth-Century Virginia." *Virginia Magazine of History and Biography* 97: 311–54.

Vaughan, Virginia Mason. 1994. *Othello: A Contextual History.* Cambridge: Cambridge University Press.

Wace, A. J. B. 1909–10. "North Greek Festivals and the Worship of Dionysos." *Annual of the British School at Athens* 16: 232–53.

1912–13. "Mumming Plays in the South Balkans." *Annual of the British School at Athens* 19: 248–65.

Waddell, Rev. Hope Masterson. 1863. *Twenty-Nine Years in the West Indies and Central Africa, 1829–1859.* London: T. Nelson & Sons.

Wallace, Edward S. 1957. *Destiny and Glory.* New York: Coward–McCann, Inc.

Walser, Richard. 1971. "His Worship the John Kuner." *North Carolina Folklore* 19: 160–72.

Waterman, Richard: 1943. "African Patterns in Trinidad Negro Music." Ph.D. diss., Northwestern University.

Webster's New International Dictionary . . . , 2d ed. 1936. Ed. William Allan Neilson. Springfield, Mass.: G. & C. Merriam Co.

Weinbaum, Paul O. 1979. *Mobs and Demagogues: The New York Response to Collective Violence in the Early Nineteenth Century.* Ann Arbor, Mich.: UMI Research Press.

Welch, Charles D., Jr. 1963. "'Common Nuisances': The Evolution of the Philadelphia Mummers Parade." *Keystone Folklore Quarterly* 8: 95–106.

———. 1966. "'Oh, Dem Golden Slippers': The Philadelphia Mummers Parade." *Journal of American Folklore* 79: 523–36.

———. 1970. *Oh Dem Golden Slippers*. New York: Thomas Nelson, Inc.

Wells, Paul F., and Anne Dhu McLucas. 1997. "Musical Theater as a Link between Folk and Popular Traditions." In *Vistas of American Music: Essays and Compositions in Honor of William K. Kearns*, ed. John Graziano, pp. 99–124. Warren, Mich.: Harmonie Park Press.

Wemyss, Francis Courtney. 1848. *Theatrical Biography; or, The Life an An Actor and Manager*. Glasgow: R. Griffin.

White, Charley. 1854. "Origin of Negro Minstrelsy." *New York Clipper*, 24 June.

White, Shane. 1988. "Pinkster: Afro-Dutch Syncretization in New York City and the Hudson Valley." *Journal of American Folklore* 102: 68–75.

———. 1994. "'It Was a Proud Day': African Americans, Festivals, and Parades in the North, 1741–1834." *Journal of American History* 81: 13–50.

Whitten, Norman E., Jr., and John F. Szwed, eds. 1970. *Afro-American Anthropology: Contemporary Perspectives*. New York: Free Press.

Widdowson, J. D. A., and Herbert Halpert. 1969. "The Disguises of Newfoundland Mummers." In Halpert and Story 1969a: 145–64.

Wilentz, Sean. 1984. *Chants Democratic: New York City and the Rise of the American Working Class, 1788–1850*. New York: Oxford University Press.

Wilkes, George. 1844. *The Mysteries of The Tombs, a Journal of Thirty Days Imprisonment in the New York City Prison; for Libel*. New York: n.p.

Willeford, William. 1969. *The Fool and His Scepter: A Study in Clowns and Jesters*. Evanston, Ill.: Northwestern University Press.

Williams, Cynric R. 1826. *A Tour through the Island of Jamaica . . . in Year 1823*. London: Hunt & Clarke.

Williams, David. 1955. *The Rebecca Riots: A Study in Agrarian Discontent*. Cardiff: University of Wales Press.

Williams, Raymond. 1958. *Culture and Society, 1780–1950*. New York: Columbia University Press.

———. 1973. "Base and Superstructure in Marxist Cultural Theory." *New Left Review* 82: 3–16.

———. 1981. *Culture*. London: Fontana.

———. 1982. *The Sociology of Culture*. New York: Schocken.

Williams-Myers, A. J. 1985. "Pinkster Carnival: Africanisms in the Hudson River Valley." *Afro-Americans in New York Life and History* 9: 7–17.

Willis, Eola. 1924. *The Charleston Stage in the XVIII Century with Social Settings of the Time*. Columbia, S.C.: State Co.

Wilmeth, Don B., and Tice L. Miller, eds. 1993. *Cambridge Guide to American Theatre*. Cambridge: Cambridge University Press.

Wilson, Arthur Herman. 1935. *A History of the Philadelphia Theatre, 1835 to 1855*. Philadelphia: University of Pennsylvania Press.

Winans, Robert B. 1976. "The Folk, the Stage, and the Five-String Banjo in the Nineteenth Century." *Journal of American Folklore* 89: 407–37.

1984. "Early Minstrel Show Music, 1843–1852." In *Musical Theatre in America*, ed. Glenn Loney, pp. 71–97. Westport, Conn.: Greenwood Press.

1995. Review of *Love and Theft: Blackface Minstrelsy and the American Working Class*, by Eric Lott. *American Music* 13: 109–12.

Winter, Marian Hannah. 1948. "Juba and American Minstrelsy." In *Chronicles of the American Dance*, ed. Paul Magriel, pp. 39–63. New York: Henry Holt.

Wittke, Carl. 1930. *Tambo and Bones: A History of the American Minstrel Stage.* Durham: Duke University Press.

Wolfe, Charles K. 1989. "Crockett and Nineteenth-Century Music." In *Crockett at Two Hundred: New Perspectives on the Man and the Myth*, ed. Michael A. Lofaro and Joe Cummings, pp. 83–96. Knoxville: University of Tennessee Press.

Wood, Peter H., and Karen C. C. Dalton. 1988. *Winslow Homer's Images of Blacks: The Civil War and Reconstruction Years.* Austin: University of Texas Press.

Woodworth, Samuel. 1825. *The Forest Rose; or, American Farmers.* New York: n.p.

Wyatt-Brown, Bertram. 1982. *Southern Honor: Ethics and Behavior in the Old South.* New York: Oxford University Press.

Wynter, Sylvia. 1967. "Lady Nugent's Journal." *Jamaica Journal* 1, no. 1: 23–34.

1970. "Jonkonnu in Jamaica: Toward an Interpretation of Folk Dance as a Cultural Process." *Jamaica Journal* 4, no. 2: 34–48.

1979. "Sambos and Minstrel," *Social Text* 1 (Winter): 149–56.

Yetman, Norman R., comp. 1970. *Life under the "Peculiar Institution": Selections from the Slave Narrative Collection.* New York: Holt, Rinehart & Winston.

Yetman, Norman R., and C. Hay, eds. 1971. *Majority and Minority: The Dynamics of Racial and Ethnic Relations.* Boston: Allyn & Bacon.

Young, Alfred F. 1984. "English Plebeian Culture and Eighteenth-Century American Radicalism." In *The Origins of Anglo-American Radicalism*, ed. Margaret C. Jacob and James R. Jacob, pp. 185–212. London: George Allen & Unwin.

Zanger, Jules. 1974. "The Minstrel Show as Theater of Misrule." *Quarterly Journal of Speech* 60, no. 1: 33–8.

Zipes, Jack. 1979. *Breaking the Magic Spell: Radical Theories of Folk and Fairy Tales.* Austin: University of Texas Press.

Index